Sociological Beginnings

On the Origins of Key Ideas in Sociology

Sociological Beginnings

On the Origins of Key Ideas in Sociology

George Ritzer
University of Maryland

McGraw-Hill, Inc.

New York St. Louis San Francisco Auckland Bogotá Caracas Lisbon
London Madrid Mexico City Milan Montreal New Delhi San Juan
Singapore Sydney Tokyo Toronto

This book was set in Palatino by Ruttle, Shaw & Wetherill, Inc.
The editors were Phillip A. Butcher and Sheila H. Gillams;
the production supervisor was Friederich W. Schulte.
The cover was designed by John Hite.
R. R. Donnelley & Sons Company was printer and binder.

SOCIOLOGICAL BEGINNINGS
On the Origins of Key Ideas in Sociology

This book is printed on acid-free paper.

1 2 3 4 5 6 7 8 9 0 DOC DOC 9 0 9 8 7 6 5 4 3

ISBN 0-07-052974-4

Text Credits
Pages 49–50, 52–59, and 68–69: Marianne Weber, *Max Weber: A Biography,* Harry Zohn (ed. and trans.). New York: Wiley, 1975. Reprinted by permission.
Pages 93, 94, and 100–102: Herbert Blumer, *Symbolic Interaction: Perspective and Method.* Englewood Cliffs, New Jersey: Prentice-Hall, 1969. Reprinted by permission.
Page 122: Andrew Beyer, © 1990, The Washington Post. Reprinted with permission.
Pages 148–149: Peter Singer, *Animal Liberation: A New Ethics for Our Treatment of Animals.* New York: Avon, 1975. Reprinted by permission.
Page 153: Lee Hockstader, © 1990, The Washington Post. Reprinted with permission.
Page 154: Richard Cohen, © 1990. The Washington Post. Reprinted with permission.
Pages 185–186: From "The Culture of Production: Aesthetic Choices and Constraints in Culinary Work," by Gary Fine, *American Journal of Sociology 97,* 1992, pp. 1280–1282 and 1286. Reprinted by permission of The University of Chicago Press.

Library of Congress Cataloging-in-Publication Data

Ritzer, George.
Sociological beginnings: on the origins of key ideas in sociology / George Ritzer.
p. cm.
Includes bibliographical references and index.
ISBN 0-07-052974-4
1. Sociology—History. 2. Sociology—Philosophy. I. Title.
HM19.R483 1994 93-23915
301'.09—dc20

Contents

Preface

This is a highly personal introduction to sociology. I have brought together in this book many of my personal favorites in sociology. I have put them together carefully in order to tell a coherent story about the beginnings of various sociological ideas. This set of beginnings offers the student a different kind of introduction to sociology and, I hope, a number of key insights into the nature of sociology. I explain why I chose to focus on beginnings, especially the beginnings of an array of sociological ideas, in Chapter 1. Here I deal with my focus on specific topics and how they hold together to form a coherent whole.

I begin in Chapter 2 with the founding of sociology in France, especially by Auguste Comte. Comte's contributions—his coining of the term "sociology," his positivism, his evolutionary theory, his distinction between social statics and social dynamics—are all important to the later development of sociology. In addition to the importance of these ideas, the relationship between these and other ideas and Comte's bizarre life makes interesting reading for beginning students. It is fun to discuss Comte because he was so nutty; and because many of his ideas, especially his later and long-discarded plans for the future, were so loony. The transition within the second chapter to a discussion of Durkheim and his contributions is striking because, in comparison to Comte, he was so sane and sensible. As a result (at least in part) of these characteristics, he was able to do what Comte had been unable to do—put the fledgling discipline of sociology on a firm footing. The contrast between the personalities of Comte and Durkheim is especially striking and engaging even though there are strong similarities in some of their most important ideas.

Next, I turn to my personal favorite among sociological theorists—Max Weber. Weber may have been as crazy, or even crazier, than Comte. As a result it is fascinating to read about him and to speculate, as I do in

Chapter 3, on the relationship between his personal problems and his social theories. However, Weber offers more than a discourse on the intriguing relationship between his life and his work. By discussing his beginnings we learn much about the beginnings of sociology in another country—Germany. Furthermore, Weber was a genius who created many interesting ideas that continue to have relevance to this day. In fact, as the reader will see, a good portion of my own thinking (and perhaps my own looniness) was shaped by Weber's theories.

Chapters 3 through 6 deal with the relationship between four more of my personal favorites, favorites that all have deep affinities with and linkages to one another. They are the Chicago School (my "pet" school), participant observation, a most admired method, symbolic interactionism (one of my preferred theories), and the sociology of work (my own substantive area of specialization). These are discussed not only because they are personal favorites but because they hang together so well. Participant observation, symbolic interactionism, and the sociology of work all emerged in an interrelated fashion from the Chicago school. Not only do they relate to one another, but they are linked to Comte's founding of sociology in France and to a number of Weber's ideas. The early Chicago sociologists were influenced by Weber's work; participant observation has strong connections to Weber's ideas on the method of *verstehen* (understanding); the symbolic interactionists were influenced by Weber's thoughts on action and interaction; and the sociology of work was strongly affected by Weber's specific focus on such issues as bureaucracies, professions, and the Protestant ethic. Beyond all of this, there are interesting stories to be told about the Chicago School, participant observation, symbolic interactionism, and the sociology of work. Finally, each of these is more easily accessible to the introductory student than most other schools, methods, theories, and substantive areas.

In Chapters 7 and 8 I get even more personal by dealing with two of my own sociological ideas. McDonaldization and hyperrationality. These ideas are drawn from Max Weber's theories, and they have particular applicability to the sociology of work. Not only do I discuss ideas that I have developed recently, but I also present for the first time the beginnings of a new idea of mine—"the creditcardization of society." I fully expect that this concept, presented in boxed exhibits, will lead to a book length discussion dealing with the revolutionary and sometimes devastating impact of the credit card on society.

Beyond all of this, *Sociological Beginnings* represents an effort to do for introductory students what I have been doing for years for a professional audience. Much of my professional work over the last twenty years has been devoted to the sociological study of sociology, or what I prefer to call "metasociology." This book can be seen as a work in the sociology of sociology, but one that is aimed at, and made accessible to, the introductory sociology student.

I love all of the ideas I have brought together in this book. I hope that students will sense some of my affection and enthusiasm for this material and come to share it, at least to some degree. I also hope that by dealing with my favorite topics I can succeed in giving students at least a taste of the essence and the excitement of sociology. Thus, I hope that this book will whet readers' appetites and lead to a desire to partake further in the veritable banquet of sociological ideas readily available to them.

Finally, I would like to thank the following reviewers for their many helpful comments and suggestions: Rebecca Guy, Memphis State University; John B. Harms, Southwest Missouri State University; Christopher Hunter, Grinnell College; Meg Wilkes Karraker, College of St. Thomas; Donald A. Maxam, Central College; Peter Melvoin, Bellvue Community College; Kenneth R. Muse, Westminster College; and Ken Westhues, University of Waterloo.

George Ritzer

Sociological Beginnings

On the Origins of Key Ideas in Sociology

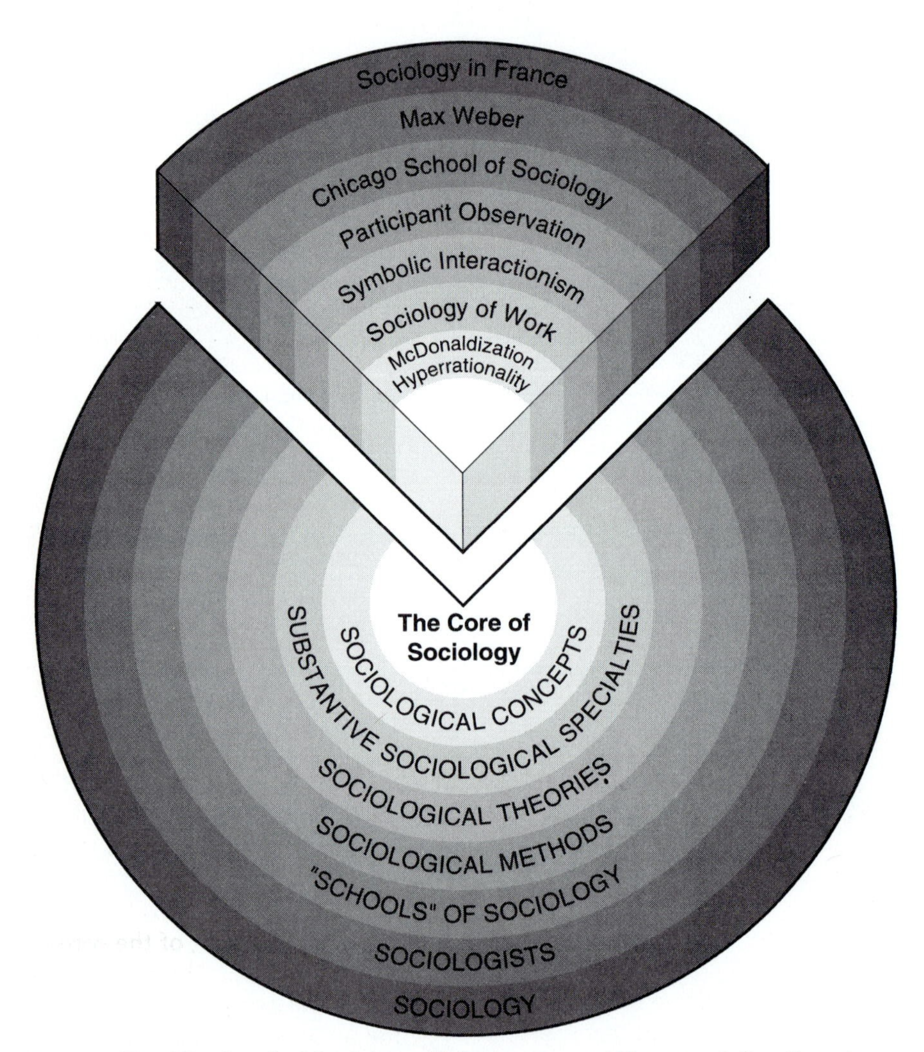

Figure 1 The "Geology" of Sociology: Major Layers and Representative Samples.

INTRODUCTION

The Author as Geologist and Archaeologist of Sociology

One way to think of me, the author of this book, is as a kind of "social geologist." Geologists, of course, are scientists who study the rocks and rock formations in the various layers of the earth. They are generally not content to remain on the earth's surface picking up rocks here and there because they are not satisfied with the amount and kind of information they can derive from surface phenomena. Thus, they often bore deep through the earth's crust to collect samples from various layers as they descend closer to the earth's core. Since their drill bits are small and limited, geologists can collect only a small sample of rocks from each layer. However, they believe they can learn a great deal about each layer from those samples. In addition, while they can never come close to the earth's core, they feel that their explorations can tell us many things about it as well.

SOCIAL GEOLOGY

What does boring through the earth's crust and its many layers in search of rocks have to do with this book? In this book, unlike most introductions to sociology, I will not remain on the surface of the field, content with picking up and discussing nuggets of sociological wisdom here, there, and everywhere. While many of those nuggets are quite interesting, they often do not give the student a sense of the various aspects (or, to return to the geology analogy, layers) of sociology, to say nothing of the core—the essence—of sociology. To get a better sense of sociology, both its various layers and its core, I will pierce the surface and descend through the major layers of the field. While the geologist uses physical tools, I will employ a variety of intellectual tools in doing a geology of sociology. As I descend—intellectually, not physically—through each layer, I will collect samples. Instead of rocks, I will collect information about specific aspects of sociology. The samples of knowledge I collect will, I think, be interesting *and* tell us a great deal about the broader layers of sociology from which they are drawn. Many other aspects of sociology exist in each layer, but my intellectual tools, like the physical implements of the geologist, permit me to deal with only a few things in each layer. Also like the geologist, I will be unable to reach (again intellectually, not physically) sociology's core. However, as is also true of a geologist, I believe that the various samples I collect as I descend through the various levels will offer considerable insight into the nature of the essence of sociology.

Of course, sociology's strata are not like the earth's layers. The layers of sociology to be explored in this effort at "social geology" include the following (see Figure 1):

- The surface level of sociology as a whole
- Sociologists as people
- Schools, or cohesive groups, of sociologists
- Methods of sociological research
- Sociological theories
- Substantive areas in which sociologists specialize
- Specific sociological concepts

An understanding of these layers of sociology, taken individually and collectively, will give the student a good sense of the nature of sociology as a whole as well as its major components.

Of course, many specific examples of each component exist in every layer, with the result that I have been forced to extract a sample from each stratum.

- While sociology has existed in various countries, I will focus on *sociology in France* (Manuel, 1962).
- From all the individuals who have practiced and continue to practice sociology, I have selected the great German social theorist *Max Weber* (Mitzman, 1970; Marianne Weber, 1975; Scaff, 1989).
- Although there have been several schools of sociology, I have opted to focus on the *Chicago School of sociology* in the United States (Bulmer, 1984).
- From the welter of methodologies, I have chosen to discuss the method known as *participant observation* (Gold, 1969).
- From a similar range of sociological theories, I have selected *symbolic interactionism* (Charon, 1985; Fine, 1990).

- There are many specialties in sociology, but I have chosen to focus on the subfield known as the *sociology of work* (Ritzer and Walczak, 1986; Abbott, forthcoming).
- Finally, among the innumerable specific concepts that are an integral part of sociology, I will concentrate on two that I created and have devoted a great deal of thought to: *McDonaldization* (Ritzer, 1983, 1993) and *hyperrationality* (Ritzer and LeMoyne, 1991).

The question immediately arises: Why these samples and not others from each layer? The answer is that these samples are all drawn from the same general region of each layer of sociology. Thus, while they are taken from different layers, there are a number of commonalities and linkages among them. Sociology, of course, is common to all the other layers. Max Weber was a theorist whose ideas influenced the development of the Chicago School of sociology (Faris, 1970:110). Participant observation, symbolic interactionism, and the sociology of work all had important origins in the Chicago School and experienced much of their early development in that school. Sociologists of work also tended to use participant observation as their research method and symbolic interactionism as their theoretical perspective. The specific concepts of McDonaldization and hyperrationality are derived directly from the work of Max Weber and are particularly relevant to the sociological understanding of work.

I hope to be able to use an analysis of each of these samples to shed light on the entire layer from which it is drawn. However, it should be clear that there is far more to each layer than can be learned from a single sample. To compensate for this limitation, I will bore through other locations on the surface of sociology in order to pass through other, usually nearby, regions of each layer and come up with additional, much smaller samples of each stratum of sociology. Thus, I will offer vignettes on the following:

- Sociology in China (Hanlin et al., 1987)
- The contemporary American sociologist of intimate social and sexual relationships, Pepper Schwartz (1990)
- The Second Chicago School (Fine, forthcoming)
- Quantitative methods in the First and Second Chicago Schools (Bulmer, 1984; Platt, forthcoming)
- Labeling theory (Colomy and Brown, forthcoming)
- The sociology of women and work (Reskin and Roos, 1990; Witz, 1992)
- Another of my concepts, the "creditcardization" of society (Ritzer, forthcoming)

These smaller samples, in concert with the much larger samples mentioned previously, reveal more about each layer and should give the reader a better and a broader sense of these layers. These smaller samples will be found in exhibits in each chapter.

ARCHAEOLOGY OF SOCIOLOGY

Another aspect of this analysis can be better thought of as an "archaeology of sociology" than as a geology of sociology. An archaeologist is a scientist who studies historical artifacts to learn more about what life was like in the past. I not only will descend through the various layers of sociology in this book, I also will touch on an array of historical periods from sociology's very beginnings to the present day. Just as I cannot discuss all the aspects of a given layer of sociology, I also cannot survey the entire history of the field in this brief book. Forced to be limited in terms of my time sample, I will operate like a "social archaeologist," focusing on artifacts that cast light on the *beginnings* of each aspect of sociology mentioned above. (I explain why I chose beginnings rather than another time frame in Chapter 1.) Thus, the focus will be on the following:

- The beginning of sociology as a whole, which is traced to the invention of the term *sociology* by Auguste Comte in 1822. (In a boxed exhibit I will deal with the beginnings of sociology in China almost a century later in the early twentieth century.)
- The origins of Max Weber as a sociologist. Weber lived between 1864 and 1920. [The exhibit in this chapter will deal with the contemporary sociologist Pepper Schwartz (1945–).]
- The founding of the Chicago School, symbolic interactionism, and participant observation, all of which came of age between 1892 and 1935. [The exhibits here will focus on the Second Chicago School (1946–1952) as well as the labeling theory of deviance and the quantitative methods that emerged from that school.]
- The development of the sociology of work between the late 1930s and the 1960s. (I will examine in the exhibit in Chapter 6 the rise in interest in women and work, especially in the 1990s.)
- The creation of the specific concepts of "McDonaldization" and hyperrationality in the 1980s and 1990s. (The exhibits in Chapters 7 and 8 will deal with the idea on which I am currently working, the "creditcardization" of society.)

Thus, in this book the reader will be exposed to *both* a sampling of the various layers of sociology *and* a selection of a number of key periods in its historical development. As a result, the student will get a sense of both the various aspects of the sociological enterprise and the historical development of sociology and its major components.

SOCIOLOGY OF SOCIOLOGY

What of the tools to be used in this geological and archaeological exploration of sociology? Clearly, I cannot use the drills and bits employed by the geologist or the hammers and chisels that are the archaeologist's tools of the trade, but I can use as my tools many ideas drawn from sociology itself to study the various layers and time periods. How can this be? How can one use sociology to study sociology? Sociology is an unusual discipline in that its own ideas can be turned on it to gain a better understanding of the field. One cannot do a physics of physics or a chemistry of chemistry, but one can do a sociological analysis of sociology. After all, sociology is a social phenomenon and therefore can be analyzed like any other social phenomenon. Thus, sociology can be studied in much the same way, and with many of the same tools, that the family, work, or politics is studied sociologically.

In fact, there is a well established and growing subfield known as the *sociology of sociology*. Furthermore, I have been a contributor to and practitioner of the sociology of sociology for almost two decades (Ritzer, 1975, 1981, 1991, 1992). There is even a journal, *The American Sociologist*, devoted to sociological studies of sociology.

In terms of the concerns of this book, the sociology of sociology leads me to use as an intellectual tool the idea that *large-scale* and *small-scale* social factors are involved in the beginnings of each of the samples of sociology mentioned above (Ritzer, 1991: Chapter 10). This intellectual tool leads me to look for certain things (and not others) in my geological and archaeological work. I will look especially for the role played in each sample by large-scale factors, those generally involving the impact of the social structure and culture of a society on the aspect of sociology under consideration. I will also seek out small-scale factors, those which involve the effect of psychological, behavioral, and interpersonal factors on those aspects of sociology. This is admittedly very abstract, so allow me to offer a few examples from the chapters that follow.

In Chapter 2 I will examine the founding of sociology in France. I will look at the role played by various large-scale factors in that development. For example, the French Revolution in 1789 led to dramatic changes in the social structure of that nation. In fact, it caused turmoil in the social structure, chaos that lasted for many decades. One of the reasons for the birth of sociology was a desire to found a discipline which might restore order to that society. At the cultural level, the intellectual movement known as the Enlightenment led to the creation of a set of ideas that helped lead not only to the French Revolution but also to the ensuing chaos. Thus, the French Revolution and the Enlightenment were historical developments that led to large-scale, social structural, and cultural changes in France, and these changes, as we will see, played a key role in the development of sociology in France.

At the small-scale, or individual, level, Auguste Comte and later Émile Durkheim played key roles in the development of sociology in France. They were, of course, affected by the changes in the social structure and culture of that nation, but their distinctive personalities, actions, social relationships, and so forth also were crucial in leading them to take the intellectual positions and actions that they did, which in turn played a crucial role in the founding of sociology in France.

To take an example from Chapter 4, the Chicago School of sociology was a product of the dynamic and changing structure of American society at the turn of the twentieth century. Chicago was at the center of the development of capitalism and a major site of the wave of urbanization sweeping the nation. Capitalism and urbanization involved, and were leading to, dramatic changes in the social structure and culture of the United States. The Chicago School was a product of those changes and sought in turn to analyze them. At the same time, at the small-scale level, individuals and their ideas, actions, and social relationships played a key role in the founding of this school. As we will see, the president of the University of Chicago, business tycoon John D. Rockefeller, who gave the university large sums of money, and various sociologists associated with the Chicago School in its early years (for example, Albion Small and Robert Park) all were crucial to the founding of the school.

Thus, this is a different kind of introduction to sociology. Most introductions give an overview of a number of the major specialty areas in sociology and some of the things that work in those areas has revealed to us about the aspects of the social world those specialties cover. In the course of surveying these areas, a little can be learned about important sociologists, methods, theories, and sociological concepts. Returning to the analogy with geology, most texts cover a wide area of sociology but do not go very deeply or get very far in investigating the core of sociology. This book opts for depth rather than breadth. Instead of ranging widely across the surface of sociology, I go deeply into a relatively narrow range of topics. Instead of voluminous names of sociologists, schools of sociology, theories, methods, specialties, and concepts, the student will be introduced to one or two major representatives of each of these. The objective is to go into detail about the beginnings of a relatively small number of key aspects of sociology and the way in which they relate to one another.

To put it another way, this is more of an invitation to you to gain a sense of sociology now and to learn more about the discipline in the future than a full-scale introduction. Specifically, you are invited to explore in the following pages a range of aspects of sociology in the hope that it will whet your appetite to learn more about sociology as a field of study and perhaps a career.

To use yet another kind of analogy, I approach sociology with a microscope while most other authors of books for introductory sociology courses use a telescope. A telescope gives a sense of the broad sweep of the field but permits the viewer to see few details. A microscope allows me to go into great detail about a few key aspects of sociology. However, even though efforts will be made to broaden the scope of coverage through the use of boxed exhibits, the fact remains that the student also needs the telescopic coverage provided by a conventional introductory textbook. Thus, this book should be used in conjunction with such a textbook. The textbook provides the big picture, while this book offers some depth. Together, they will provide the student with a fuller sense of the nature of sociology.

In addition to offering samples of the beginnings of various layers of sociology and going into depth on a limited number of issues, this book is devoted to giving the student a sense of the excitement of sociology. Much of that excitement is derived from a focus on the beginnings of each of the major components of sociology mentioned above. This discussion is based on the idea that beginnings are inherently exciting. It is to the issue of beginnings and what make them so interesting that we turn in Chapter 1.

CHAPTER 1

On Beginnings

Having introduced you to the general approach I will take in this book, I now turn to some introductory comments on the book's substance: the beginnings of the specific aspects of the layers or domains of sociology outlined in the Introduction. The first issue to be addressed here is, Why focus on beginnings?

SOCIOLOGICAL BEGINNINGS

The beginning of a social phenomenon—a friendship, a love affair, a business, a nation—is often its most interesting and exciting time. On the one hand, beginnings are usually highly positive, frequently involving optimism, excitement, creativity, and great promise. On the other hand, there are often problems and difficulties such as tension, anxiety, and fear of failure. Because of the confluence of such powerful positive and negative forces, the beginning of any social phenomenon is often a fascinating period.

Beginnings not only are interesting and exciting, they are also very revealing. That is, it is at its beginning that we often can learn the most about any social phenomenon. Because it is new, there is little opportunity for those involved to erect defenses or plausible but untrue explanations that obscure fundamental realities.

For example, two people falling in love for the first time have little chance to obscure and little interest in concealing the realities of their relationship. Although there are certainly exceptions, such couples tend to be very open about themselves and their feelings toward one another. This is true for three reasons. First, the relationship is so new that the couple have had no time to erect defenses around themselves. Second, they are too deeply immersed in their blossoming relationship to bother with camouflaging it from outsiders. Third, because it is such a wonderful experience for them, they are unable to fathom why anyone would be critical of it. Hence, they feel little need to conceal it from others and outside observers can learn a great deal about such a couple with relative ease.

In contrast, two people involved in a long-running relationship are likely to have erected all sorts of barriers around, and false explanations about, themselves and the relationship. This is so for three reasons. First, they have been together for a substantial period and therefore have had the time to create such barriers. Second, they are not likely to be as deeply involved in the relationship as they were when they first fell in love. Third, it is more likely that the motivation is there to conceal things from outsiders since problems such as frequent arguments and physical abuse are likely to arise as time goes by. These barriers and rationalizations make it far more difficult to learn about people involved with one another for a long time.

The same point can be applied to many other areas of social life, including those which are the concern of this book: academic fields. Those involved in the founding of new disciplines are ordinarily far too full of enthusiasm, energy, and optimism and far too busy trying to help the field become established to conceal fundamental realities (especially problems such as mistakes and gaps in knowledge) about the discipline and themselves. Those involved in long-established fields, in contrast, often have an interest in obscuring and concealing knowledge gaps and past mistakes from outside scrutiny. For example, the medical profession has long been accused of seeking to convey the impression that it understands more than it actually knows; in other words, it conceals gaps in knowledge from the public (Freidson, 1970; Starr, 1982). Similarly, practicing medical professionals, especially physicians, are often accused of concealing past mistakes such as botched surgery and erroneous diagnoses from the public. Because they are actively engaged in trying to protect and expand their fields, those in established disciplines are usually interested in hiding such things from outsiders, especially negative things that would tend to reduce the discipline's status in the eyes of other professionals as well as the larger society (Geison, 1983). More generally, a mythology such as the all-knowing doctor tends to be created about the field, concealing not only problems but the basic workings of the field. Thus, we look at beginnings not only because they are very interesting, but also because it is far easier to penetrate to the basic and fundamental realities of a discipline and its various components at its beginnings.

A third reason for focusing on beginnings is that it is a good way to learn about the principles that lie at the base of any social phenomenon, especially an academic discipline. Beginnings are by definition formative periods. Many of the later directions of a field are defined during its formative period. A field's founders define the domain of the discipline, and while that domain is likely to change over time, its basic parameters are likely to remain. Founders also define problems, develop concepts, generate theories, and create methods that have a profound effect on later generations. For example, one of the founders of sociology, Max Weber (Chapter 3), created the concept of rationalization, and that notion affected the thinking of many later sociologists, including my own on McDonaldization (Ritzer, 1983, 1993) and hyperrationality (Ritzer and LeMoyne, 1991). To take another example, as we will see in Chapter 7, the work of another founder, Georg Simmel, especially his book *The Philosophy of Money* (Simmel, 1907/1978), affected my thinking on the creditcardization of society as well the thinking of many others on the modern world (Frisby, 1992).

Thus, by studying beginnings we are also getting a feel for contemporary realities within a discipline. In terms of the academic field of concern in this book—sociology—it is my view that many basic insights into and fundamental principles of sociology can be effectively communicated in a book that deals with various types of beginnings in that discipline.

Because of its beginnings and because it is still in many ways at its beginning, sociology constitutes an exciting field of study. As mentioned in the Introduction, the term *sociology* was invented in 1822 by Auguste Comte (1798–1857) (Heilbron, 1990; Lenzer, 1975). While a number of important but isolated works were produced throughout the nineteenth century, sociology as a discipline did not really come into existence until roughly the turn of the twentieth century. Thus, in comparison to fields such as philosophy and physics, sociology is still in its infancy. Despite its relative youth, sociology today possesses a wide array of perspectives, theories, methods, and bodies of knowledge about an immense variety of social phenomena. Thus, sociology has clearly grown and progressed since the turn of the century. Nevertheless, it is clear that there is an enormous—indeed, a never-ending—amount of work to be done in the future. Sociologists know many things, but the social world is so vast and complex that there is infinitely more to be known than is currently comprehended. Furthermore, because the social world is constantly expanding and changing, there are ever more things to know and learn. Because of its vastness and everchanging character, sociologists are destined to know a great deal about only a minute portion of the social world. In addition, what they know is ordinarily only provisional and tentative. This is true of many fields, especially the sciences, but it is especially true of sociology and the other social sciences because the social world is in a state of continual change and flux. Thus, what we know today will need to be revised in terms of tomorrow's social realities. In a very real sense, then, sociology is destined to be *always* at its beginnings. This represents a constant challenge and a continuing source of excitement.

Because it is at its beginnings and perhaps always will be, sociology is characterized more by approaches, points of view, ways of looking at the social world, theories, and methods than by the wide range of answers it has to offer to questions raised about the social world. Thus, a student who is interested in—who needs—answers to each and every question might be better advised to seek out another field of study. Sociology is for those who have a high tolerance for ambiguity, for not knowing many things, and perhaps for never knowing certain things. Sociology is for those who love the search for answers to the riddles of social life but who know that those answers are highly elusive. Even when an answer is found, it is likely to hold for only a given time and place. As conditions change or as one finds oneself in a different setting, the answers may be quite different.

Sociologists do know many things about the social world. Furthermore, there are general principles and perspectives that hold from one time or place to another. We will encounter many of these principles and perspectives in this book; we will encounter some of the things known to sociologists. However, this knowledge is destined to constitute only a small proportion of that which can be known, and much of it will be altered, if not made obsolete, by the changing nature of the social world.

A good example of this point involves the work of the great German social theorist Karl Marx (1818–1883) (McLellan, 1973). Marx developed a brilliant theory of capitalism that was quite accurate for the economic system of the mid-1800s (Marx, 1867/1967). In other words, his theory helped us understand better the workings of the capitalist system and come to know new things about capitalism. For example, Marx's theory helped us understand the ways in which capitalists exploit workers and learn that labor is the source of value. However, over the years capitalism has changed dramatically, with the result that Marx's theory, while still important, is not nearly as accurate it once was. In other words, Marx's theory needs to be revised in light of recent changes in the capitalist system.

To take one example, the capitalists of Marx's time often engaged in cutthroat competition with one another, usually by undercutting the prices of competitors in order to acquire a larger share of the market. Over the years, however, the capitalist market grew less competitive, especially in terms of prices. Instead of engaging in the often self-defeating process of price competition, American capitalists of the 1950s and 1960s preferred to compete on the basis of sales and marketing campaigns

(Baran and Sweezy, 1966). Thus, the competition was over who could come up with advertising campaigns that would lead to increases in market share. The beauty of competing in this way was that the costs of advertising could be passed on to the consumer in the form of higher prices. This was obviously far better from the capitalists' point of view than price competition in which the lower prices came out of their own pockets.

Interestingly, in the last few decades we have witnessed something of a shift back to price competition, although it does not come close to the cutthroat competition of the early days of the capitalist system. This competition is now found in many American industries, including automobiles, home computers, and fast food (Lev, 1990). Companies in these and other industries have been forced to compete on a price basis because of substantial competition from the industries of other nations (for example, the Japanese in the automobile industry) or because many companies are fighting over a limited number of consumers (as in computers and fast food). While there is more price competition today than there was two decades ago, the major form of competition still occurs in the area of sales and advertising.

Let me offer another example of the impact of social change on sociological thinking. In the 1960s modernization theory became very popular among sociologists as well as other social scientists (Parsons, 1966; Hoselitz, 1960; Eisenstadt, 1965). The basic premise of modernization theory was that the world was evolving from a traditional form to a modern form. While traditional societies tended to be characterized by social inequality and authoritarianism, modern societies inclined toward equality of opportunity and democracy. Many modernization theorists tended to see America as the lead society and modernization as largely equivalent to Americanization (Antonio and Akard, 1986). In other words, all the less developed countries in the world had to do was copy what the United States had done, and they too would magically become modern societies.

There were many problems with modernization theory, such as its failure to recognize that one model of development cannot fit the needs of different nations, at different historical stages, with different traditions, and in very different parts of the world. However, the key point in terms of this discussion is that given the relative decline of the United States in the last two decades, especially in terms of its position in the world economy, it is difficult to think of the United States as *the* model of modernization for the rest of the world. Indeed, other nations, especially Japan (Womack, Jones, and Roos, 1990; Ritzer and LeMoyne, 1991), are now the countries that other nations seek to emulate. In fact, even the United States is seeking to learn from Japan's economic success and adopt some of its industrial and economic innovations.

Today many sociologists are studying Japan in an effort to uncover the reasons for that nation's economic success (Lincoln and Kalleberg, 1990). In effect, Japan (as well as Germany) has become the new lead society, displacing the United States. However, change will proceed, and sooner or later Japan will be displaced as the world's economic model (Amsden, 1989). When that occurs, sociologists will once again need to revise their perspectives. In summary, because of the continually changing nature of the social world, sociological perspectives are always provisional and subject to revision as social realities change.

SOCIOLOGICAL IDEAS

In addition to being a book about beginnings, this is a book about *ideas.* In fact, as I will demonstrate later in this chapter, the two themes are combined in that much of our focus is on the beginnings of a number of important sociological ideas.

I hasten to point out that the creation of sociological ideas is not the exclusive province of professional sociologists. Clearly, thinkers were coming up with conceptualizations that we now define as sociological ideas long before there was a field of sociology. Even today many nonsociologists are creating ideas that are clearly sociological and in fact have been picked up and developed by sociologists. Examples of ideas created outside sociology include "future shock" (Toffler, 1970) and more recently "technopoly" (Postman, 1992). *Future shock* means that people are overwhelmed by the rapidly changing nature of society and as a result suffer physical and psychological distress. *Technopoly* is defined as "the submission of all forms of cultural life to the sovereignty of technique and technology" (Postman, 1992:52). It is clear that the generation of such ideas will continue whether or not there is a field of sociology. While the generation of sociological ideas outside the discipline is welcome, the vast preponderance of useful and important ideas will be created within the field of sociology.

Whatever else one might say about sociology, it is itself an idea that encompasses a wide range of ideas about the social world. The founders of sociology, especially Comte, believed that the social world needed to be studied systematically. After all, there were already distinct fields devoted to the study of biology, physics, and chemistry. Thus, given its importance, perhaps its ultimate importance, the view emerged that there *also* needed to be a field devoted to the study of society. Furthermore, society had to be studied from the vantage point of a new discipline that was free of the biases and constraints of academic fields, such as philosophy and psychology, that concerned themselves partly with social issues.

Sociology was therefore, at least at first, an idea, a notion that has now come to be institutionalized as a distinct field within the scholarly world.

In addition to having the idea for a new field, the founders of sociology generated a number of specific sociological ideas about the social world. In the ensuing years later sociologists both explored those original notions and created innumerable other ideas. Thinking about and doing studies using ideas inevitably generate new sets of ideas. In this way, ideas in sociology and every other field grow geometrically. The result is that today sociology is a field loaded with an almost inexhaustible array of interesting, exciting, often counterintuitive, and almost always provocative ideas that help us understand the social world. In studying sociology, the beginning student is introduced to some of these ideas, and the further one advances in the field, the more of these sociological notions one encounters.

In the following few pages I offer for illustrative purposes just a few sociological ideas. These ideas illustrate what sociology has to offer as well as the distinctive ways in which sociologists look at some very common social phenomena.

Dramaturgy

A number of sociologists, most notably Erving Goffman (1922–1982), believe that the social world is like a stage on which people put on a variety of theatrical performances. We are all performers on this stage and are involved in a variety of different shows; we put on disparate performances for different audiences. We put on one kind of show at home for our parents, another for our boyfriend or girlfriend, and still another at school or work. To succeed in the social world, we all need to become adept actors who are able to alter our performances from one setting to another. The fact is that a performance that works in one setting (the home, for example) may not be appropriate in another locale (socializing with one's friends).

One of the key problems for people as performers is to be sure that what takes place in the *back* stage does not intrude in the *front* stage. The front stage is the setting in which we put on a particular performance. Let's say that the front stage is the performance you are putting on at home to explain to your parents why you did so poorly on your midterm examination. Your explanation is that the professor was inept and failed to explain things properly. Your parents accept this explanation, but the next day they run into some friends of yours who are taking the same course. In other words, they now have access to the back stage (the class) of the performance you had put on at home the day before. Your friends rave about the professor. They also inquire about your health and tell your parents they are concerned because they haven't seen you in class during the semester. Such revelations clearly shatter your front stage performance of the previous day. As a result of such revelations, it is often in people's interest to keep their front and back stages separated and keep people from the front stage from intruding in the back stage (Goffman, 1959).

The idea of dramaturgy has wide applicability. For example, sociologists have examined the way in which physicians put on performances to satisfy their patients (Haas and Shaffir, 1982). A doctor may define a patient as a hypochondriac, or someone who imagines various illnesses, but nonetheless will prescribe placebos (pills that actually contain no medication) to keep the patient happy. The physician may act as if the medications were very important to the health of the patient and must be taken exactly as prescribed, even though the pills will have no physical effect on the patient. To take another specific example, Kitihara (1986) examined how the American Commodore Perry opened Japan to the West between 1853 and 1854. Basically, he put on a threatening performance by brandishing his fleet's weapons and deploying its ships to intimidate the Japanese. The performance worked, and Japan opened itself to Western trade and cultural influences. As with all important sociological ideas, the notion of dramaturgy has wide and continuing applicability to the social world.

Charisma

The concept of charisma has come to be widely used in American society. We generally think of someone with charisma as having an extraordinary personality or other unusual characteristics. Thus, we think of people such as John F. Kennedy, Ronald Reagan, Elvis Presley, Madonna, and Michael Jordan as charismatic because of their extraordinary abilities. However, sociologists take a very different view of charisma.

The source of modern thinking about charisma is once again Max Weber. Unlike our conventional view of charisma, Weber argued that the source of charisma is not necessarily the individual who is thought to be charismatic but rather the followers and disciples of that individual (Weber, 1921/1958). What is most important is *not* the characteristics of the individual but the definitions of that person by the followers. If the followers define a person as charismatic, then that person *is* charismatic no matter what the person's individual qualities and characteristics. This view of charisma has at least two strengths. First, it allows us to see charisma as a social, not an individual, phenomenon; that is, it is the social group of followers and their social definitions that make a person charismatic. Second, it allows us to understand how ordinary individuals can come to be defined as charismatic. For example, to an outsider the great leader of modern India, Mahatma Gandhi, appeared to be quite unexceptional. He was not handsome, a great public speaker, or the possessor of a magnetic personality. Yet he came to be defined by his followers as a charismatic leader, and eventually millions of people came to follow him. A more recent example is the billionaire Texan Ross Perot, who despite his squeaky voice and homely appearance was defined as charismatic by the millions of people who desperately wanted him to be elected President in 1992.

Dyads and Triads

We often think of large groups as being very different from couples or small groups of people. However, another major German social theorist, Georg Simmel (1858–1918), had the idea that the crucial change in group size occurs when we move from a two-person (a dyad) group to a three-person (a triad) group (Simmel, 1950). Simmel's point is that many things (see below) become possible in a triad that are not possible in a dyad. Furthermore, the things that become possible in a triad can also occur in far larger groups. Thus, if we understand the triad and how it differs from the dyad, we can understand much about larger groups.

For example, a coalition is impossible in a dyad, but it becomes possible for the first time in a triad. Thus, two parties can join forces—form a coalition—against the third party in a triad. In a triad a person can also become an arbitrator or mediator trying to settle a dispute between the other two parties. Also, in a three-person group an authority structure can emerge in which one person becomes the leader of a group (in this case composed of two people) of followers. Coalitions, arbitration, mediation, and authority structures exist in triads and are characteristic of far larger groups. On the surface, it is not obvious that the addition of one person to a dyad is of the great sociological significance that was uncovered by Simmel.

Looking Glass Self

When we consider our self-concepts, we usually think about how we view ourselves. That is, we think of the self as something personal, something of concern only to the individual. However, Charles Horton Cooley, an important early American sociologist and key member of the Chicago School, had the idea that the self is a social phenomenon (Cooley, 1902/1964). That is, others are involved in what we come to think of ourselves. He called this idea the "looking glass self." Cooley saw the looking glass self as involving three elements or steps. First, we imagine how we appear to those around us. Second, we come to a conclusion about how they judge us. Third, we develop a series of feelings about ourselves as a result of imagining other people's judgments. In short, what we think of ourselves is a product of how we think others assess and judge us. Other people become in effect looking glasses (mirrors) in which we see ourselves reflected. Thus, the development of a self-concept is not an individual but a social phenomenon.

As was pointed out in the beginning of this section, later sociologists often pick up and extend earlier sociological ideas. Rosenberg (1979) extended Cooley's ideas on the self in various ways, including the formation of the idea that the self-concept extends to objects outside ourselves. For example, our automobiles and clothes are seen both by us and by others as extensions of ourselves. Thus, we are very conscious of the way others judge the cars we drive and the clothes we wear. We feel good about ourselves if those judgments are positive and not so good when they are negative.

Anomic Suicide

When we think of someone committing suicide, we think of it as a highly individual act: A distraught person, acting on his or her own, takes his or her life. Again, sociologists, in this case the great French social theorist Émile Durkheim (1858–1917), look at suicide as a social phenomenon (Durkheim, 1897/1951). That is, Durkheim was not concerned, at least as a sociologist, with a single individual committing suicide but rather with the *suicide rate* for a given social group. Groups tend to have rather stable suicide rates, but various social changes can cause the rate to rise or fall, in other words, can cause more or fewer people to kill themselves.

Durkheim differentiated among four types of suicide, but our focus here will be on only one of those types: anomic suicide. *Anomie* is defined as a feeling of rootlessness or, as it is often called, normlessness. Increases in such feelings may lead to increases in the rate of anomic suicide. Thus, a war or an economic depression leads to massive disruption in society and to people feeling uprooted. For example, wars and depressions can cause massive migrations of people from one part of a nation to another or from one country to another, and such migrations often make the participants feel uprooted. Unable to hold on to the stable social realities to which they have become accustomed, more people are likely to kill themselves; the rate of anomic suicide is likely to rise. Specifically, more people may commit suicide because they have lost their jobs as a result of migration and see little prospect of finding a new way of earning a living or may commit suicide in large numbers because their families have been dispersed by war and they feel alone and adrift in the social world. Durkheim's point is that such changes can lead to changes in the overall rate of suicide. It is this rate and the changes in it, not the individual act of suicide, that interest Durkheim.

These, of course, are just a few major sociological ideas. There are literally thousands of such ideas dotting the sociological landscape. What many of them share is a demonstration that many things that we think of as individual are in reality social phenomena. Dramaturgy requires a performer and an audience, charisma requires followers, a triad has the characteristics of much larger social realities, the self is defined by how others view it, and even suicide is related to larger social changes. Because all these ideas are social in character, they are considered part of sociology.

SOURCES OF SOCIOLOGICAL IDEAS

There are many sources of sociological ideas, and a number of them will be explored in this book. First, of course, there is the field of sociology. Without such a field, many sociological ideas would never have been created. (Of course, there had to be some ideas in place, such as Comte's idea of sociology, for the field to develop in the first place.) That is, the development and institutionalization of sociology (Oberschall, 1972) as a discipline led to generation after generation of sociologists who used the sociological perspective to create new ideas about the social world. Without a disciplinary base, many of those ideas would never have been developed. Working within a clear intellectual domain and tradition, sociologists have been able to develop new ideas, usually building on the concepts of their predecessors. We have already encountered a number of ideas; we will encounter more, and *none* of them would have been created if there had not been a field of sociology.

There are many other sources of sociological ideas. For example, ideas come from individuals and their experiences. The biographical experiences of individual sociologists intersect with both the history of sociology and the history of their societies at a given point to lead to the creation of new sociological ideas. Thus, individuals make a difference, especially people with strong viewpoints and powerful insights into the social world. Throughout this book we will discuss a number of these individuals, including Auguste Comte, Émile Durkheim, Max Weber, Robert Park, and Everett Hughes.

Georg Simmel offers a good example of the importance of biographical experiences (Frisby, 1984). Simmel was a Jew in anti-Semitic turn-of-the-twentieth-century Germany and as a result was relegated to marginal positions within the academic world. Jews were marginal to German society, and as a Jew Simmel was marginal not only to the academic world but also to the larger society. This was the case despite the fact that Simmel was a wonderful teacher and a brilliant thinker whose work was very popular in his day and is still widely read. Simmel was also marginal because of the style of his work. He wrote mostly popular essays, or what today is called "pop sociology," rather than heavy tomes, and he often wrote about exotic topics such as prostitution and the coquette.

In spite of, or perhaps because of, his marginality, Simmel (1908/1971) is famous for the creation of innumerable sociological ideas (I have already discussed his thoughts on the dyad and triad), many of which continue to be important. Another of those ideas is the *stranger.* The stranger is a type of person who is neither too involved in a group nor completely removed from it. This peculiar relationship allows the stranger to have a distinctive relationship with the group. For example, since he or she is not too involved in the group, the stranger can be more objective about it than is someone who is deeply enmeshed in it. Simmel offers many other insights into the stranger, but the key point here is that this concept can be traced to Simmel's biographical situation. That is, it can be argued that Simmel was a stranger to German society and German academia and that this led him to develop this idea as well as many other unparalleled insights into society.

Sociological ideas can also be traced to schools of sociological thought, that is, to formal and informal groups of sociologists who share a common perspective on the world (Tiryakian, 1979, 1986). These schools create a climate and a pattern of interaction among their members that often lead to the generation of a distinctive set of ideas. Indeed, different schools in the history of sociology have tended to produce unique sets of ideas.

As was pointed out in the Introduction, one of the most important schools in the history of American sociology is the Chicago School of sociology (Bulmer, 1984). As the name suggests, the Chicago School developed at the University of Chicago, beginning in the 1890s and reaching its peak in the 1920s. Many famous sociologists were either founders of this school or products of it. One of the early ideas of the school was the importance of *role taking:* the idea that people have the capacity to anticipate how others will respond to what they are doing. One of the implications of this idea is that people tend to do what they think will please others. In other words, this view tends to portray people as conformists. Ralph Turner (1968), a later sociologist working within the tradition of the Chicago School, created the idea of *role making.* In this perspective, people do not merely conform to role expectations but actively and more innovatively create their social roles. It is clear that people engage in *both* role taking and role making. For example, many readers of this book may have at one time or another occupied the social role of baby-sitter. Role taking associated with being a baby-sitter would involve getting the child to bed and making sure nothing bad happens to the child. However, many of you may have gone beyond role taking to role making by engaging the child in creative games or teaching the child something new. By working within the tradition of the Chicago School, Ralph Turner was able to extend our understanding of these processes and show that there is more to social roles than role taking.

Sociology is also divided into major domains, such as theory (a set of ideas that provide explanations for a broad range of social phenomena), research methods (the tools used by sociologists to study the social world), and substantive areas (for example, the sociology of the family or of race relations). Ideas are generated within each of these domains, and many of the best ideas have an impact on all those areas as well as on the field as a whole.

For example, one of the key theories in contemporary sociology is structural functionalism (Colomy, 1990). As the name suggests, this theory is concerned with the *structures* (regular patterns of social interaction, persistent social relationships) of society and the *functions* (positive consequences) such structures have for the rest of society. The system of social stratification is one such structure. A stratification system is a hierarchical order of positions within a society. We often think of the stratification system as involving a series of social classes, for example, the upper, middle, and lower classes. It is functional in the sense that it motivates people to move higher in the stratification system, because the higher one moves, the more likely one is to have high status, power, and income (Davis and Moore, 1945).

Working within the tradition of structural functionalism, a contemporary sociologist, Robert Merton (1949/1968), realized that in focusing on functions, structural functionalists were ignoring the negative consequences of social structure and as a result created the idea of *dysfunctions,* or negative consequences, within structural functional theory. For example, while the system of stratification can have positive consequences such as motivating people to improve their social class position, it can also have an array of negative consequences, such as relegating some people, and therefore the lower classes, to a lifetime of poverty. Thus, Merton reasoned that structural functionalists must look at both functions *and* dysfunctions. It is highly unlikely that he would have come up with the idea of dysfunctions if he had not been working within the domain of structural functionalism.

To take another example of the creation of new sociological ideas, this time within a substantive area known as the sociology of work, a great deal of attention has been devoted to the study of careers within various occupations (Glaser and Strauss, 1971). Careers are the various steps associated with an occupation. For example, in the military there are a large number of career steps, starting with private and ending with five-star general (Janowitz, 1960). One of many interesting ideas developed by sociologists dealing with careers is *career contingencies* (Ritzer and Walczak, 1986:168). These are events, often unforeseen, that have a crucial effect on one's career prospects. For example, a key career contingency for a graduate of a military academy is whether a war is taking place. If there is no war and therefore no place to demonstrate one's capacities as a soldier, one's career progress is likely to be slow. However, *if* there is a war, *if* one performs well in it, and *if* one survives the war, one's career progress is likely to be swift (Janowitz, 1960). There are similar, although not usually as dramatic, career contingencies in all occupations.

Finally, it should be made clear that the creation of ideas is not merely something that defines the history of sociology: New ideas are constantly being generated within the field. Thus, new ideas are being created as you read this book, and untold numbers of additional notions will appear in the future.

In the following chapters I will deal with all the aspects of idea generation in sociology that were mentioned above. In fact, we have already encountered a number of these ideas: dramaturgy, charisma, dyads and triads, the looking glass self, anomic suicide, functions, dysfunctions, the stranger, role taking and role making, and career contingencies. This of course does little more than scratch the surface of the enormous body of sociological ideas.

In sum, sociology is an exciting field not only because of its beginnings but also because it is loaded with ideas. As is clear from the few ideas discussed above, an understanding of those ideas will give the student new ways of looking at and thinking about the social world. While some of these ideas will illuminate aspects of the social world that have remained hidden to the student, others will challenge the student to think about the social world in very different ways. Readers of this book will not accept all these ideas, but they almost certainly will come to accept some of them. No matter how many ideas are accepted, readers will surely come to think of the social world differently than they did before they had contact with the field of sociology and its distinctive sets of ideas.

BEGINNINGS OF SOCIOLOGICAL IDEAS

Thus, this is a book about sociological beginnings, especially the beginnings of an array of sociological ideas. It is at this point that the ideas of social geology and social archaeology, as discussed in the Introduction, come into play. As a social geologist, I will examine samples drawn from the various layers of sociology outlined in the Introduction and in Figure

1. As a social archaeologist, I will focus on specific time periods, in this case beginnings, as they relate to each layer and to the samples drawn from them.

At the surface level, I will examine in Chapter 2 the founding of sociology as a distinctive discipline in France, especially by Auguste Comte and Émile Durkheim. However, in many senses sociology is still at its beginnings; thus, contemporary sociology is still part of the opening phase of what will eventually become a long history for the discipline.

As was pointed out above, sociology itself is an idea. While Comte created the idea of sociology, it was Émile Durkheim who gave sociology a base on which to build with his idea that the field had a subject matter that was different from that of all other existing disciplines. Thus, for example, while psychology involved the study of psychological facts, Durkheim (1895/1964) created the idea of a *social fact* to distinguish the subject matter of sociology from that of psychology (Gilbert, 1992). While psychology studied facts that were internal to individuals, sociology was to study facts that were *external* to individuals and also *coercive* over them. This led sociology into a focal concern with collective phenomena such as groups, societies, and culture. Thus, it was Durkheim's idea for sociology which set it on a course that led to its present focal concern with such collective phenomena.

Not only will I examine the beginnings of sociology as a whole, I also will examine the beginnings of various components of the sociological enterprise as we descend through other layers and periods. One type of beginning relates to the individual sociologist and how he or she became a sociologist. I could examine any number of sociologists from this point of view (I have already discussed, at least briefly, in this way Georg Simmel and the biographical roots of his concept of the stranger), but I have opted to focus on the biography of another key figure in the early years of the discipline: Max Weber (Chapter 3). There are several reasons for this decision. First, Weber was a German sociologist, and a focus on him allows us to shift the spotlight from France to Germany. Chapter 2 gives a feeling for the founding of sociology in France, while in Chapter 3 we get a similar sense of events in Germany since Weber was a key figure in the formal creation of the field in that nation. Second, Weber produced most of his important work in the early twentieth century, the formative years for contemporary sociology. Third, Weber is the focus not only because of his importance as a sociologist but also because there is an interesting story behind his early development. Weber had an unusual and even outlandish life, including a period of seven years when he suffered from severe mental illness and was almost totally unable to work. In fact, many of the early giants in sociology led fascinating lives, and an understanding of their experiences and how they affected their work makes for interesting reading. To take another example, Comte had bizarre relationships with women, including a prostitute whom he lived with and who supported him for a time. Ultimately, in his later work, he came to accord women a central role in his ideal world of the future. While not all sociologists are as interesting or important as Weber and Comte, it is revealing to look at the relationship between life experiences and intellectual accomplishments.

In terms of intellectual accomplishments, our main concern in the case of Weber is with some of his distinctive sociological ideas, especially that of *rationalization*. Rationalization may be defined provisionally as the process of searching for the most efficient means to whatever goals we happen to choose. Weber saw the Western world growing increasingly rational in this sense of the term, and the epitome of that rationality was the bureaucracy. That is, bureaucracy is a form of organization devoted to achieving the most efficient means to the goals it sets for itself. While rationality (and bureaucracies) brought with it enormous advantages, it also created terrible problems for society. For example, instead of being treated as humans, people in a rational society tend to be treated as automatons to be exploited as much as possible in the pursuit of the most efficient means to an end. The process of rationalization that Weber described has continued to expand and proliferate.

Moving to another layer and time period, another type of beginning relates to the development of a particular school of sociological thought. As was pointed out earlier, there have been a number of schools of sociological thought, including the Durkheimian School (Besnard, 1983), but it will be the origins of the already mentioned Chicago School that will concern us here (Chapter 4). As the name suggests, this school developed at the University of Chicago (Bulmer, 1984). It had its beginnings in the late nineteenth century and began to decline in the 1930s. In spite of its eventual demise (although, as you will see, a strong argument can be made that a Second Chicago School developed between 1946 and 1952), the Chicago School left an indelible mark on the development of sociology. I will look at the early years of the school, the people involved in it, and why the school developed as it did in the city of Chicago. Once again, there is an interesting story to be told here involving the relationship between the dynamism of Chicago during this period and the explosion of work in sociology at the university bearing that city's name. Another reason for focusing on the Chicago School is that many of its intellectual products, as we have already seen, continue to be important in sociology.

In the next chapter (Chapter 5) I look at two other layers and some of the key elements of the Chicago School, particularly its distinctive theoretical and methodological orientations. Theoretically, the Chicago School was the source of an idea or, more specifically, a theoretical perspective known as symbolic interactionism (Fine, 1990), while its best-known methodological idea came to be called participant observation (Bruyn, 1966). Briefly, *symbolic interactionism* is a theory that views social phenomena primarily in light of the interaction among individuals that takes place largely at the symbolic level. *Participant observation* is a method that typically involves the researcher directly in the lives and events of the people being studied; the researcher is *both* participant *and* observer. Interestingly, this theory and method developed at about the same time and in a parallel fashion. Furthermore, there are strong affinities between them. That is, the use of symbolic interactionism as a theoretical perspective fits well with the use of participant observation as a method of collecting information. A discussion of why this is so and the nature of symbolic interactionism and participant observation will have to wait for Chapter 5. As with other aspects of the Chicago School, this theory and method continue to be important. That is, many contemporary sociologists (for example, Fine, 1992a) continue to use symbolic interactionism as a theory and employ participant observation as a method for collecting data on the social world.

Moving on to the next layer, sociology, as was mentioned above, is characterized by a number of substantive fields. In this book, as was the case earlier in this chapter, I will be concerned with the beginnings of the sociology of work (Chapter 6). I chose this field because it had its origins in the Chicago School and because an analysis of it therefore makes for greater continuity in this book. The early sociologists of work also often adopted symbolic interactionism as their theory and used participant observation as their preferred method. Furthermore, I selected work because of its crucial importance not only to society but also to the student reading this book. Many of you hold part-time jobs during the school year and work during the summer. Most of you are in school to get the education that is needed to hold a "good" job in American society. Finally, most of you are concerned about the kind of work you will do, the kind of economy you will encounter, and the economic future of American society. The sociology of work is a subfield which helps students better understand the work world and the economy that will exist once their education has been completed and they take their places in the American work force.

Up to this point in the book I will be examining the early history of sociology. However, as was pointed out above, various aspects of sociology are still at their beginnings. In the next two chapters the focus shifts to the layer of sociological concepts and to more contemporary beginnings. In addition, I shift from discussing aspects of sociology in which I was not involved (for example, I was not born until five years after the Chicago School had passed its prime and begun its decline) to work in which I was, and am, intimately involved. I will devote the next two chapters (Chapters 7 and 8) to the beginnings of two of my own sociological concepts: McDonaldization (Ritzer, 1993) and hyperrationality (Ritzer and LeMoyne, 1991). I will trace the origin of these two concepts to earlier work in sociology, my personal biography, and my work in sociology. These are two new sociological concepts that I hope and believe will have an impact on sociology in the future. Thus, it is hoped that the creation of these concepts will lay the groundwork for the beginning of additional sociological work on them in the future.

In brief, McDonaldization is a concept derived from the theories of Max Weber. As we have seen, Weber was concerned with the rationalization of society and viewed bureaucracy as the epitome of that process. However, the world is now far more rationalized than it was in Weber's day. Furthermore, the best model of rationality is no longer the bureaucracy but the fast-food restaurant, especially the leader in that field, McDonald's. As we will see, the rational principles and techniques (for example, the drive-through window, which is a highly efficient means to attain the goal of obtaining a meal) that lie at the base of McDonald's have spread throughout the United States and are now spreading across much of the rest of the world. As with rationalization in Weber's day, McDonaldization is bringing with it major advantages *and* serious problems.

The second new concept to be discussed is hyperrationality (Chapter 8). Like the concept of McDonaldization, it is derived from the work of Max Weber. In this case it is based on the fact that Weber identified four types of rationality (Chapter 8). In Weber's view, what came to define the Western world was its reliance on one of these types of rationality. While this reliance on only one type gave the West a number of advantages, over the years its disadvantages have come to outweigh its advantages. While this is true of the West in general, it is particularly true of Western industry, especially the automobile industry. The failure of the Western, particularly the American, automobile industry in recent years is traced to its overreliance on one type of rationality and its failure to exploit the advantages of utilizing the other three types as well.

A hyperrational system is one that simultaneously employs all four types of rationality. The argument is made that it is the Japanese who have developed such a hyperrational system and that this accounts for the economic success of many Japanese industries, especially its automobile industry. Thus, the ability to develop hyperrationality accounts for Japan's economic successes, and simultaneously, the failure to develop such a high level of rationality explains American economic failures. (While Japanese industries have been highly successful in an economic sense, they have their problems. For example, Japanese workers are highly exploited, and a growing problem in Japan is *karoshi*, or death from overwork.)

I should reiterate that all these chapters are concerned not only with beginnings but also with ideas. The ideas to be dealt with include, among others, sociology, social facts, rationalization, symbolic interactionism, participant observation, the sociology of work, McDonaldization, and hyperrationality. As we will see, these not only are ideas in their own right, they are also productive of additional sets of ideas (for example, creditcardization, an outgrowth of McDonaldization, will be discussed in Chapters 7 and 8). As is often the case, one idea begets many other ideas.

The book will close with a chapter (Chapter 9) in which I look at contemporary sociology as a field still in its relative infancy. I will discuss some of the promise of contemporary sociology, the excitement that continues to pervade a field still at its beginnings. I will also look at some of the dangers that confront this still-fledgling discipline and the things that need to be done to overcome those dangers. While the dangers enhance the sense of excitement in sociology, they also pose a potential threat to the survival of the field. Thus, sociology will need to overcome these threats if it is to have a future. In my view, sociology *will* overcome these dangers and not only survive but thrive as a discipline. Observers will look back on the current period as another, particularly exciting phase in the beginning of sociology.

CHAPTER 2

In the Beginning: The Founding of Sociology in France

It is impossible to give a precise date for the founding of sociology. If in its broadest connotation sociology means thinking about and studying the social world, then it has been practiced informally since the appearance of humans on the planet. In order to survive and progress, the earliest humans had to be students of the social world; that is, they had to be amateur sociologists.

BEFORE SOCIOLOGY

Early humans certainly had to devote a great deal of time to coping with their physical environment. There were berries to be gathered, animals to be hunted, and vicious beasts to be avoided. While people could do many of those things alone, such activities were better carried out collectively. Thus, early humans also had to cope with their social environment. As amateur sociologists, they had to find people they could work with to provide food, clothing, and shelter as well as people who could help them deal with the dangers of the wild. Early humans had other social needs as well. For example, they had to be able to find potential mates in order to procreate and had to figure out who their enemies were and how to deal with them. They had to be able to band together with their peers to ward off their adversaries. To this day, we all need the ability to engage in these social behaviors and many more in order to survive. Engaging in these social behaviors requires us to be students of the social world; in other words, all humans, both primitive and modern, need to be at least part-time amateur sociologists.

While there have been amateur sociologists since the beginning of human existence, it was not until many centuries later that people emerged who devoted themselves to thinking about and studying the social world and communicating to others what they learned. However, these early social thinkers were *not* sociologists because there was as yet no distinctive field of sociology. Rather, it was religious leaders and philosophers who created the first works in what is today known as sociology. Insight into the social world was also provided by poets, novelists, biographers, and artists. Because they had a lot to say about the social world, one can learn a great deal about sociology by studying the works of a philosopher such as Aristotle (384–322 B.C.), reading the novels of Charles Dickens (1812–1870), and viewing the engravings of William Hogarth (1697–1764). However, none of these thinkers and artists was first and foremost a sociologist: The sociological insights they provided were by-products of their work as philosophers, novelists, and artists. In the work of sociologists such insights are not by-products but the direct and intended result of their life's work.

Because so many early scholars can be considered amateur sociologists, it is impossible to identify the first true sociologist. Some might argue that the very first was Abd-al-Rahman ibn-Khaldun (Azadarmaki, 1992). Ibn-Khaldun lived between 1332 and 1406 and resided in various places in southern Europe, northern Africa, and the Middle East. He eventually obtained an academic base as a lecturer at the center of Islamic study, the Al-Azhar Mosque University in Cairo, Egypt. Ibn-Khaldun produced a body of work that has much in common with contemporary sociology. First, he was committed to the *scientific* study of society, and most contemporary sociologists see themselves as being involved in such a science. Second, instead of restricting themselves to armchair theorizing about the social world, ibn-Khaldun urged sociologists to go out and study the social world on a firsthand basis, experiencing it with their own senses rather than through imagination or speculation. In other words, sociologists were urged to do what is now known as empirical research. Finally, in their research, sociologists were to search for the causes of social phenomena.

Ibn-Khaldun devoted considerable attention in his work to the study of what we now call social institutions, or sets of groups and organizations that center on the most basic needs of society. Ibn-Khaldun was particularly interested in politics and the economy as well as the analysis of the interrelationships among such social institutions. Most contemporary sociologists focus on the study of one or more social institutions (Douglas, 1986). For example, one of my concerns is the sociology of the economy (Ritzer, 1989). Ibn-Khaldun was also interested in comparative social research, particularly comparing primitive societies to those which existed in his time. Once again, many contemporary sociologists follow ibn-Khaldun in this and are interested in comparing various contemporary (let's say, the United States and Japan) societies with their predecessors [for example, Japan in the modern era compared with what it was like during the earlier Tokugawa era (Bellah, 1957)].

Given his interests, which were surprisingly in tune with contemporary sociological interests, why isn't ibn-Khaldun considered the founder of sociology? The answer lies in the fact that his work did *not* lead to the development of a field of sociology in the fourteenth and fifteenth centuries in the Middle East. Rather, his work and ideas were lost to the Christianized West, although not to the Islamized East, for a long period and are only now being rediscovered by Western scholars interested in the early sources of sociology. There were many other social thinkers who also could be seen as precursors of sociology, but they are not considered founders of the discipline because no field of sociology grew directly out of their work. This failure may be traced in part to weaknesses in their ideas, but it is more a result of the fact that the times were simply not right for the founding of sociology; the necessary social conditions did not yet exist.

THE ROOTS OF SOCIOLOGY IN FRANCE

The confluence of necessary social conditions did come into existence in the nineteenth century, especially in France. (See exhibit on pp. 38–40 for a discussion of the beginning of sociology in another nation—China.) It is customary to use 1822 as the date for the "official" founding of sociology, for it is in that year that, as was mentioned earlier, Auguste Comte first coined the term *sociology*. Comte not only created the term, he developed a significant sociological approach to the world that came to be expressed in a variety of highly influential works (Comte, 1830–1842/1974, 1851–1854/1976). Comte's ideas were picked up by others in France in the nineteenth century; it is of special importance that Émile Durkheim carried on the Comtian tradition and successfully institutionalized sociology as a distinctive academic field in France by the late nineteenth and early twentieth centuries. Thus, in the remainder of this chapter I focus on the founding of sociology in France, especially the contributions of Comte and Durkheim in the nineteenth century (Manuel, 1962).

While Comte is accorded pride of place in the founding of sociology, it would be wrong to conclude that his ideas developed in a vacuum. Profound social and intellectual developments provided the impetus and the background for many of Comte's ideas. Those developments also afforded the base for the formal creation and later development of sociology as well as the context that permitted a number of Comte's intellectual heirs, especially Durkheim, to develop ideas based on Comte's pioneering work.

The major social context for the founding of sociology as well as for much else that took place in nineteenth-century France was the French Revolution in 1789 and the profound social disruption that ensued. When the impact of the French Revolution is discussed by scholars, most of their attention is devoted to its positive consequences, especially the liberty, equality, and fraternity that played a key role in the spread of democracy around the world. Yet these positive effects had only a secondary bearing on later sociologists who were more directly and deeply influenced by the disruptions that affected French society for decades after the revolution (Wright, 1960).

Whatever else might be said of pre-1789 France, it had political stability under the leadership of a succession of kings backed by a small aristocracy. Prerevolutionary France was a reasonably stable society, although tensions simmered below the surface. The growing middle class resented the economic privileges and enormous political influence of the aristocracy. The peasantry's fortunes ebbed and flowed with the quality of the harvest, and the peasants also resented the aristocracy, especially because of the dues that had to be paid to them. These resentments and tensions came to a head on July 14, 1789, with the storming of the Bastille. After the successful rout of the aristocracy and its military supporters, a National Assembly was put in place. The National Assembly, dominated by the middle classes, stripped the aristocracy of many privileges and relegated the king to a secondary role in government. However, surrounding nations such as Austria and Prussia, which were still dominated by the aristocracy and threatened by the events in France, pressured the National Assembly to restore the powers of the king, and when that did not occur, the Prussian Army invaded France in September 1792. On September 22, 1792, while the Prussian Army was being held at bay by French forces, France declared itself a republic with power residing in a Constituent Assembly. The assembly was dominated by the most radical group of revolutionaries, the Jacobins.

Disorder continued in France into 1793. The king was tried and executed in January of that year. War was being waged against various counterrevolutionary armies, there were proroyalist uprisings in various parts of the country, and the economy was in a shambles. As a result of these disorders, the Assembly appointed a Committee of Public Safety, and to restore "order" a reign of terror was instituted in which approximately 40,000 "enemies of the revolution" were guillotined. In 1794 the counterrevolutionary armies were defeated, but the Jacobin dictator, Robespierre, was overthrown and executed. A more moderate Executive Directorate took power in 1795. However, the popularity of the directorate declined, and in 1799 Napoleon led a coup that overthrew it and allowed him to gain power. During the next fifteen years France under Emperor

Napoleon engaged in a series of wars throughout Europe. However, after crushing military defeats and years of disruption caused by uninterrupted warfare, Napoleon was forced to abdicate on April 11, 1814. However, in 1815 Napoleon briefly regained power, only to lose it once and for all with the defeat of his army at Waterloo and his subsequent exile to the island of Saint Helena in the South Atlantic.

Whatever else may be said of this period, which lasted a little more than a quarter of a century, it clearly was characterized by cataclysmic changes in French society. Furthermore, the disruption did not cease with the defeat of Napoleon. Rather, the events of those years ushered in a period of social dislocation which was to characterize France for decades to come. As we will see later, Comte and later Durkheim attempted to develop theories that could explain these disruptions in the social world.

While the French Revolution clearly disrupted France socially, the *Enlightenment* led to intellectual disorder in that country as well as many other countries. Just as Comte and Durkheim were influenced by the social changes and disorder wrought by the revolution, they were also profoundly affected by the intellectual changes and disorder caused by the Enlightenment.

The Enlightenment, an intellectual development that began in the seventeenth century, preceded the French Revolution and can be seen as one of its causes (Hawthorn, 1976; Zeitlin, 1990). While it occurred in a variety of nations, the Enlightenment was centered in France and was represented by the work of a number of philosophers (as well as that of a wide range of authors and artists), especially Charles Montesquieu (1689–1755) and Jean-Jacques Rousseau (1712–1778). What unified the Enlightenment thinkers was a commitment to the use of reason, rational thinking, and a belief in scientific thinking and its applicability to the social world. Enlightenment thinkers were opposed to irrationality, superstition, traditional knowledge, and accepted wisdom. It is in the latter sense that the Enlightenment can be seen as a precursor of the French Revolution. When these thinkers examined traditional values and institutions, they often found them to be irrational, that is, contrary to human nature and inhibitive of human growth and development. The French monarchy in particular was seen as traditional and irrational, in need of being supplanted by a more rational republican form of government.

In addition to providing the intellectual base for the dramatic changes brought about by the French Revolution, the Enlightenment was disruptive in its own right. Enlightenment thinkers such as Rousseau and Montesquieu, like some of their predecessors, tried to think rationally about the social world, but what distinguished them was the desire to combine rational thinking with empirical research. The model for this was science, especially Newtonian physics. The revolutionary development here was the idea that the scientific model could be applied to the social world. This application of the scientific model implied that there were laws of the social world just as there were laws of the physical world. It was up to the social thinker, using reason and empirical research, to discover those laws. Thinkers were to test out their ideas in the social world and derive new ideas from such research. Ideas were not only to be applied to and derived from the social world, they were also to be used in the social world, especially in critical analysis and efforts to reform the social world by eliminating the problems uncovered by thinking and research.

The Enlightenment tended to undermine many of the intellectual moorings on which societies had been built up to that point in history. For example, a belief in the importance of tradition had been dominant in the social world. Tradition was comforting to people and permitted society to function in a highly predictable manner. The Enlightenment thinkers rejected this belief in tradition and substituted a belief in that which was rational and reasonable. People were asked by these thinkers to give up the comfort of tradition for a more rational society, the parameters of which were still unclear and ambiguous. Furthermore, the new, more rational society was to be subjected to continual rational scrutiny and empirical research. When this research found society wanting, it was to be altered so that it would function in a more rational manner. This meant that rather than a traditional society that people could count on year after year and generation after generation, people were to be faced with a society that would be subjected to continual change. This was quite unnerving to people who had been raised in and had come to value traditional society.

Similarly, another traditional aspect of society—religion—came under the scrutiny of Enlightenment thinkers and was subjected to a blistering attack as an irrational social institution. People, rather than God, came to be seen as the source of society. These criticisms of both religion and the idea of God were threatening to people for whom religion, the church, and a belief in God brought stability and order to their lives. Without these moorings, many people felt adrift and unable to deal with the vagaries and dangers of life on their own. They had little faith in the idea that rationality and science would replace God and religion as ways of dealing with the world.

These fears helped give birth to an intellectual movement known as the *Counter-Enlightenment* (Zeitlin, 1990). In France this took the form of what was called French Catholic counterrevolutionary philosophy headed by Louis de Bonald (1754–1840) and Joseph de Maistre (1753–1821). These men were reacting against not only the Enlightenment but also the French Revolution, which they saw partly as a product of the thinking characteristic of the Enlightenment. De Bonald, for example, was disturbed by the revolutionary changes taking place around him and yearned for a return to the world that had existed before the Enlightenment and the French Revolution, in other words, a return to what he regarded as the peace and harmony of the Middle Ages. In that world God was seen as the source of society, and as a result, reason was considered inferior to religious belief systems. Furthermore, since God was the source of society, mere mortals ought not to tamper with it; they should not try to change a holy creation. By extension, de Bonald opposed anything that undermined traditional institutions such as patriarchy, the monogamous family, the monarchy, and the Catholic Church.

More generally, Counter-Enlightenment thinkers turned away from what they considered to be the "naive" rationalism (not to be confused with Weber's concept of rationalization discussed in Chapter 1) of the Enlightenment. For example, they rejected the rational belief in science, scientific laws, and empirical research. They not only recognized the irrational aspects of social life, they assigned them positive value. Thus, they regarded such "irrational" phenomena as tradition, imagination, emotionalism, and religion as useful and necessary components of social life. Since they abhorred upheaval and sought to restore an earlier form of social life, they deplored developments such as the French Revolution and the Industrial Revolution, which they saw not as progress but as disruptive developments.

It is in the context of the French Revolution, the Enlightenment, and the reaction against both that we once again encounter Auguste Comte and the formal beginnings of sociology. Both Comte's thinking and much of early sociology were shaped by the political and intellectual ferment described above.

AUGUSTE COMTE AND BEGINNING OF SOCIOLOGY IN FRANCE

Auguste Comte was born in Montpelier, France, on January 19, 1798 (Manuel, 1962; Sokoloff, 1975). While he was born after the French Revolution, he matured and came of age during the ferment of the Napoleonic era and its disorderly aftermath. Intellectually, he came of age during the post-Enlightenment era and the negative reaction to it, especially in the work of de Bonald and de Maistre. These social and intellectual disruptions had a profound effect on the nature of his work.

While Comte was a precocious student, he never received a college degree, and this was to have a severe negative effect on his ability to obtain and maintain an academic appointment. At the age of twenty, Comte took a position as secretary to another famous French social thinker, Claude-Henri Saint-Simon (1760–1825), who was nearly forty years Comte's senior. Comte became not only Saint-Simon's secretary but also his disciple. In fact, their relationship grew so close that he came to be labeled as Saint-Simon's "adopted son" (Manuel, 1962:251). Comte worked with Saint-Simon for six years, but they parted ways in 1824 because Comte felt that Saint-Simon was not giving him sufficient credit for his intellectual contributions. Comte grew hostile to Saint-Simon, labeling him a "depraved juggler," but he also acknowledged his intellectual debt to Saint-Simon (Durkheim, 1928/1962:144).

Like Comte, Saint-Simon was the somewhat ambiguous product of both the Enlightenment and the reaction against it. On the one hand, he accepted the Enlightenment's emphasis on science and its applicability to the social world. On the other hand, he wanted to preserve society as it was, though he did not seek a return to life as it had been in the Middle Ages, as did de Bonald and de Maistre. Comte shared these seemingly conflicting ideas with Saint-Simon, but the latter was more influenced by Enlightenment thinking than Comte was. For example, Saint-Simon believed, like Karl Marx, although less extremely, that socialist reforms were required in society, primarily in the form of centralized economic planning. While Saint-Simon is an important transitional figure, Comte was far more significant in the beginning of sociology.

Crucial to our story is Comte's coining of the term *sociology* in 1822, and we can take this date as *the* founding of the discipline. Comte also labeled sociology "social physics." This, of course, reflected Comte's alignment with the Enlightenment view that the social world could be studied scientifically in the same way that the natural world was subjected to such study. Yet Comte sought to distance his scientific view from that of Enlightenment thinkers by labeling it "positivism," or "positive philosophy" (Turner, 1985, 1989, 1990). For him, sociology was to be a positive science in contrast to what he considered the negative and destructive philosophy of the Enlightenment. Thus, Comte's sense of a positivistic sociology employed an uncomfortable mix of Enlightenment and anti-Enlightenment ideas.

Similarly, Comte only partially associated himself with the counter-revolutionary Catholic theorists de Bonald and de Maistre. On the one hand, like de Bonald and de Maistre, Comte was appalled by the negative effects of the Enlightenment and the French Revolution, but he did not think it possible to return society to what it had been in the Middle Ages. Comte wanted to create a stable society, but it was to be based more on modern scientific principles than on outmoded ideas. On the other hand, Comte, unlike the others, was willing to accept the Enlightenment idea of a science of society.

Within sociology, Comte distinguished between the study of existing social structures ("social statics") and the study of social change ("social dynamics"), a distinction that remains important in sociology today. In studying *both* social structures and social change, sociologists were to approach them as scientists seeking out the invariant laws that dominated them and permitted sociologists to understand them better. That is, existing social structures and social changes obeyed a series of social laws, and it was up to sociologists to discover them. While Comte dealt with both social structure and social change in his science of sociology, he emphasized change because it fit better with his desire not just to study society but to reform it. Comte's desire for change was primarily oriented to dealing with the disruptions caused by the French Revolution and the Enlightenment.

While Comte desperately wanted to change society, he did *not* favor revolutionary change. This was the case because he accepted the view that society was undergoing a natural *evolutionary* process and would of its own accord move beyond the negative phase in its existence during his lifetime and toward a more positive state. Then why Comte's interest in social reform? The reason lies in the fact that he believed that while the course of social evolution was unalterable, it could be helped along by various social reforms.

Given his views on evolution and social reform, Comte was clearly opposed to revolutionary change. Indeed, he traced the evils in society to political (the French Revolution) and intellectual (the Enlightenment) revolutions. To Comte, revolutions only served to derail the historical movement toward a better society. Thus, Comte was quite conservative and was willing to accept only modest reforms in the existing system.

Comte's uniqueness and importance to the later development of sociology lay not only in his self-proclaimed "discovery" of sociology but also in the fact that he placed sociology at the pinnacle of the positivistic sciences. He developed a hierarchy of the sciences ascending from the most general, abstract, and remote from people to those which are most complex, concrete, and interesting to people. That hierarchy begins with mathematics and ascends in the following order: astronomy, physics, biology, chemistry, and ultimately sociology. This was a breathtaking claim for the newly discovered science of sociology. Not only was it to be a science, it was to be the *leading* science. It occupied this position, in Comte's view, because it was the most difficult of the sciences and because it dealt with the most important subject matter of all—human society. In Comte's work, then, sociology not only was created, it immediately ascended to pride of place among all the sciences. It is little wonder that future sociologists were drawn to and felt an affinity with Comte's work.

Comte was not content to define sociology as a science; he also sought to delineate the basic methods to be used by the scientific sociologist in studying the social world. The methods delineated by Comte continue to be used by contemporary sociologists. The first is *observation,* a method by which the sociologist directly inspects aspects of the social world (Fine, 1992a). The second is *experimentation,* or the process by which a part of the social world is manipulated in order to study its impact on other aspects of that world (Cook et al., 1983). The third is *comparative research,* which can involve comparisons between human and lower animal societies, between societies in different parts of the world (Kohn, 1989), and, most important from Comte's perspective, the different stages in the development of society over time. The latter, which can be separated out and labeled *historical research,* has become the most important type of comparative research in contemporary sociology (Wallerstein, 1974, 1980, 1989). This type of research has achieved that status because it often deals with the broadest and most essential sociological issues over time and across many societies.

While Comte delineated various research methods and made the case for the empirical study of the social world, the fact is that he did little if any empirical research. He is best known for his abstract thoughts about the social world; in other words, he is recognized primarily as a *social theorist.* That is, Comte most often speculated about the social world and the invariant laws that dominated its evolution. He did not derive his sense of those laws from observational, experimental, or comparative studies of the social world. Rather, he deduced them from his own theory of human nature. Thus, while Comte was a positivist in the sense that he believed that the social world was dominated by invariant laws, he was not in the sense that he did not do empirical studies of the social world.

A good example of this can be found in Comte's famous "law of the three stages," stages that were *not* discovered through careful empirical study but rather were derived by Comte from his general philosophy of human nature. Comte argued that human history passed through three invariant stages. In the first, or theological, stage people are dominated by the belief that all phenomena are created, regulated, and given their purpose by supernatural forces or beings (gods). While Comte praised this stage as being orderly, he critiqued it for blocking social progress. The second, or metaphysical, stage is a transitional phase in which abstract forces such as nature replace supernatural beings as the explanation of all phenomena. This stage was objectionable to Comte because while it offered progress, it was disorderly. In fact, Comte associated the Enlightenment and the French Revolution with this stage. The final stage is the positivistic stage, in which people give up the vain search for supernatural beings and mysterious forces and look instead for the invariable natural laws that govern all phenomena. This was the ultimate stage as far as Comte was concerned because it promised *both* order *and* progress. That is, invariant laws would provide order and scientific research would lead to progress.

Comte saw the world evolving toward a positivistic stage. This development was inevitable, although it could be helped along, as was pointed out above, by reforms initiated by people such as Comte (see below). It promised both a way out of the disorder caused by the French Revolution and the Enlightenment and future progress rather than the regression to an earlier state offered by the French counterrevolutionaries. At the pinnacle of the sciences in this ultimate stage in human history was to be the science of sociology. From their lofty heights sociologists could speculate on and study the newly emerging society. They could also offer reforms that would hasten the evolution of a perfect positivistic society. Here was an evolutionary theory that for obvious reasons was to prove very attractive to later sociologists. While they came to reject the specifics of Comte's evolutionary theories, sociologists generally accepted positivistic methods and the goal of becoming the "queen of the sciences."

Later in his life Comte (1851–1854/1976; 1891/1973) moved from theoretical work to more practical proposals for the reform of society and the hastening of the movement toward a positivistic society. Some would say that by this point in his life Comte had grown embittered and perhaps insane. In fact, as early as 1826 Comte had had a nervous breakdown, and he continued to suffer from psychiatric problems throughout the remainder of his life. In 1827 he had tried to commit suicide by throwing himself in the Seine.

Comte came to declare positivism a religion of humanity and pronounced himself the founder of that religion. The following are some of Comte's plans for his positivistic religion that were never implemented. Instead of worshiping supernatural beings or gods, positivism worshiped humanity, or what Comte called the "Great Being." Comte created a large number of public holidays to reaffirm positivism, its basic principles, and its secular heroes. He also designed what were to be the new positivistic temples, specifying the number of priests and vicars required in each temple. Forty-two of the vicars were to be chosen as the priests of humanity, and from that group the high priest ("the Pontiff") was to be chosen. While the Catholic pontiff resided in Italy, the positivist pontiff was supposed to be a resident of Paris. Needless to say, Comte designated himself as the pontiff of positivism and worried greatly about who was to be his successor.

While this all seems more than a little mad, it did imply an exalted place for sociology. After all, if positivism was the religion of humanity and sociology was the ultimate form of positivism, then sociology was clearly to reign over the social world. While no modern sociologist would share Comte's grandiose ambitions, those dreams were important in their

Sociology in China: Beginning Again and Again

Sociology in China has had a number of new beginnings. As in many other countries, academic fields in China are responsive to political changes, and this is especially true of a socially and politically relevant field such as sociology. The result is that sociology in China has had a series of ups and downs, of new beginnings, in the twentieth century (Hanlin et al., 1987). The likelihood is that this will continue for the foreseeable future as sociology ebbs and flows with the prevailing political winds.

Sociology in China can be traced to the early twentieth century, when Chinese sociologists trained in Europe and the United States returned to their homeland. A number of sociological classics, for example, Durkheim's *Division of Labor in Society,* were translated into Chinese. Chinese sociologists were interested in theory and methods, but given the difficulties in their society, their prime interest was in the study of social problems, especially overpopulation, poverty, and the problems of rural life.

However, the fortunes of sociology in China took a dramatic turn for the worse in 1949 when the communists took power. Soon departments of sociology throughout China were shut down, and within a few years sociology, at least as a formal discipline, had disappeared. There are a number of reasons why the communists were hostile to sociology, but two are of the utmost importance. First, they saw Marxism as an alternative to Western-style sociology and one that was better able to not only understand but solve the kinds of problems mentioned above. In any case, sociology was associated with hated capitalism, especially the type found in the United States. Second, sociology was seen as a field that could provide a base for critiques of communist society and the Communist party. Thus, it was feared as a potentially counterrevolutionary force.

In 1957 an effort was made by a few sociologists to revive the discipline. These sociologists had survived mainly as members of other academic departments. However, their efforts were severely criticized by the party and its supporters and were labeled as part of a right-wing conspiracy. As a result, sociology lost its foothold in Chinese academia.

Although they lacked academic homes, the Chinese sociologists who survived into the 1960s suffered, like other academicians and intellectuals, from the excesses of Mao Zedong's Cultural Revolution. This was a misguided effort to revive the revolutionary spirit of 1949 by, among other things, forcing professors out of their academic "ivory towers" and into the "real world," where they were forced, for example, to do manual labor on farms. Many older academicians, including a number of sociologists, died as a result of the harsh conditions associated with unaccustomed manual labor in such places as rice fields.

However, after the death of Mao China moved in a more liberal direction. In 1979 a symposium was held in which the president of the Chinese Academy of Social Sciences announced that sociology had been "rehabilitated." The Chinese Sociological Association was founded the very next day. However, Chinese sociology was confronted with a daunting task. Nothing had taken place in Chinese sociology since the early 1950s, and almost three decades of work in sociology in the rest of the world was unknown in China. Most of the early Chinese sociologists were now dead or too old to start anew. The lack of well-trained teachers, facilities, and written materials made it difficult for young students drawn to the newly reviving field.

In spite of these difficulties, Chinese sociology made dramatic progress in the 1980s. This included formal ties between Chinese and Western universities, visits by foreign scholars to teach and do research, the translation into Chinese of many works in Western sociology, and most important, large numbers of Chinese students studying abroad, especially in the United States. As a result, Chinese scholars were beginning to produce their own distinctive brand of sociology.

It is in this context that I visited China in late 1988 to lecture in Shanghai and Beijing. It was an exciting time for sociology, and large numbers of students turned out for my lectures. The young faculty members and students were filled with enthusiasm for sociology and felt sure that it had bright future in China. I was named an honorary professor at Shanghai University with the idea that I would return on a regular basis. I was also invited by Beijing University to return the following year for an international conference on Max Weber. However, that conference did not take place, and I have yet to return to Shanghai University.

The reason is that in May 1989 the government brutally crushed the democracy movement in the infamous Tiananmen Square massacre. Sociology students, faculty members, departments, and institutes all played central roles in the democratic movement and were singled out for particularly severe reprisals. The sociology that remains in China today must conform to the demands of the state and those of Marxian theory. I recently received a letter exploring the possibility of having me visit Shanghai University again. However, I am reluctant to do so because I am told that I would be closely monitored by party officials and would not be able to speak freely, as I had been able to do in 1988.

As of this writing (early 1993), Chinese sociology is on hold. It is not being destroyed as it had been in the 1950s, but it is not being allowed to progress. Chinese sociology, like much else in China, awaits the next major political change. If and when the Communist party is ousted, as it was in the former Soviet Union, sociology in China will experience yet another new beginning.

---

time. Even though it was not yet an accepted field, sociology was granted by Comte and his followers an exalted status and a preeminent place in the society of the future. Such an image surely gave the next generation of sociologists an enormous boost. While they were destined to fall far short of Comte's ambitions, later sociologists were at least given a grand goal. Even in failing to achieve the Comtian ambition, sociologists were to make a number of notable advances in the coming decades (see the discussion of Durkheim's work below).

What is interesting about Comte's plans for the future in light of the previous discussion is that they resemble the ideas of the French counterrevolutionary Catholics de Bonald and de Maistre, who sought a return to the comfort of the Middle Ages. Comte did not propose such a return, but he did propose a new religious system that would move the medieval structure of Catholicism, with its Pope and priests, into the modern world. Comte fused this reactionary move with the then-progressive idea of positivism to produce a distinctive system of ideas that formed the base for the emergence of sociology.

As important as Comte's ideas were, he failed to develop a following or an institutional base for sociology. While widely read in their day, Comte's works did not lead directly to the institutionalization of sociology. It was Émile Durkheim, who accepted Comte's conservativism and positivism but not his outrageous plans for a future society, who came to legitimate and institutionalize sociology as a distinctive field in France and ultimately in much of the rest of the world (Clark, 1973). While Comte's work decreased in influence over the years, Durkheim's work had a profound influence on the development of sociology; indeed, it remains highly relevant to the present day (Alexander, 1988).

ÉMILE DURKHEIM AND THE INSTITUTIONALIZATION OF SOCIOLOGY IN FRANCE

Émile Durkheim was born on April 15, 1858, a year after the death of Comte, in Epinal, France (Lukes, 1972). Durkheim had none of the inspired craziness of Comte. Rather, he was more of a scientific sociologist; indeed, he became, and to many still is, *the* model for the modern scientifically oriented sociologist. He rejected religion (even though he was descended from a long line of rabbis) and philosophy and sought training in scientific principles that could be used in the moral guidance of society. In these objectives Durkheim was little different from Comte, but as he developed his ideas, Durkheim moved far from the excesses of Comte's theory, especially Comte's plans for a positivistic society. While Durkheim rejected philosophy, he obtained his first university teaching job in philosophy at the University of Bordeaux in 1887. Durkheim was unable to teach in a sociology department at that time because there simply were no sociology departments anywhere in the world. (The first sociology department was created in the United States at the University of Kansas in 1889.) However, it was in the philosophy department at Bordeaux that Durkheim taught the first course in France that can legitimately be labeled a sociology course. This was a particularly notable achievement because only a decade before a furor had erupted at a French university merely because Auguste Comte's name had been mentioned in a student dissertation.

The years that followed were characterized by a series of successes for Durkheim and the publication of a number of works that were destined to become landmarks in the history of sociology, including *The Division of Labor in Society* (1893/1964), *The Rules of Sociological Method* (1895/1964), *Suicide* (1897/1951), and *The Elementary Forms of Religious Life* (1912/1965). As a result of these accomplishments, Durkheim was named a full professor at Bordeaux in 1896. In 1902 he was summoned to the most famous French university, the Sorbonne, in Paris. In 1906, he was named professor of the science of education (he had always been very much interested in teaching moral education to schoolteachers) at the Sorbonne and, most important, his title was changed to professor of the science of education *and sociology* in 1913. Thus, Durkheim was able to achieve the kind of institutionally important position that was denied to Comte, in part because Comte was a man far ahead of his time and in part because Comte was at times as mad as a hatter.

Durkheim's institutional significance extended far beyond the achievement of his professorate in sociology in 1913. He also attracted a number of disciples who both disseminated and extended his ideas. He founded the journal *L'Année Sociologique,* which served as a major outlet for his work, that of his students and disciples, and that of sociologists in general (Besnard, 1983). Furthermore, his ideas influenced not only sociologists but also anthropologists, historians, linguists, and psychologists. This influence on already established fields was a great aid to sociology in its effort to become established as a recognized field in France and many other nations.

Durkheim (1895/1964) self-consciously sought to carve out a place for sociology within French academia. In so doing, he saw that he had to position sociology as a field distinct from the neighboring and already established fields of philosophy and psychology. Complicating matters was the fact that practitioners in those fields and many others were interested in defending their turf and resisting the incursion of sociology or any other field into the academic world.

To separate it from philosophy, Durkheim, given his scientific and even positivistic orientation, argued that sociology should be oriented toward the empirical study of the social world. That is, sociologists were to go out and experience the social world. Most often, this translated into going into the field and collecting *data* about society. Such an orientation was contrasted by Durkheim to that of philosophers, who generally think only about the social world. While they may think about the same social world studied empirically by sociologists, philosophers never engage in research in that world. Thus, in Durkheim's mind there was a clear distinction between philosophy and sociology, or at least such a distinction had to be made in order to carve out an academic niche distinct from that held by philosophy.

However, Durkheim had a problem in making this distinction. Comte, as was discussed above, while designating himself a sociologist, had been content to speculate, to philosophize, about the social world rather than study it empirically. Thus, Durkheim had to distance sociology not only from philosophy but also from Comte's philosophical style of sociology. While Comte sat in his armchair and thought about society, Durkheim went out and collected data, most notably on suicide rates in different countries. Durkheim attacked Comte for substituting his preconceived ideas about social phenomena for the actual study of those phenomena in the real world. Thus, Comte was guilty of assuming theoretically that the world was evolving in the direction of a perfect society rather than engaging in the hard, rigorous, and basic work of studying the changing nature of various societies. If the field continued to move in the direction pioneered by Comte, Durkheim felt that it would become nothing more than a branch of philosophy.

To help sociology further distinguish itself from philosophy and give it a clear and separate identity, Durkheim argued that sociology should have a distinctive subject matter, one he called social facts. Social facts are social phenomena that are to be treated as things, are to be studied empirically, and are external to and coercive over the individual. Let us look at each element of this definition.

Crucial to the separation of sociology from philosophy is the idea that social facts are to be treated as "things." That is, social phenomena are to considered as things just as we consider a chair, a tree, and a mountain to be things.

As things, social facts must be studied empirically, not philosophically. That is, to study social facts we need data drawn from outside the mind; they cannot be known through introspection. Thus, it is far more productive for a botanist to go out and study a tree carefully than it is for that botanist to sit in his or her armchair and philosophize about trees. We learn far more about trees through empirical research than we do from philosophizing about them. The same is true, as far as Durkheim was concerned, in the study of social facts such as laws, families, businesses, and nations.

Having differentiated sociology from philosophy through the idea that social facts were to be treated as things and studied empirically, Durkheim was confronted with the problem of distinguishing sociology from psychology. Although a far more recent creation than philosophy, psychology was already well entrenched in French academia. Furthermore, it seemed to deal with the same general subject matter as sociology: human life. To distinguish sociology from psychology, Durkheim argued that social facts are "external to" and "coercive over" the individual actor. Sociology was to study these external and coercive social facts, while psychology was to be content with the study of psychological facts which exist *within* the minds of actors.

What are some examples of such external and coercive social facts? Some social facts take a *material* form. For example, the physical structure of a room, a house, or a building is external to us and coercive over us in the sense that it allows us to do certain things but not others. Thus, a huge lecture hall may permit the professor to lecture to large numbers of students, but it discourages personal interaction between the professor and the students. Similarly, the law and legal institutions are material social facts. The law exists in codified law books and the legal apparatus; the police, courts, judges, and prisons are all material phenomena that are external and coercive. People may violate the law, but if they do, there is a good chance that, acting on behalf of codified law, the police will arrest them, court officers will try them, and prison officials will incarcerate them.

Other social facts exist in a *nonmaterial* form but are also external and coercive. For example, culture is composed of a series of unwritten rules about what we are and are not supposed to do. We generally follow those rules, and if we do not, the people around us will coerce us into following them. For example, if students repeatedly speak out and disrupt a class, eventually the professor and their classmates will enforce the rules by acting to stop the actions that violate the unwritten rules of classroom behavior. Culture is also composed of ideas about things we are supposed to value, such as economic and material success. If we ignore those values, at least some of those around us are likely to ridicule our behavior.

Durkheim defined sociology as the study of social facts in a book published in 1895, *The Rules of Sociological Method.* While Comte had invented sociology almost three-quarters of a century earlier, it was this work which put meat on sociology's bones. Sociology now had not only a name but also a well-defined subject matter. Furthermore, it was now clearly differentiated from its main competitors, philosophy and psychology. With a name and a niche within academic life, the foundation had been laid for the future development of sociology.

However, it was not enough that sociology had an intellectual base; it also had to have a more material infrastructure in order to develop. Durkheim was also crucial in the creation of this infrastructure. First, he helped here by having his professorship at the Sorbonne changed so that it included "sociology" in the title. Second, he created the journal *L'Année Sociologique,* which served as an outlet for work in sociology. Third, he had a set of followers who extended his ideas within sociology and in many other disciplines. Let us look at each of these developments in more detail.

First, it is clearly important for a field to have its own academic base. Sociology could not progress very far if it were little more than a minor subarea within a larger field such as philosophy or education. Thus, by having sociology appended to his academic title, Durkheim helped that field move toward the status of an independent discipline in France. In fact, however, as was pointed out above, sociology had already achieved that status in other societies, most notably in the United States with the founding of a sociology department at the University of Kansas in 1889. Thus, not only did the United States have professors of sociology long before Durkheim succeeded in getting his title changed, more importantly, there were sociology departments in the United States decades before this momentous development. The establishment of professorships and departments was far more difficult in Europe than in the United States. The European academic world in general, and that of France in particular, was well entrenched and difficult to change, while the new world of American academia was far more fluid and open to new developments. With professors and departments of sociology, the field had a necessary base on which to develop.

A second necessary development was the creation of a journal devoted to the publication and dissemination of work in sociology. Durkheim was the key figure in the founding of *L'Année Sociologique* in 1896. (It is interesting to note that this development was preceded in 1895 by the founding of the *American Journal of Sociology* in the United States. The German *Archiv für Sozialwissenschaft und Sozialpolitik* was created in 1904.) With the creation of a journal, fledgling sociologists had an outlet for their work. Without such an outlet, sociologists would have had to struggle to publish their work in the journals of fields such as philosophy and education. Such journals were far less likely to be receptive to the work produced in this new field than was a journal exclusively devoted to work in sociology.

Third, *L'Année Sociologique* also was set up to be and ultimately became the center around which Durkheim's followers in sociology revolved. In fact, Durkheim explicitly created *Année* with the intention of encouraging collaborative work among sociologists. Durkheim not only created a "school" of sociologists around *Année,* he succeeded in recruiting what came to be considered the most brilliant group of young scholars ever gathered in the history of sociology. Among the leading figures associated with the Durkheimian school were Durkheim's nephew, Marcel Mauss, and Lucien Lévy-Bruhl, who became leading anthropologists; François Simiand, who created French economic sociology; and Celestin Bouglé, who is best known for his studies of the history of socialist doctrines. Many of these brilliant young minds stayed with the school and made contributions over many decades to sociology as well as other academic fields. Durkheim exerted strong personal control over the journal and provided its intellectual focus with his definition of sociology as the scientific study of social facts. This strong personal and intellectual leadership helped give the Durkheim school, and ultimately sociology, a clear and well-defined identity.

CONCLUSION

This chapter has been devoted to the beginning of sociology. While sociology had other beginnings in other nations (see the exhibit in this chapter for the story of sociology in China), I chose to focus on France for several reasons. First, it was Auguste Comte who first coined the term *sociology* in 1822. Second, Comte also developed a number of foci for sociology, especially the concern with social statics and social dynamics, that remain with us to this day. Third, Comte laid the groundwork for the development of Durkheimian sociology with its focus on the scientific study of social facts. Fourth, Durkheim was important not only for giving sociology a distinctive focus but also for succeeding in having his academic title changed to include "sociology," for the founding of *L'Année Sociologique,* and for the development of a brilliant group of disciples around that journal who played key roles in the development and expansion of sociology. Thus, between 1822 and 1913 in France sociology, professors of sociology, a sociology journal, and a community of sociologists had been created. While this cannot be considered a meteoric rise, by 1913 sociology had a firm intellectual and institutional foundation in France.

It should also be mentioned that a number of important ideas were created during this period. The most important, of course, is the idea of sociology itself. Beyond that, other, more specific ideas mentioned in this chapter include social physics, social statics, social dynamics, positivism, invariant laws of the social world, social evolution (particularly the law of the three stages), sociological methods [observation, experimentation, comparative (and historical) research], and social facts (material and nonmaterial). Some of these ideas have been lost (for example, the law of the three stages), others have been transformed (social statics and social dynamics), and still others (positivism, sociological methods, and social facts) remain much as they were during this period. Whatever their current status, the creation of these ideas had a profound effect on the development of sociology, and they remain useful in attaining a better understanding of the contemporary social world.

CHAPTER 3

The Beginnings of a Sociologist: A Brief Biographical Sketch of Max Weber

In Chapter 2 I focused on the beginning of sociology in a particular nation, France. While there was some discussion of specific individuals, notably Comte and Durkheim, my main concern was with the development of sociology in a specific country. In this chapter the focus shifts from a nation to an individual, Max Weber (1864–1920). In describing Weber's journey into sociology, I am able to trace the beginnings of a sociological perspective and a number of important sociological ideas to the biography and personality of an individual sociologist. (For a comparison with the life experiences of a contemporary sociologist, see the exhibit on Pepper Schwartz.) While sociology was shaped by large-scale social and intellectual developments such as the French Revolution and the Enlightenment, it was, and still is, also shaped by the personalities and personal experiences of important and not so important individual sociologists (Mills, 1959).

Max Weber was certainly an important sociologist, and as the reader will see, his journey into the field is particularly interesting and instructive. In learning a bit about Weber's sojourn into sociology, the reader will also pick up insights into some of his important sociological ideas. Furthermore, because he was German and played a key role in the development of sociology in that nation, a role that parallels that played by Durkheim in France, a look at Weber's life also allows us to learn something about the beginnings of sociology in a second nation: Germany (Salomon, 1945).

In looking at Weber's biography, we are immediately confronted by the fact that in Weber's day in Germany, just as was the case in France and almost all other nations (the United States was an exception), there was *no* field known as sociology, no journals devoted to the publication of sociological works, and neither professors nor students of sociology. Thus, in those days the careers of people interested in sociological questions were quite different from what they are today. In the contemporary world there are national and international associations of sociologists, innumerable departments of sociology in universities and colleges, and graduate training programs leading to advanced degrees in sociology. Once one has such an advanced degree, there are set career paths, most of which are found in the academic world.

None of this existed in Weber's early years as a scholar in Germany. There were no associations of sociologists, no training specifically in sociology, and no jobs or career paths for sociologists. Indeed, what is crucially important about Weber is that as a result, at least in part, of his work and his activities on behalf of the field, sociology was created in Germany. Furthermore, Weber's work played a key role in the development of sociology not only in Germany but also in many other countries, including the United States.

WEBER'S LIFE

Max Weber was born in Erfurt, Germany, on April 21, 1864, and died on June 14, 1920 (Marianne Weber, 1975). Perhaps the most striking thing about Weber's personal life was his long battle with mental illness. This illness is often traced to the tensions that existed between his parents and to his conflicts with his father (Mitzman, 1970). In fact, Weber first manifested his mental illness in 1897 after a fight during which he asked his father to leave his home. Not long after the fight Max Weber, Senior, died and the younger Weber undoubtedly felt some responsibility for his death. In any case, Max Weber began to experience various symptoms of mental illness: depression, agitation, inability to work, and insomnia. From 1897 to 1904, Weber's mental illness was almost totally incapacitating and he produced little work. His mental health began to improve in the early 1900s, coincident with a trip to the United States in 1904. Weber had been invited to give a talk at the Universal Exposition held in Saint Louis. His excitement over his experiences in the United States and the talk in Saint Louis marked a turning point in Weber's life: He began to cope better with his illness. As a result, over the next decade and a half he was able to produce his most important work. While Weber was to suffer many setbacks and recurrences of mental problems, they never again created the problems that they had between 1897 and 1904. What is most important for our purposes is that his work, which had always had a sociological dimension (as we will see below, Weber was trained in law and economics), grew more and more overtly sociological, as did his identity as a sociologist.

The defining struggle between Weber's mother and father not only played a central role in his personal life, it also served to define his sociology. Thus, it is worth taking some time to examine this conflict and its effects on Weber.

Max Weber's father was a politician, although not a leading one, and a bureaucrat in the German government. For example, he held a salaried position as municipal councillor in Berlin, in charge of construction projects such as planting trees along roads, and at various times held positions in the regional and national parliaments. As a result of this political involvement, the Weber household became a center of political discussion and was frequented by many leading politicians. This gave young Max a lifelong interest in politics, both from a practical and an intellectual point of view. Furthermore, in addition to politicians, the Weber home was frequented by leading academicians and intellectuals. The precocious Weber was undoubtedly inspired by his early contact with leading scholars.

Weber's father is described as being middle-class, self-satisfied, and perhaps even lazy. He was very much interested in creature comforts; he is often depicted as being hedonistic or "pleasure-loving" (Mitzman, 1970:21). If he was interested in anything, it was politics and his position within the German political system. His sole ambition seemed to lie in the sphere of his chosen vocation, but even there he was averse to taking risks and making personal sacrifices. He seemed uninterested in the "serious problems of life" and "closed his eyes to suffering and did not share the sorrows of others" (Marianne Weber, 1975:63). He was also very patriarchal, believing that he had the final authority in all family matters. In fact, one cousin described him as "a genuine despot" (Mitzman, 1970:20).

In contrast to his hedonistic and this-worldly father, Max Weber's mother was oriented to self-denial and to the religious and supernatural world. Thus, in many senses Weber's mother and father were opposites. It is worth quoting at length from Weber's biography (written by his wife, Marianne) about his mother:

> There was his mother, in whom the powers of the gospel were active, to whom loving service and self-sacrifice to the last were second nature, but who also lived in accordance with burdensome heroic principles, performed her inordinate daily tasks with a constant expenditure of moral energy, never "left well enough alone," and quietly placed every significant event in the context of eternity. She was dynamic in all she did, energetic in coping with her everyday chores, joyously open to everything beautiful in life, and had a liberating laugh. But every day

Pepper Schwartz: On Becoming a Sociologist of Intimate Sexual Relationships

Pepper Schwartz is one of the leading contemporary sociologists of intimate relationships, especially sexual relationships. Schwartz (1990:363) traces her interest in sexual relationships to her childhood; indeed, she says: "I have been studying intimate relationships all my life . . . being unduly intrigued with the topics of sex, love, and commitment, and being voyeuristic about the lifestyles of others whether or not I felt I could, or should, share them." Her progressive parents exposed her to a wide range of adult books, including the work of leading sex experts such as Havelock Ellis and Alfred Kinsey. When she was ten her parents gave her "sex books," "the usual egg-and-sperm chases and drawings of denuded vulvas and penises—but they were hot stuff to my peer group. I would hold educational sessions where these books were presented and explained" (Schwartz, 1990:365).

At about that time she reassured her girlfriend Sally, who had been caught masturbating by her mother and scolded for it. Schwartz heartened her friend by showing her what scholars said about masturbation and by telling Sally that her (Schwartz's) "mom said it was okay as long as you did not do it in class" (Schwartz, 1990:365). When she was eleven Schwartz organized a "sex information club": "I remember one day we discussed sanitary belts and napkins and passed around products that my mother had provided. Another time we discussed french kissing, but we decided that it did not really happen because it was too yucky" (Schwartz, 1990:365).

In high school, Schwartz (1990:365–366) describes herself as "obsessed with my hormones" and "definitely in heat." She also began to narrow her career choices: "Sometime in this period I decided I wanted to be either an actress, a writer or a *sociologist*. I do not know how sociologist got in there . . ." (Schwartz, 1990:366; italics added). She attended

---

> she plunged into the depths and was anchored in the supernatural (Marianne Weber, 1975:62–63).

Overall, Weber's mother was oriented to religion, was otherworldly, and was energetic, while his father was not religious, was oriented to success and pleasure in this world, and was often quite indolent. Given her religious orientation, Weber's mother was interested in the suffering of others, while his father was concerned with little more than himself and his own well-being. As Mitzman (1970:21) sums it up, there was a fun-

Washington University in Saint Louis because it had an excellent sociology department.

While she dabbled in other fields, Schwartz eventually gravitated back toward sociology, in large part because of the sponsorship of a female professor of sociology, Helen Gouldner:

> Dr. Gouldner decided I was worth spending time on. She submitted a paper of mine (on my theater experiences) to Erving Goffman, who thrilled me by commenting on it. She encouraged me to deliver a paper at an undergraduate sociology conference . . . soon, at her urging, I was interacting with graduate students and taking graduate classes. All this was in my freshman year. . . . Her [Gouldner's] efforts are the real reason I am a sociologist by training as well as by inclination (Schwartz, 1990:368).

Schwartz completed her M.A. at Washington University and moved on to Yale for her Ph.D. At that time Yale was virtually all-male, and Schwartz was stung by the sexism rampant throughout the university: "Until Yale, I had never understood the nexus between sex, sex-role, power and privilege" (Schwartz, 1990:369). Among other things, she became involved with one of the early undergraduate sexuality courses in the United States, and this led eventually to a volume to which she was one of the contributors, *A Student's Guide to Sex on Campus.* By the end of her years at Yale Schwartz had become committed to the sociological study of gender, the family, and sexuality.

Schwartz eventually took a position at the University of Washington in Seattle, where she has remained to this day. She has coauthored several books of note, including *American Couples* (with Philip Blumstein), *Sexual Scripts* (with Judith Long Laws), and *Gender in Intimate Relationships* (with Barbara Risman). In addition, "from time to time I write articles on love, sex, marriage, or sex roles for magazines like *Ladies' Home Journal, New Woman,* or *Redbook*" (Schwartz, 1990:380). Schwartz is currently working on a new book, *A More Perfect Union,* dealing with intimate relationships among modern egalitarian couples.

---

damental conflict between "the pleasure-loving Berlin politician [and] his pious wife." It is hard to think of a man and a woman as different from one another as were Max Weber's father and mother.

The conflict between Weber's mother and father is important for two reasons. First, it made for a tense household, and it is easy to surmise that these tensions laid part of the groundwork for Weber's later mental illness. Second, the conflict between mother and father was transformed into a broader tension between an otherworldly religious orientation (the mother) and a this-worldly, practical orientation (the father). The conflict between otherworldliness and this-worldliness later came to be a defining theme of Weber's lifework. Thus, Weber's personality *and* work were profoundly shaped by the tensions that marked his childhood and young adulthood. Weber evidently had to choose between the orientations of his mother and father. At certain points in his life he opted in his father's direction, while at others he was more oriented to his mother's lifestyle. The choice that he made at any given time affected both his personality and his work.

Early in his life Weber seemed to opt for his father's orientation. His father fancied himself something of an intellectual or at least chose to surround himself with intellectually stimulating people. Intellectuality defined Max Weber from the beginning. As a youth he was a voracious reader. For example, at age twelve he was reading Machiavelli's *The Prince.* At fourteen he demonstrated his propensity for research by creating a map of what Germany looked like in 1360: "The map costs me a lot of effort, because I have to gather the material for it from all sorts of genealogies, territorial histories, and encyclopedias" (Marianne Weber, 1975:46). At fifteen Weber said: "I don't daydream, I don't write poetry, so what else shall I do but read? So I am doing a thorough job of that" (Marianne Weber, 1975:46). Weber not only was doing serious reading at an early age, he also was precocious in his writing. *Before* his fourteenth birthday he wrote historical essays on topics that were to concern him throughout his life: German and Roman history. Two years later he was writing works which reflected his philosophy of history and his views on the patterns that govern historical development.

At eighteen Weber finished gymnasium (similar to high school in the United States), and in 1882 he enrolled at the University of Heidelberg. Reflecting his identification with his father, Weber chose his father's field—jurisprudence—as his major subject and made the law his career objective. However, it is important to our later discussion to make it clear that Weber took a wide range of liberal arts courses at Heidelberg, especially in history, economics, and philosophy. He took no sociology because, of course, there was as yet no sociology in Germany.

Weber not only sought to fulfill his intellectual needs at Heidelberg, he also sought to act out his father's hedonistic side, with which he identified at the time. He became involved in fraternity life, especially his father's old fraternity, where he led a libertine lifestyle defined by heavy beer drinking and dueling. Here is the way his wife describes Weber's lifestyle at this time:

> He . . . attended the obligatory drinking parties two evenings a week, and increasingly lived the life of a fraternity brother. In his third semester he fought the customary duels and received the ribbon. He now indulged

> wholeheartedly in the gaiety of student life, became a jolly good fellow, and soon distinguished himself by his outstanding capacity for alcohol. This was of no small significance in those days, because it was part of a brother's education for manhood that he should be able to pour in the greatest amount of alcohol without losing self-control. The increase in his physical girth was even more striking than the expansion of his intellect . . . he inclined toward corpulence (Marianne Weber, 1975:69).

At Heidelberg, Weber also acquired what was then considered a sign of manhood—a dueling scar. The added weight and the scar were overt reflections of the influence of his father's lifestyle. When his mother first saw him after his initial exposure to university life, overweight and scarred, her immediate reaction was to slap him resoundingly across the cheek. With the slap, she seemed to be rejecting both her husband's lifestyle and her son's identification with it. At the same time she was expressing her outrage over the fact that Max had chosen this course rather than her pious style of life.

The next year, 1883, Weber moved to Strasbourg in order to spend the required year in the army. Weber found the constraints, the monotony, and the meaninglessness of the highly routinized and bureaucratized army life oppressive. As Weber described it, he reacted against "'the tremendous waste of time that is used to turn thinking beings into machines that react with automatic precision upon command'" (Marianne Weber, 1975:72). As we will soon see, this reaction against bureaucratic control was to become another dominant theme in his work. This period also might be seen as the beginning of a reaction against his father because the elder Weber seemed quite content to operate within the constraints of the bureaucratized German political system.

However, another side of Weber and another theme in his work appeared the year after he completed basic military training. In 1885 he returned to Strasbourg for officer training. He was now moving up the military hierarchy, and as a result, he adopted a different view of the system. While he still regarded the military as a "machine," he developed a desire to occupy a leadership position in it and to lead his company into battle on behalf of the "fatherland." This reflected Weber's deep sense of patriotism and desire to see Germany occupy a leading position in the world.

However, it was also during this period that Weber began to shift more in the direction of his mother's values. While not religious, Weber began to devote himself to what he called the "gods of this world" (Marianne Weber, 1975:90), especially the fatherland and science. While these gods were different from the religious one worshiped by his mother, Weber shared his mother's desire to throw himself wholeheartedly into devoted service to a higher purpose. In accepting his mother's willingness to sacrifice herself, Weber was simultaneously rejecting his father's indolent and self-satisfied attitude toward life. Devotion to these larger values inhibited Weber's yearning, derived from his father, to surrender to his hedonistic desires.

When he had completed his first year of military service in 1884, Weber resumed his studies and lived at his parents' home during the year before he returned to Strasbourg as an officer. Although moving away from his father in terms of values, Weber continued to follow his father's career course and interest in the law.

In the winter of 1885–1886 Weber was to take the exam that would make him a junior barrister. However, he first spent a semester at Göttingen. What is notable during this period was his remarkable self-discipline and self-denial, a continuation of his rejection of his father's indolence (even though he was still planning on a career in the law) and his acceptance of his mother's lifestyle:

> He continued his strict work routine, regulated his life by the clock, divided his day into exact segments for the various subjects on instruction, and "saved" after his fashion by preparing his evening meal in his room—a pound of chopped raw beef and four fried eggs [no concern for cholesterol in Weber's day!]. The last hour of his day was reserved for a game of skat. . . . For the rest, he was tempted neither by the winter fun that jingled past his windows nor by spring wanderlust; from the time he stopped dueling, he got no exercise of any kind (Marianne Weber, 1975:105).

Weber had become, much like his mother, an ascetic, or someone who lives a life of rigorous self-denial.

In 1886 Weber passed the required examination to become a junior barrister and took such a position, which carried with it no pay. Weber came to hate the routine, clerical character of this work, saying: "I can look back on part of my period as a [junior barrister] only with horror" (Marianne Weber, 1975:146). As a result of his lack of income, Weber was forced to move back home, where he lived, in the midst of the titanic struggle between the lifestyles of his mother and father, until his marriage seven years later.

During this period Weber embarked on a six-year program to get his law degree. En route, he wrote a lengthy doctoral dissertation dealing with legal and economic history. Soon after defending his first dissertation, Weber began a *second* dissertation, which was required of those who wished to obtain a faculty position at a German university. The second thesis dealt with the agrarian history of ancient Rome.

As he was completing this study in 1892, Weber also began to teach courses in Roman, German, and commercial law. At this point Weber accepted an invitation to study the situation confronting agricultural workers, a study which combined his interests in law, economics, and politics. Weber designed the questionnaire to be completed by landowners and wrote within a year's time a 900–page treatise on agricultural labor. At the time this work was associated with the field of political economy, but today we can see it as Weber's first major step in the direction of sociology. We can think of political economy as a field concerned with the relationship between politics and economics, especially the impact of economics on the political structure of society. In fact, many early sociologists were thought of as political economists, and their work was heavily influenced by the work of their predecessors in political economy. Thus, for example, while we now think of Karl Marx primarily as a sociologist, in his day he was considered a political economist and his thinking was heavily influenced by the work of such notables as Adam Smith, David Ricardo, and J. B. Say. In any case, the study of agrarian workers gave Weber a reputation outside of the law as a political economist and an expert on agrarian labor.

By 1893 Weber had created for himself the possibility of a major career as a professor of law at the University of Berlin. However, his interests had already begun to shift away from law and toward political economy and ultimately sociology. In 1894 the University of Freiburg offered him a professorship in political economy. Weber took that position, but within two years he was offered and accepted a far more prestigious chair in political economy at a much more noted school, the University of Heidelberg.

The following year, 1897, marked the major turning point in Weber's life, as was mentioned at the beginning of this chapter. The unresolved conflict in Weber's life between his mother's and father's lifestyles—otherworldliness versus this-worldliness—came to a head, and he opted for his mother and against his father. In fact, years of pent-up hostility toward his father burst forth, and during a heated argument Weber banished his father from his house. A short time thereafter, perhaps seven weeks later, the elder Weber died, and Max must have felt enormous guilt over this event. As Mitzman (1970:152) says: "It was the first time that Weber had ever revealed to his father the full depths of his bitterness. And he never saw the old man alive again."

At first Weber appeared to take his father's death in stride, but within a short period he began to manifest the psychological symptoms that were to lead to his mental breakdown. On a trip to Spain he was irritable and restless. On the trip home "he was feverish and felt apprehensive" (Marianne Weber, 1975:234). However, by the start of the fall semester he seemed to improve: "'Max is better now, he lives sensibly, goes walking a bit, and several times went to bed early; he sleeps a lot'" (Marianne Weber, 1975:234). There were brief periods of good health followed by periods of psychological distress, but these periods seemed to increase in duration and intensity. He was subject to crying fits and to bouts of insomnia that were to plague him for the rest of his life.

Finally, on doctor's orders, Weber spent a few months the following summer in a sanatorium. In spite of the treatment, his condition did not improve. Most notably, he still suffered from bouts of insomnia.

He was well enough to pick up his teaching responsibilities the next fall term, but after only a few weeks his psychological problems returned. Every lecture became a torment. He was forced at times to suspend lecturing so that he could regain his strength. In 1899 he asked for permission, which was granted, to be relieved of lecturing altogether and concentrate on his small seminar. Of his inability to lecture, Weber said: "'My inability to talk is purely physical, the nerves break down, and when I look at my lecture notes, my head simply swims'" (Marianne Weber, 1975:239). After another failed effort to lecture, Weber asked to be dismissed from his position. However, the authorities were loath to lose him completely and rejected his request, although they did grant him an extended leave without pay. While he was relieved of his duties, things did not improve for Weber: "Everything was too much for him; he could not read, write, talk, walk, or sleep without torment. All his mental and some of his physical functions failed him" (Marianne Weber, 1975:242). His mental condition appeared to reach its low point in 1900. From that point on there was some improvement, although it was very slow at first, with many painful setbacks.

Gradually Weber began to read again, and even more gradually he began to write anew. However, he continued to feel guilty about the fact that he was still receiving his pay as a professor even though he was unable to teach. He renewed his request to be relieved of his professorship, and this time, in spite of great reluctance on the part of the authorities, his request was accepted. In the prime of his life, Weber was without an academic position. It appeared that his career was behind him.

In 1903 Weber was invited to be one of the coeditors (another scholar who was to become well known in sociology—Werner Sombart—was the other) of the *Archiv für Sozialwissenschaft und Sozialpolitik,* which began publication in 1904. In spite of misgivings about his ability to undertake such a task, Weber accepted. This is a key development from our point of view because Weber was now identified, at least in this instance, with social science rather than law or political economy. In the prefatory note to the first issue of the journal Weber declared that it would focus on the factors involved in and the significance of the development of modern capitalism. To deal with this question, Weber sought out the work of people in "general political science, the philosophy of law, social ethics, social psychology, and the research usually grouped together as *sociology*" (Marianne Weber, 1975:278; italics added). The journal was to focus on both empirical and theoretical work in the social sciences.

Weber not only performed an editorial role for the journal, he was also one of its major contributors. In 1904 he published an important essay on methodology that was relevant to an array of social sciences, including sociology. (This essay is still widely read and of great influence in contemporary sociology.) As he neared the completion of this essay, Weber's wife wrote: "Max's study is almost completed. To be sure, his sleep now leaves a lot to be desired; he again eats Camembert every night, has to take soporifics, but is quite pleased that he has accomplished this thing" (Marianne Weber, 1975:279). More important, at the end of 1904 he published in his journal the first part of a work that to this day, for reasons to be discussed later in this chapter, is one of the leading works in the history of sociology, *The Protestant Ethic and the Spirit of Capitalism* (Weber, 1904–1905/1958). From this point on Weber's work became more and more clearly sociological; it became increasingly appropriate to think of him as a sociologist.

Later, I will deal with the significance of this work and related works that were to be produced by Weber to sociology both in its early years and to this day. I will also discuss how this body of work, like the rest of Weber's life, reflected the tension between his parents' lifestyles and philosophies of life. But for now, let us pick up the thread of the rest of Weber's biography.

The publication of the first part of *The Protestant Ethic* coincided with the invitation to Weber to attend a scholarly conference that would be held in conjunction with the Saint Louis World's Fair. The excitement of seeing on a firsthand basis the United States, *the* center of capitalism, allowed Weber to overcome, at least in part, his concerns about his mental health and depart for America in August 1904.

In Manhattan Weber was impressed with America's "capitalistic spirit" and, among other things, the skyscrapers that could be produced as a result of it. However, while he was impressed by the capitalist spirit and its products, he was also put off by the inhumanity of this system. For example, he was critical of American hotels, which seemed to him to be "loveless barracks for traveling salesmen in which everyone was a number. . . . Undoubtedly one could take ill and die without anyone caring!" (Marianne Weber, 1975:281). As we will see, this ambivalence toward capitalism, and more generally toward the modern world, was to be the defining theme of his postbreakdown work. It also reflected yet again the conflict between his father's uncaring careerism and his mother's concern for broader human values.

Moving on to Chicago, Weber saw on a firsthand basis labor violence, crime, racism, the intensity of work in the slaughterhouses, and accidents caused by the public transportation needed to move large numbers of people to and from work. Shaken by what he saw, Weber said, "'Look, this is what modern reality is like'" (Marianne Weber, 1975:287).

At the American colleges and universities he saw continuing signs of the religious spirit that had helped give rise to the spirit of capitalism. However, both of these "spirits," of religion and capitalism, were seen to be on the decline: Only the capitalist structures that the spirit of capitalism had helped to produce were left. This too was to become a major theme in his work. Weber's experiences were directly manifested in the second half of *The Protestant Ethic*, which was published in 1905.

Weber's lecture at the World's Fair went well and was not followed by a major increase in his mental problems. After more traveling in the United States, Weber returned to Germany and enjoyed a new burst of productivity. It was in the post-1904 period that Weber was to produce his most notable work. This work not only solidified his reputation as a sociologist, it did much to help sociology develop in Germany and the rest of the world.

The heart of Weber's work during this period was broadly in the sociology of religion even though Weber was not a religious person. Rather, he had an academic and intellectual interest in the role played by religion in social change. He sought to complement his study of Protestantism in the West with studies of religion in China, especially Confucianism and Taoism (Weber, 1916/1964), and studies of Hinduism and Buddhism in India (Weber, 1916–1917/1958) as well as other world religions (Weber, 1921/1963). As was true of his work in the West, his main interest was in the relationship between religious ethics and economics. More specifically, he was interested in why Protestantism had contributed to the rise of capitalism in the West while the rest of the world's religions seemed to have served as an impediment to the rise of capitalism. More generally, Weber saw capitalism as one manifestation of the process of *rationalization* (see the Introduction and Chapters 8 and 9 for a discussion and extension of this key concept in Weber's work). The West developed not only a rational economy (capitalism) (Weber, 1927/1981) but also rational science (Weber, 1919/1946), political systems (Weber, 1921/1968), cities (Weber, 1921/1968), and even music (Weber, 1921/1958). Thus, the broader question addressed by Weber was why the West was able to rationalize while large parts of the rest of the world were inhibited in the rationalization process. As was the case with capitalism, religious systems clearly played a central role in the development of or the failure to develop all other types of rational systems.

While Weber was now able to produce his most important work, it would be wrong to conclude that his mental problems disappeared after 1904. He continued to suffer from these problems, especially insomnia, throughout the rest of life. In fact, he was often forced to take long vacations in order to retain his mental well-being. It is remarkable that even with the seven-year hiatus (1897–1904) during which Weber was able to do little work and the recurrent bouts with mental illness in his later years, interrupted often by long vacations to help him recoup his psychological strength, Weber was able to produce a monumental amount of work. Even more astounding was the breadth of Weber's ability to deal with many different societies and many different areas of the social world. One can only imagine what he would have been able to accomplish if he had been mentally sound all his life.

A key development in the history of sociology occurred in 1909 when Weber, along with Georg Simmel, Werner Sombart, Ferdinand Tonnies, and others, participated in another important beginning: the founding of the German Sociological Society. The society held its first meeting in 1910. Weber participated in all the substantive discussions and gave a business report in which he defined his image of what sociology ought to be and do. Among other things, he presented his position that sociology ought to be "value-free"; that is, sociologists' personal values should not be allowed to distort their work: "'The question shall be asked as to what *is* and why something is exactly the way it is, but there shall be no judgment as to its desirability or undesirability'" (Marianne Weber, 1975:422). Weber adopted this value-free position because he feared that the sociologists of the day were using their research and teaching to espouse their personal and political values. However, Weber soon withdrew from a leadership position in the German Sociological Society because its members and leaders refused to adhere to his ideas of value-free sociology and insisted on expressing their personal values in their professional statements. Nonetheless, the German Sociological Society had been established, and Weber had played a key role in its creation and in setting it on its future course. While he no longer played a leadership role in the society, Weber retained an interest in it and tried to help further its growth and development.

Over the next decade Weber produced most of his sociology of religion and other work relevant to sociology and was also able to hold teaching positions at Vienna and Munich, to be active in World War I organizing military hospitals, to be involved in German politics, to travel much, and to experience periods of mental distress and disorder. Weber died on June 14, 1920, at fifty-six years of age. While he had a strong reputation as a scholar in general and a sociologist in particular during his lifetime, his reputation has grown dramatically since his death. Today he is regarded as one of the greatest sociologists, if not *the* greatest sociologist, in the history of the discipline. His work is much translated and widely read. It continues to be of enormous and perhaps even increasing influence in sociology.

When exactly did Weber become a sociologist? At one level, the answer is never because he continued to be interested in a wide range of issues in political science, law, and other fields. At another level, the current identity of Weber as a sociologist can be traced to two events. The first was the publication of *The Protestant Ethic* in 1904–1905 and the associated journey to the United States. The second was his key role in the founding and definition of the German Sociological Society in 1909. It is to these two dates and two events that we can trace Weber's sociological beginning. However, it is clear that long before those times and events Weber was doing work that had strong sociological aspects.

Having traced Weber's biography and beginnings as a sociologist, I turn now to a very brief discussion of the central ideas in his sociology. As with his life, I will organize the discussion of his work around the theme of the conflicting influences of his parents.

WEBER'S WORK

Weber produced an enormous amount of work that was to be influential in a number of areas in sociology. His work on bureaucracies had a profound effect on the sociology of organizations. An essay on what Weber called "class, status and party" (in Gerth and Mills, 1946:180–195) played a central role in the sociological study of the ways in which societies are stratified. His thoughts on the city (Weber, 1921/1968) influenced urban sociology. The way sociologists go about doing research has been affected by Weber's (1903–1917/1949) ideas on methodology. Most generally, sociological theory has been strongly affected by his theoretical orientation (Collins, 1985). I cannot go into all his work in this brief section but will focus largely on his work on religion and the theory of rationalization that emerged from it.

In his sociology of religion Weber distinguished between innerworldly and otherworldly religious sects. This distinction may be traced, at least in part, to his father's commitment to his career and satisfaction in this world (inner-worldliness) and his mother's orientation to otherworldly religion. In Weber's sociology of religion, religious sects that led people in the direction of inner-worldliness, especially if it was coupled with ascetic self-denial, were more likely to lead to the modernization and rationalization of the world. In contrast, otherworldly religions led people away from such developments.

The religion Weber focused on in *The Protestant Ethic* was Calvinism, a variety of Protestantism which strongly inclined its followers in a decidedly inner-worldly direction. That is, Calvinists were oriented more to deeds in this life than to reflections on the next life. However, unlike his father's hedonistic orientation to this world, Calvinism induced an inner-worldliness that was subordinated to larger human values. In its commitment to such values, Calvinism was far closer to Weber's mother's values than to his father's. Furthermore, Calvinism preached *asceticism,* or self-denial, which clearly was in line with Weber's mother's orientation to life, an orientation that Weber later adopted. In fact, Weber's mother was a Calvinist. Thus, Weber's interest in Calvinism can be traced to his mother's influence. His ultimate argument that Calvinism was decisive in the rise of the spirit of capitalism in the West can be linked to the fact that in the end he came to identify with his mother rather than his father. This argument is made in *The Protestant Ethic,* and it is to a brief discussion of that work that I now turn.

Weber did not directly link the idea system of the Protestant ethic to the economic structures of capitalism (for example, the marketplace for goods and labor) but was content to link it to another system of ideas, "the spirit of capitalism." Thus, *The Protestant Ethic* is not about the rise of modern capitalism but about the origin of a distinctive spirit that eventually made a capitalist economy possible.

Calvinism, as we have seen, was the version of Protestantism that interested Weber most. One feature of Calvinism was the idea that only some people are chosen for salvation. In addition, Calvinism entailed the idea of predestination; people were predestined to be among the saved or the damned. Calvinists were taught that it was impossible to earn salvation by anything they did. Nevertheless, they naturally had a deep interest in attempting to learn during their lifetimes whether they were to be among the saved or the damned. Hence, they developed the idea of *signs* that could be used as indicators of salvation. People were urged to work hard because if they did, they would uncover the signs of salvation, which were to be found in economic success. In other words, if people were successful in business, it was likely that they would go to heaven.

The Calvinists, like Weber's mother, believed in self-control and an ascetic way of life. They were not to pursue pleasure in this world. Furthermore, they were not to use their business profits to pursue pleasure. Rather, they were to plow those profits back into their businesses so that they could grow even more successful. All these things were not to be isolated acts but rather were to be developed into a whole style of life.

In Weber's view, it was these aspects of Calvinism that led to the spirit of capitalism. As he put it, "the religious valuation of restless, continuous, systematic work in a worldly calling, as the highest means of asceticism, and at the same time the surest and most evident proof of rebirth and genuine faith, must have been the most powerful conceivable lever for the expansion of . . . the spirit of capitalism" (Weber, 1904–1905/1958:172).

It was the spirit of capitalism, a product at least in part of the Protestant ethic, that gave birth to the capitalistic economic system. The Protestant ethic also provided a series of more specific supports to the rise of the capitalist economy. First, capitalists could ruthlessly pursue profit because it was seen not as mere selfishness but as the fulfillment of their ethical duty to seek signs of salvation. Second, it provided the early capitalists with a ready and eager work force. Like their bosses, the workers were eager to succeed at their work so that they too could obtain signs of salvation. Third, it was a comfort to the capitalists to believe that they deserved their rich rewards because they were among the saved. They did not need to feel guilty about the comparative poverty of the workers. Those laborers who failed to prosper deserved such a fate because they were among the damned, and their impoverishment provided evidence of that fact.

Once the worldly economic system of capitalism was in place, it no longer needed Calvinism or any other religious system. Compared to capitalism, any religion, even Calvinism, was otherworldly. Anything that led workers, managers, and owners away from the economic concerns of this world was an enemy of capitalism. Thus, while capitalism was the indirect creation of the Protestant ethic, the capitalist system proved not to be receptive to it or to any other religious system. More strongly, capitalism turned its back on many of the religious ideas that had contributed to its development. Thus, many Calvinists came to be appalled by many of the practices, such as the ruthless pursuit of profit rather than salvation, that came to characterize capitalism.

In a way, the triumph of capitalism over Protestantism represented in the social world the triumph of the viewpoint and lifestyle of Weber's hated father over those of his beloved mother. However, while Weber recognized the advance of capitalism in the modern world as well as the advantages brought about by capitalism, he was a severe critic of it and thus, indirectly, of his father. Note the following critique of the kinds of people produced by capitalism, which also could stand for Weber's criticisms of his father: "specialists without spirit, sensualists without heart; this nullity imagines that it has attained a level of civilization never before achieved" (Weber, 1904–1905:182). Weber would certainly have thought of his father as a spiritless specialist, a heartless sensualist, and a nullity.

Weber not only asked why capitalism arose in the West, he also was interested in why it did not arise in other societies. As was true of his study of the West, the key factor was religion, specifically religious ethics, which in those other societies functioned as a barrier to capitalism. Thus, while the Protestant ethic was a spur to capitalism in the West, Confucianism and the Confucian ethic served as a barrier to capitalism in China (Weber, 1916/1964) and Hinduism and the Hindu ethic played a similar role in India (Weber, 1916–1917/1958). Let us look briefly at these two cases.

The key to understanding Confucianism as a barrier to capitalism in China is the fact that it encouraged a highly bookish literary knowledge. Confucians had to know a body of literature, and movement up the hierarchy was based on performance in tests of that knowledge. This knowledge was bookish and had little or nothing to do with the demands of the position held by the individual. Administrative tasks were seen as being beneath Confucians, things to be delegated to underlings. Confucians were men of culture, not practical men of business. Thus, they emphasized clever puns, euphemisms, and allusions to classical quotations. All this, of course, stood in stark contrast to the Calvinists, who focused on success in the practical world of business. The world view of the Confucians ultimately came to dominate Chinese society, with the result that there was little interest in business or the rational development of the business world.

Confucians also tended to accept things as they were; they were not much interested in changing things. In contrast, Calvinists were interested in any changes that would expand commerce and increase the profitability of their businesses.

Finally, Confucianism did not have within it the kinds of inherent tensions that would impel people to act. In Calvinism that tension was produced by the desire to know whether one was among the saved and to seek signs that that was the case. There was no such tension in Confucianism; indeed, the idea of salvation was foreign to Confucianism. Instead, Confucians were quite content with the world as it was and with their position in it.

The Hindu religion in India posed similar barriers to capitalism. The key idea here was reincarnation. To the Hindu a person is born into the caste in which he or she deserves to be by virtue of behavior in a past life. Meritorious behavior in a past life leads to a high caste in a future life; conversely, misbehavior leads to a lower caste. Salvation could be achieved by faithfully following the rules, and this stood in stark contrast to the innovative behavior brought into being by Calvinism. In any case, activity in this world in Hindu society was not considered important. This world was seen as merely a transient abode and an impediment to the larger and grander spiritual quest. Such a system was highly unlikely to foster the beliefs and behaviors that would lead to a capitalistic economic system.

In the last few pages I have offered a sense of Weber's sociology of religion, especially as it relates to the role played by religions in the development of or the failure to develop capitalism. Actually, this is only part of a broader concern: the rationalization process. The rise of capitalism is only one aspect of a far broader question: Why did the rationalization process proceed in the West while it was inhibited in other societies?

One of the major products of the rationalization process is bureaucracy. The modern bureaucracy was another distinctive development in the West, and organizations in other societies did not measure up to the Western bureaucracy in one way or another. Returning to Weber's biography, it is interesting to note that the bureaucracy was the home of Weber's father. He was a politician, a political bureaucrat deeply committed to the German state. Thus, Weber's interest in the bureaucracy represents an interest in the setting which did so much to define his father.

Needless to say, Weber was deeply ambivalent about the bureaucracy, much as he was about his father. Weber praised many rational characteristics of the bureaucratic form of organization: its efficiency, precision, stability, reliability, calculability, and utility in a variety of areas. Yet while he praised its virtues, Weber was even stronger in his criticisms of bureaucracies. For example, he believed that the bureaucracy "reduces every worker to a cog in this bureaucratic machine and, seeing himself in this light, he will merely ask how to transform himself into a somewhat bigger cog. . . . The passion for bureaucratization drives us to despair" (Weber, 1921/1968:1iii). It is impossible to read this quotation without thinking that Weber had his father in mind. After all, Weber's father is often described as a consummate German bureaucrat eager to make his way up the political hierarchy. Just as bureaucratization in general drove Weber to despair, his father created at least as powerful a negative emotion in him.

Weber's biggest fear was the "iron cage" that he saw as being produced by rationalization and as being best exemplified by the process of bureaucratization. He described bureaucracies as "escape proof" and "practically unshatterable" and among the hardest of institutions to destroy once they are established. Along the same lines, he felt that individual bureaucrats could not "squirm out" of the bureaucracy once they were "harnessed" in it. Weber concluded that "the future belongs to bureaucratization" (1921/1968:1401), and time has borne him out. Society today is far more bureaucratized than even Weber might have imagined.

Finally, the titanic struggle between Weber's mother and father is reflected in his work on the conflict between two major types of rationality: formal and substantive rationality (for more on this, see Chapter 8). Formal rationality is basically the search for maximum efficiency without regard to human values. The bureaucracy would be a good example of formal rationality. The Nazi concentration camp would be an extreme example of Weber's worst fears, a bureaucratic system that was so inhuman that it actually led to the death of millions of people. Substantive rationality, by contrast, is rational action guided by and subordinated to human values. Weber saw a major struggle taking place in the modern world between these two forms of rationality, but he believed that formal rationality was destined to win out.

Returning to Weber's parents, it seems clear that his father represents formal rationality and his mother is an example of substantive rationality. While it would be a simplification, it could be argued that at the broadest level in his sociology and at the widest scale in the social world, Weber played out the terrible conflict between his parents and the incompatible value systems they represented. It might even be said that writing about this struggle in academic terms was a kind of psychotherapy that allowed Weber to emerge from the depths of his mental problems in the last two decades of his life and produce his important work on the relationship between religion and capitalism and on the rationalization process.

CONCLUSION

My goal in this chapter has been to trace the beginnings of Weber's most important sociological ideas to important developments and tensions in his personal life. In discussing the beginnings of Weber's ideas, I have also dealt with the beginning of sociology in Germany. It is because of Weber's sociological work and practical work on behalf of the sociological society that sociology in Germany had its beginnings.

I should close by making the point that Weber's beginnings have been the starting point for generations of later sociologists. That is, many sociologists have taken several of Weber's ideas (value-free sociology, the Protestant ethic, the spirit of capitalism, inner-worldliness, otherworldliness, rationalization, bureaucracy, the iron cage, formal and substantive rationality) as the starting points for their own work. This will be illustrated in terms of some of my own work later in this book (Chapters 7 and 8). Thus, powerful sociological ideas have a long life, providing the starting point for generations of sociologists to follow. Today's sociologists have little difficulty returning to Weber's work and finding insights that set them off in new directions (Sica, 1988; Scaff, 1989). This is one of the things that makes Weber a genius and one of the founders of modern sociology.

CHAPTER 4

The Beginnings of a Sociological School: Chicago Sociology from 1892 to 1935

In Chapters 2 and 3 I dealt with some of the major aspects of the beginnings of sociology in France and Germany. In this chapter I turn my attention to the beginnings of sociology in the United States. In the discussion of the situation in France the unit of analysis was the field of sociology, while in Germany I focused on a specific individual—Max Weber. In this chapter the focus shifts to what is called a school. That is, I will focus on a group of sociologists who shared a common time and place, had a high degree of interaction with one another, and had a common way of doing sociology (Bulmer, 1984). The specific school is the Chicago School of sociology as it existed between 1892 and 1935 (Bulmer, 1984; Mathews, 1977; Faris, 1970; L. Kurtz, 1984). These specific dates were selected because the school was founded in 1892 and had begun to decline by 1935. (For a discussion of the existence of a second Chicago School between 1946 and 1952, see the exhibit in this chapter.)

It should be pointed out that other schools have been significant in the development of sociology. As we have seen, the Durkheimian School developed around Émile Durkheim and his journal, *L'Année Sociologique* (Besnard, 1983). Another can be said to have evolved at Harvard at about the same time the Chicago School began its decline. The Harvard School developed around Talcott Parsons and his major theoretical orientation, structural functionalism. While there have been other schools, the Chicago School will be the focus of attention in this chapter.

Why should we concern ourselves with the beginnings of a sociological school, specifically the Chicago School? The key reason is that the success and influence of the Chicago School were crucial to the initial development of sociology in the United States: "Viewed in historical perspective, the Chicago school was the first great flowering of sociology in the United States" (Bulmer, 1984:8). While there were various developments in sociology before the rise of the Chicago School, it was that school which was of key significance to the rise of American sociology. The Chicago School was of great importance during that period, and it continues to have a powerful and lasting impact on sociology.

As I will detail below, there were a variety of specific reasons for the early influences and success of the Chicago School. First, it succeeded in attracting a number of sociologists, both professors and students, who had a tremendous influence on the field. In many cases their work is still influential in sociology. Second, a journal for the publication of sociological ideas, *The American Journal of Sociology,* was begun in Chicago's sociology department as early as 1895. That journal continues to be one of the most important sociology journals, and its influence is felt throughout the world. Third, the Chicago sociologists influenced many areas of sociology, including theory, methods, and innumerable substantive areas, most notably the sociology of the city, work, deviance, and race. In short, many of the specific areas that characterize modern American sociology can trace their roots to the Chicago School. Finally, the members and products of this school played a central leadership and administrative role in the rise of sociology in the United States. They played a central role in the founding of a national society of sociologists and provided an extraordinary number of presidents of that association through the first half of the century. Thus, in a very real sense, the story of the founding of the Chicago School is to a large extent the story of the beginnings of sociology in the United States. Before I proceed to a more detailed discussion of that school, a little background is needed.

It is difficult to give a precise date for the founding of sociology in the United States. A course in social problems was taught at Oberlin College in Ohio as early as 1858, Comte's term *sociology* was used by George Fitzhugh in 1854, and William Graham Sumner taught social science courses at Yale beginning in 1873. During the 1880s courses specifically bearing the title "sociology" began to appear. The first department with "sociology" in the title was founded at the University of Kansas in 1889. [This department recently celebrated its hundredth anniversary (*Mid-American Review of Sociology,* Spring 1991).] However, the most important date in the history of the founding of sociology in the United States is usually considered to be 1892, when Albion Small moved to the University of Chicago and set up its first department of sociology. (Even Kansas's department, which was founded three years *before* Chicago's, eventually came to be shaped by the Chicago School, as many graduates of Chicago came to hold professorships at Kansas and at many other universities in the midwest and throughout the United States.) This chapter begins with Albion Small's arrival at Chicago.

THE EARLY YEARS

One question worth considering at the outset is, Why Chicago? What was it about the city of Chicago and the University of Chicago that made them the center of the development not only of a significant school of sociology but of schools that were influential in many other fields as well? The short answer is that the youth and dynamism of both the city and the university made them conducive to new and important developments in many domains, including academic fields.

The city of Chicago had grown dramatically during the half century before the founding of sociology at the University of Chicago, and it continued to increase in size significantly throughout the heyday of the Chicago School. Not only was the city of Chicago growing in size, it was being transformed physically. The great fire of 1871 and the subsequent rebuilding of the city played a key role in this transformation, as did the city's emerging role as the rail and stockyard center of the United States. Chicago also boomed as an industrial and finance center, bringing migrants from the rural midwest as well as foreign immigrants from innumerable nations. This "melting pot" played a central role in giving the city its dynamic quality. In addition to lending dynamism to the city, all the changes mentioned above created lots of urban problems that were to play a key role in the development of the Chicago School.

Interestingly, Max Weber, on his visit to the United States, was struck by the nature of the city of Chicago, and it influenced his thinking about the spirit of capitalism. It is worth quoting Weber at length on his feelings about Chicago:

> Chicago is one of the most incredible cities. By the lake there are a few comfortable and beautiful residential districts . . . and right behind them are little wooden houses. . . . Then come the "*tenements*" of the working-men and absurdly dirty streets. . . . In the "*city*" among the "*skyscrapers,*" the condition of the streets is utterly hair-raising. And they burn soft coal . . . everything is haze and smoke. . . .
>
> It is an endless human desert . . . on the horizon all around . . . the city continues for miles and miles, until it melts into the multitude of suburbs. . . .
>
> All hell had broken loose in the "*stockyards*": an unsuccessful strike, masses of Italians and Negroes as strikebreakers; daily shootings with dozens dead on both sides; a streetcar was overturned and a dozen women were squashed because a "*non-union man*" had sat in it. . . . Right near our hotel a cigar dealer was murdered in broad daylight; a few streets away three Negroes attacked and robbed a streetcar at dusk, etc.—all in all, a strange flowering of culture.
>
> There is a mad pell-mell of nationalities . . . the whole tremendous

> city—more extensive than London!—is like a man whose skin has been peeled off and whose intestines are seen at work. For one can see everything—in the evening, for example, on a side street in the "*city*" the prostitutes are placed in a show window with electric light and the prices are displayed! . . .
>
> Everywhere one is struck by the tremendous intensity of work—most of all in the "*stockyards*" with their "ocean of blood," where several thousand cattle are slaughtered every day. . . . There one can follow a pig from the sty to the sausage and the can.
>
> When they finish work at five o'clock, people must travel for hours to get home. . . . Around 400 people are killed and crippled in accidents every year (Marianne Weber, 1975:285–287).

In his casual observations about Chicago Weber anticipated many of the concerns of the Chicago School, including the city itself; its neighborhoods; its racial and ethnic diversity; its problems, such as pollution, crime, and violence; its work settings, such as the stockyards; and its occupations, even deviant occupations such as prostitution. In his analogy between what could be seen when human skin is stripped away and what could be seen readily in the city of Chicago, Weber even anticipated the Chicago School's later interest in using the city as a laboratory to get at basic human processes. If he had chosen to stay in Chicago, Weber would have been a welcome addition to the Chicago School. In any case, at least some members of the school came to be intimately familiar with his work and were influenced by it. Finally, in the above quotation Weber gives the reader a vivid feel for Chicago at the turn of the century.

In addition to all its other characteristics, Chicago was a cultural center, and this contributed to the founding of the University of Chicago in 1890, with the first students being admitted in 1892. Thus, Albion Small arrived at a brand-new university (see below), and the sociology department got its start with the opening of the university. The newness of the university made it open to fresh ideas and to innovative fields such as sociology. Sociology had a far harder time gaining a foothold in more established universities in the United States. Some older Ivy League universities, for example, refused to have sociology departments for many decades. In Europe, with its far older and more traditional universities, sociology had even tougher sledding. As we saw in Chapter 2, it was not until 1913 that Durkheim succeeded in having sociology added to his title, and even then it was only a secondary part of that title. Thus, the establishment of sociology at Chicago, and ultimately in the United States, was aided greatly by the fact that it was a new and open university.

Another important fact about the University of Chicago was that it was, from the beginning, well funded (initially by Rockefeller money) and dedicated to becoming a center of research and graduate training. For example, on the issue of research, the first president of the university, William Rainey Harper, said:

> It is only the man who has made investigation who may teach others to investigate. Without this spirit in the instructor and without his example, students will never be led to undertake the work. Moreover, if the instructor is loaded down with lectures he will have neither time nor strength to pursue his investigations. Freedom from care, time for work and liberty of thought are prime requisites in all such work. . . . It is expected that Professors and other instructors will, at intervals, be excused entirely for a period from lecture work, in order that they may thus be able to give their entire time to the work of investigation. Promotion of younger men in the departments will depend more largely upon the results of their work as investigators than upon the efficiency of their teaching, although the latter will by no means be overlooked. In other words, it is proposed in this institution to make the work of investigation primary, the work of giving instruction secondary (Harper, cited in Bulmer, 1984:15).

Harper did more than encourage his faculty to publish; he also established what was to become the University of Chicago Press to serve as an outlet for the work of Chicago professors and others. Similarly, he urged academic departments at the university to set up their own academic journals.

Furthermore, unlike most other colleges and universities of the day, the focus at Chicago was not on educating undergraduates but on the education of graduate students. Harper said that the goal of higher education was "not to stock the [graduate] student's mind with knowledge of what has already been accomplished in a given field, but rather so to train him that he himself may be able to push out along new lines of investigation" (Harper, cited in Bulmer, 1984:15). Thus, faculty members at the university were oriented to producing new ideas and training the next generation of intellectual and academic leaders. The department of sociology, like the others, shared in this orientation and vision, and this is a major reason why it took the lead in the production of new sociological ideas and the creation of the next generation of sociology professors. It was through these twin influences that Chicago's department influenced sociology not only in the United States but throughout the world.

The importance of the nature of the city and the character of the university came together in the development of empirical research in the university in general and in the sociology department in particular. As was pointed out above, the university encouraged its departments and faculty members to do original thinking and research and to publish their results. Furthermore, the university encouraged public service and involvement in what was taking place in the city of Chicago. Thus, the city became in effect a grand laboratory for social research. In 1893 a sociology department document said: "The city of Chicago is one of the most complete social laboratories in the world. . . . No city in the world presents a wider variety of typical social problems than Chicago" (cited in Fitzgerald, 1990:41). In doing such research, sociologists were satisfying the demands of the university to do innovative work and to be involved in the community and were simultaneously doing the kind of work that would further their own careers as well as the field of sociology. Furthermore, it was hoped that all this research would be of assistance in coping with the social problems that were becoming increasingly evident in this exploding metropolis. In fact, as we saw above and in Chapter 3, Max Weber was stunned by the problems he encountered in Chicago and other American cities during his visit in 1904.

Compared to some other departments at Chicago, the sociology department was, at least at first, slow to develop. However, it was aided ultimately by the early successes of those other departments. For example, the philosophy department under the leadership of the world-famous thinker John Dewey almost immediately became an important force in that field. Dewey and the man he brought with him when he came to Chicago in 1894, George Herbert Mead, played crucial roles not only in the development of Chicago sociology but also in the later development of sociology. The psychology department, in which one of the later leading figures in Chicago sociology, Ellsworth Faris, was trained, also had an influence on developments in sociology.

At the opening of the university in 1892 sociology and anthropology were combined into one department with a grand total of four faculty members. Of the four, only Albion Small was committed to the development of sociology as an academic discipline. Like the sociologists discussed in previous chapters—Comte, Durkheim, and Weber—Small had no background in sociology because of the simple fact that there was little or no sociology, especially departments of sociology focally concerned with the training of graduate students, before the founding of Chicago's department. Small had an undergraduate degree from Colby College in Maine, where he had studied Greek, mathematics, and moral philosophy. He then obtained a degree as a Baptist minister from the Newton Theological Seminary. However, Small did not want to become a minister and instead journeyed to Germany, where he was exposed to sociological ideas. When Small returned to Colby College as a professor in 1881, he began teaching history and political economy (a familiar forerunner of sociology), but he was reading sociology. By 1889 Small had obtained a Ph.D. in constitutional history from Johns Hopkins. Immediately afterward, in 1889, Small was named the head of Colby College, and one of the first things he did was change the course traditionally taught by the president from moral philosophy to *sociology*. Because there were no suitable texts, Small wrote and privately printed *Introduction to a Science of Society* (1890). Sociology in the United States had one of its first leaders, one of its early courses, and its first textbook!

The president of the University of Chicago, William Rainey Harper, invited Small, while Small was president of Colby College, to come to Chicago. Small responded by saying that he indeed wanted to come to Chicago to create a department of sociology: "The academic work which I would do for the rest of my life, if perfectly free to select for myself, would be to organize such a department of sociology as does not exist to my knowledge" (Small, cited in Bulmer, 1984:32). Harper liked the idea of such a new department in the new university. Small's ambitions for the department fit nicely with Harper's ideas for the university in general. The sociology department and ultimately sociology itself were on their way.

Small became the head of the department of sociology at the University of Chicago in 1892, a position he retained until he retired at the age of seventy in 1924. Small's leadership of that department was crucial to the development of sociology in the United States, but he made other contributions as well. For example, when one of the magazines sponsored by the University of Chicago Press folded in 1895, Small suggested that its funds be used to found a sociology journal. This led to the creation of *The American Journal of Sociology*, with Small not only as founder but also as editor and leading contributor. *The American Journal of Sociology* not only led the field for decades, it is still in the forefront of the discipline. In fact, at first it had the field all to itself, for it was not until the early 1920s that other sociology journals were founded. The most important current journal, *The American Sociological Review*, was not founded until 1935 (more on this later in this chapter).

Another key role played by Small was in the founding of the American Sociology Society (ASS, an embarrassing set of initials) in 1905. While its name was subsequently changed to the American Sociological Association (ASA), in part to come up with less awkward initials, that society remains the largest and most important society of sociologists in the world. Small not only occupied a central place in the founding of the society, he played a key administrative role in its development. As a reward for his service to the society as well as his many other contributions to sociology, Small was elected president of the ASS for two terms: 1912 and 1913 (Faris, 1970). Interestingly, Small also played a leading role in the social scientific efforts associated with the 1904 World's Fair in Saint Louis, efforts that were instrumental in bringing Max Weber and others to America.

Thus, in a variety of different ways Albion Small was crucial to the beginnings of sociology at Chicago and in the United States. However, Small's significance lay in administration, *not* in his sociological writings, which have had little lasting impact on the discipline. However, Small created an environment at Chicago and in the nation that was conducive to the rise of other sociologists whose work was to be crucial to the development of the field.

There are various objective indicators of the early success of Chicago's sociology department. Between 1895 and 1915 about a hundred Ph.D.s in sociology were produced in the entire United States, and more than a third of them came from the University of Chicago. Almost half of the first forty presidents of the ASS had been on the faculty or had been graduate students at the University of Chicago. However, such numbers tell only a small part of the story. As we will see in this chapter and the next two, the strongest evidence for the influence of Chicago sociology is its impact on the way sociologists theorized, their research, and their substantive concerns.

To continue the story of the development of the Chicago sociology department, I turn to the contributions of other early leaders of that department. While the contributions of Albion Small were mainly in the area of the organization and institutionalization of sociology, W. I. Thomas's (1863–1947) significance lies much more in his substantive contributions. Following the usual pattern of the day, Thomas was not trained in sociology but received a Ph.D. in literature and classics from the University of Tennessee in 1886. A subsequent year in Germany, where he was exposed to psychology and ethnology (a branch of anthropology concerned with the comparative study of various cultures), led to a change in his orientation. When he returned to the United States, he took a job teaching English at Oberlin College, but his interests continued to move in the direction of the social sciences in general and sociology in particular. Thus, at thirty years of age, in 1893, he began doing graduate work at the University of Chicago. He taught in Chicago's department of sociology and anthropology from 1895 to 1918.

Unfortunately, Thomas's tenure at the university was cut short by scandal. Thomas had always been a controversial figure at Chicago. He seemed to lead a fast lifestyle, including relationships with a number of women. In addition, he did what was at the time considered quite daring research into sexual behavior. On public issues he argued for making illegitimate children legitimate and for disseminating information on birth control. The controversies surrounding these activities came to a head in April 1918, when Thomas was arrested in a Chicago hotel in the company of a woman. He was charged with false hotel registration and with violating the Mann Act. The Mann Act was passed by Congress in 1910 and prohibited the interstate transportation of women for immoral purposes (what was known as "white slavery"). The charges were ultimately thrown out of court (Clarence Darrow was Thomas's lawyer), but the publicity, especially in light of his other activities, led to Thomas's dismissal from the university.

It is said that Albion Small wept when he heard of Thomas's firing, but Small nonetheless seemed to do little to prevent it from occurring. Thomas spent most of the rest of his life as a free-lance researcher, and while he did more significant work, he never again approached the contributions he had made during his years at Chicago. After Thomas was cut off from his institutional base at Chicago, with its colleagues, graduate students, and funds, the significance of his work declined. His career was cut short, and his contributions to sociology were abbreviated by the prudishness and vindictiveness of Victorian American society in the early twentieth century.

While Thomas made a number of contributions to sociology, I want to focus here on his contributions to the methods used by sociologists in their research. Those contributions are mainly embodied in a five-volume work published between 1918 and 1920, *The Polish Peasant in Europe and America,* which Thomas coauthored with a Polish scholar, Florian Znaniecki (Thomas and Znaniecki, 1918–1920). This work was pathbreaking in a variety of ways. Up to that time sociology had been dominated by abstract theorizing (the work of Georg Simmel is a good example) or library research (Marx did much of his later research on the workings of capitalism in the British Museum; Weber and Durkheim got their information on religion in various societies from studying the research and analyses of other scholars).

The Polish Peasant was distinguished by the fact that it involved empirical research, with researchers actually venturing forth into the social world to collect their own original data. Furthermore, the study was not merely a collection of bits of information; rather, it was driven by a variety of theoretical orientations. As a result, the various pieces of data fit together in a broader framework. Thus, it set the standard in America for empirical sociological research driven by a strong theoretical perspective. [Durkheim had made a similar contribution earlier in France with his theoretical statement in *The Rules of Sociological Method* (1895/1964) and then with his application of those theoretical ideas to an empirical study in *Suicide* (1897/1951).] This orientation toward and commitment to empirical research was to become a defining characteristic of the Chicago School and ultimately of American sociology. Unfortunately, as that research evolved, it was not always based on a solid theoretical foundation.

The Polish Peasant was instrumental in the development of sociology in the United States for a number of reasons (Wiley, 1986). First, it gave sociology some distinctive methods and enabled it to set itself apart from fields that relied on historical or library research. Second, its integration of theory and data allowed its authors to make scientific generalizations, and this helped solidify the reputation of sociology as a social *science.* Third, it focused on immigrants, an important topic at a time when this nation was in the midst of massive immigration. No other academic field focused on this important issue, and this aided sociology in achieving the status of a distinct discipline. Fourth, it launched sociologists in the direction of seeking large grants to carry out their research (Turner and Turner, 1990). Thomas had received the then-enormous grant of $50,000 to undertake his study, money that allowed him, among other things, to spend about eight months a year in Europe between 1908 and 1913. To this day sociologists spend a good deal of time and effort seeking out private and federal grants that will allow them to do research. Doing large-scale research was expensive in Thomas's day, but it has grown infinitely more expensive since. As a result, it has become increasingly necessary for sociologists interested in doing large-scale research projects to follow Thomas's model and seek outside funding. Some of this funding comes from private agencies, while the government constitutes a second important source of funds.

Thomas ultimately decided to focus on Polish immigrants rather than other immigrant groups, but not because he had great sympathy for the Poles. In fact, at one point he described them as "very repulsive people on the whole" (cited in Bulmer, 1984:47). However, what attracted him was the fact that a great many documents and other data sources were already available on them. Thus, Thomas's interest in the Polish peasants was animated in large part by the availability of data and the requirements of empirical research.

The distinctive methodology of *The Polish Peasant* was its reliance on documents: "letters, data from newspapers, records of court trials, sermons, pamphlets issued by the clergy and by political parties, the records of peasant agricultural societies," and so on (Bulmer, 1984:51). All in all, during his visits to Poland to gather relevant data, Thomas collected about 8,000 documents or items of information of one kind or another.

Additional information was collected in the United States. A major source of information was 762 letters written to and from Polish immigrants in this country. Here is the way Bulmer (1984:52) describes how Thomas decided to use this research method and this data source:

> Thomas is supposed to have decided to use them [letters] when walking one day down the back alley behind his house, he had to leap aside to

> avoid rubbish being thrown from an upper window. Among the rubbish was a long letter, which he picked up, took home, and discovered was written in Polish by a girl taking a training course in a hospital, to her father discussing family matters. It then occurred to Thomas that such letters could be used as research material.

To obtain the desired letters, Thomas advertised in Polish newspapers in Chicago. Said Thomas, "The idea was mainly to find here and there a big bunch of letters extending over a period of years from the same person, showing changes of attitudes over time" (cited in Bulmer, 1984:52). Eventually fifty sets of such letters were published verbatim in *The Polish Peasant*. The authors' sociological insights were derived *inductively* from the letters. Induction of insights from data, rather than the deduction of such ideas from general theories, eventually came to dominate American empirical research, indeed American sociology. While few contemporary researchers use letters and almost all would find such research "unscientific," the inductive methods employed by Thomas greatly influenced their way of doing sociological research.

A second distinctive method employed by Thomas was the use of the self-reported life history of one Wladek Wiszniewski. Wiszniewski's account of his life experiences was published in *The Polish Peasant*, requiring 312 pages of text. While it was in Wiszniewski's words, the account was edited by Thomas and Znaniecki. The use of this life history allowed the authors to present a subjective viewpoint, a look at the social world from the vantage point of the subject, and this orientation came to dominate a good portion of the distinctive ethnographic research produced by the Chicago School over the following decades.

Interestingly, Thomas did *not* use the specific methods that were to come to dominate later Chicago research: face-to-face observation and interviewing. In fact, Thomas was critical of such methods, especially the interview, for distorting results. From his point of view, the beauty of using documents such as letters and life histories was that they were in the words of the respondents, undistorted by the researcher. In fact, Thomas and Znaniecki felt "safe in saying that personal life records, as complete as possible, constitute *the perfect type of sociological material*" (cited in Bulmer, 1984:55; italics added).

While Thomas and Znaniecki had a valid point, their position did not win the day: Their documentary methods were eventually deemed too unscientific by sociologists. Other methods, especially the interview and the questionnaire, were considered to be productive of far more scientific data. Aware of the possibility of the distortions pointed to by Thomas, researchers have sought to limit them in varying ways and with varying degrees of success.

THE LATER YEARS

In addition to the influence of *The Polish Peasant* and many other works involving substantive insights and theoretical ideas, Thomas was important in bringing another important figure to the University of Chicago, Robert Park (1864–1944). Park had a varied background. Although exposed as a student at the University of Michigan to philosophical ideas, Park felt a strong need to work in the real world. As he said, "I made up my mind to go in for experience for its own sake, to gather into my soul . . . 'all the joys and sorrows of the world'" (Park, 1927/1973:253). Upon graduation, he began his working life as a journalist. He particularly liked to explore the real world, "hunting down gambling houses and opium dens" (Park, 1927/1973:254).

Park wrote about city life in vivid detail. He would go into the field, observe and analyze, and finally write up his observations. In fact, he was already doing in a primitive way the kind of research ("scientific reporting") that came to be one of the hallmarks of Chicago sociology, that is, urban ethnology using participant observation (a method by which the researcher participates directly in the lives of the people being studied) techniques (Chapter 5). It was *this* method, *not* Thomas's documentary approach, that was to come to define the Chicago approach.

However, Park had deeper intellectual and practical ambitions, especially social reform. He became disenchanted with reporting and in 1898, at the age of thirty-four, enrolled in the philosophy department at Harvard. A year later he went to Germany, where he encountered Georg Simmel, whose sociological theory was to have a profound effect on Park's thinking and research. In fact, Simmel's lectures constituted the *only* formal sociological training Park received. Instead, as Park put it, "I got most of my knowledge about society and human nature from my own observations" (Park, 1927/1973:257). By 1904 Park had completed his doctoral dissertation at the University of Heidelberg, but disappointed with that work, he refused a teaching job at the University of Chicago and turned away from academia for a time.

His desire to reform society led him to the Congo Reform Association, which was set up to alleviate the brutality and exploitation of the native people in the Belgian Congo. During this period he met Booker T. Washington and was attracted to the cause of improving the lot of black Americans. He became Washington's secretary and played a key role at the Tuskegee Institute. In 1912 W. I. Thomas came to Tuskegee to give a lecture. Impressed with Park, Thomas invited him to give a course on "The Negro in America" at Chicago, and Park took him up in 1914. The course was successful, and he offered it again the next year. At this point

Park joined the American Sociological Society (he became its president only a decade later). He gradually worked his way into a full-time position at Chicago but did not become a full professor until 1923, when he was fifty-nine years old.

Robert Park played a number of key roles in the beginnings of sociology. He became the leader of Chicago's department during its heyday (1915–1930), a period in which it dominated American sociology. He also played a central role in the American Sociological Society. He was crucial to the graduate program at Chicago and to the training of many graduate students who went on to play key roles in sociology. In his teaching and writing Park was instrumental in bringing European theoretical ideas, especially those of Georg Simmel, to America. In 1921 he coauthored with another Chicago sociologist, Ernest W. Burgess, an important introductory sociology textbook, *An Introduction to the Science of Sociology* (Park and Burgess, 1921), a book that was to shape the views of beginning sociology students for decades to come. Perhaps most important, given his experiences as a reporter, Park was instrumental in the development of the ethnographic study of various aspects of social life in Chicago. Because this ethnographic work involving participant observation was of such great importance to the early years of American sociology, I look at it in some detail in Chapter 5.

The other early leader of the Chicago School, George Herbert Mead (1863–1931), was, ironically, not even a member of the sociology department but rather a professor of philosophy. Although he received no graduate degrees, Mead was hired, as was mentioned earlier, in 1894 by John Dewey as a professor of philosophy at the University of Chicago. A number of graduate students in sociology gravitated to his courses, especially the course entitled "Advanced Social Psychology." Over the years Mead developed a distinctive theoretical position that was of great relevance and significance to sociology. Although he wrote very little, he influenced many sociology students and others through his teaching. In fact, after his death his students pooled their notes from his lectures and published posthumously *Mind, Self and Society* (1934/1962). As the title suggests, the book was concerned with the emergence of mind and self in the process of social interaction. This book became one of the most important texts in the history of sociology.

It was largely through the influence of Mead's thinking that the distinctive theoretical product of the Chicago School, symbolic interactionism (Chapter 5), emerged. Interestingly, the term *symbolic interactionism* was not created until 1937. Said one prominent member of the Chicago School: "'Students at Chicago in the 1920's never heard the term *symbolic interactionism* applied to their social psychology tradition and no member of the department either attempted to name it or encouraged such naming.

Every consideration was given to open exploration, none to naming or defending doctrine'" (cited in Rock, 1979:26). Here is the way Mead's most important disciple, Herbert Blumer, describes Mead's influence:

> [Mead's] influence was along the line of giving to students a clearer picture of the nature of social interaction between human beings, an understanding that the environment or social world of human beings consisted of meaningful objects, a recognition that human beings constructed their action through processes of self-interaction, and an appreciation that group life took the form of fitting together diverse lines of conduct. These features of Mead's social-psychological thought exercised great influence on the research and scholarly perspectives of the so-called Chicago school (Blumer, cited in Kurtz, 1984:36).

While others disagree with Blumer and feel that Mead was less influential during his lifetime, the fact remains that today Mead's work is of overwhelming significance to symbolic interactionism. Symbolic interactionism remains one of the most important theories in contemporary sociology, and I will have much more to say about it in Chapter 5.

REASONS FOR THE DECLINE OF THE CHICAGO SCHOOL

Given its preeminent position in sociology, why did the Chicago School begin to lose that position in the mid-1930s? Several reasons have been put forth to explain this decline (Matthews, 1977). First, a number of the leading figures of the Chicago School departed in the 1930s, if not long before. As we saw above, Small had retired by 1924 and Thomas had been forced to resign long before that. Additionally, in the early 1930s Mead died and Park retired. While Chicago's department retained strong sociologists and other important additions were made to the faculty, it was difficult to compensate for the loss of the early giants of sociology.

Second, by the mid-1930s sociology as a whole had become preoccupied, as it is to this day, with being scientific, that is, with using increasingly sophisticated methods and employing more and more advanced statistical analyses. However, the Chicago School was viewed as emphasizing descriptive, ethnographic studies, often focusing on the subjects' personal orientation. In fact, Thomas had given sociology one of its most famous and enduring ideas in arguing that a major concern of the field was the subjects' "definition of the situation" (Thomas and Thomas, 1928). This means that what matters most is the way in which people, not sociologists, define their social lives. Additionally, it means that people's definitions matter as much as or more than the actual situation. If people

The Second Chicago School?: 1946–1952

This chapter focuses on the Chicago School, but recently a number of scholars have raised the issue of whether a Second Chicago School of sociology can be said to have emerged after World War II and to have existed between 1946 and 1952 (Fine, forthcoming). The presumption is that the original Chicago School ended in the 1930s with the death of Mead and the retirement of Park and later with the departure of many students to participate in World War II. After the war, and with an influx of new students, some argue that a Second Chicago School emerged. While there is considerable debate as to whether it can actually be called a school, there is no doubt that a group of people and activities existed at Chicago during this period that were quite consistent with those which have been associated with the original Chicago School.

Two people who have been or will be discussed—Herbert Blumer and Everett Hughes—are the major links between the Second Chicago School and its predecessor. Both Blumer and Hughes had been trained in the First Chicago School. Blumer stayed on at Chicago, and when the first-generation leaders (especially Mead and Park) had died or retired, he acceded to the leadership position. Hughes had left Chicago for a time but returned to lead the notable group of postwar Chicago sociologists interested in the study of work (Chapter 6).

Among the members of the Second Chicago School whose work I have discussed or will discuss were Erving Goffman, Howard Becker, and Eliot Freidson. These and other products of the postwar Chicago sociology department were identified not only with Chicago but also with its theoretical and methodological orientations: symbolic interactionism and participant observation (or, more generally, qualitative methods, which include anthropological fieldwork). Thus, this group would appear to have many of the qualities of a second school: clear leadership, a coherent group of scholars, a theoretical focus, a methodological orientation, and a significant influence on later generations. As to the latter, Fine (1992b:1) says that for the later generation of sociologists of which he is a member, "this was our *charter*, our legitimation, our history." Thus, it would appear that the Chicago School did have a second new beginning after the end of World War II.

However, it is difficult to be sure that there was any such thing as a Second Chicago School. First, it is not so easy to define the school's time parameters. Blumer had been at Chicago long before 1946, and Hughes did not retire until 1962. Second, there was far more going on in the Second Chicago School (and even the first) than is caught by the labels "symbolic interactionism" and "participant observation." Methodologically, Platt (see Chapter 5) argues that there was far more methodological diversity at Chicago during this period than is usually assumed to be the case. For example, considerable work in advanced statistics and statistical analysis took place at this time as well as in the First Chicago School. In addition, substantively there was also surprising diversity, as reflected in the fact that there was strong interest in population studies (demography) during this period.

Thus, there is doubt that there really was any such thing as the Second Chicago School, but the definition of a school is *always* ambiguous. Even the original Chicago School of sociology had its ambiguities, and the same is true of other schools (the Frankfurt School, the Durkheimian School, and so on). In the end, the issue is: Is there more that serves to make a group of sociologists coherent than serves to separate them? There certainly was a great deal of coherence in the original Chicago School. There was somewhat more diversity in the Second Chicago School, but nonetheless, there is enough coherence for us to be able to call it a school. There was certainly enough of a distinctive impact on later work to think of it as a new beginning in the history of sociology.

Fine (forthcoming) tries to deal with the ambiguities of defining the Second Chicago School by arguing that the whole issue needs to be addressed and interpreted from a symbolic interactionist perspective. That is, what is important is not the "objective" events surrounding the Second Chicago School but rather the way in which they were defined, or socially constructed, by both participants and outsiders at the time. The point is that many insiders and outsiders defined it as a school. And as one of the members of the original Chicago School, W. I. Thomas, taught us many years ago, if people define situations as real, they are real in their consequences. Similarly, contemporary sociologists are also likely to see the people and work associated with Chicago during the postwar period as sufficiently coherent to warrant defining them as part of a distinctive school. The fact that most people would accept the definition of the Second Chicago School and orient their thoughts and actions around that definition is probably at least as important as whether there was objectively any such thing as the Second Chicago School.

However, if we assume that there *was* a Second Chicago School, did it make any difference? Did it lead to important new advances? Colomy and Brown (forthcoming) are among those who argue that it did, that the contributions of that school represented "progress" in sociology. They find progress in various topics to be discussed later in this book, including symbolic interaction theory, the sociology of occupations, and the sociology of deviance. Colomy and Brown are among those who not only accept the idea of a Second Chicago School but also feel that it was of substantial importance to the future of the discipline.

Assuming that it existed, the end of the Second Chicago School can be traced to Blumer's departure for the University of California at Berkeley in 1952. Goffman also left Chicago for Berkeley, and their arrival marked the beginning of what has become a leading, some would say *the* leading, department of sociology in the United States. It also reflected the growth of a new power center in sociology, the Far West.

---

define a given situation in a particular way, then that is what matters. This kind of subjective orientation leads the sociological researcher in the direction of ethnography and away from the kinds of studies (for example, questionnaires) that are easily analyzed statistically.

Given his background as a reporter, Park came to despise statistics, ultimately labeling statistical analyses "parlor magic." To Park, statistical analyses prevented sociologists from analyzing not only subjectivity but also the idiosyncratic and the peculiar. All these things tended to be washed away, he felt, when the researcher was dealing only with a sea of numbers. Interestingly, the fact that important work in quantitative methods (see the exhibit on quantitative methods in Chapter 5) had been done at Chicago by William Fielding Ogburn and others tended to be ignored in the face of the department's association with qualitative methods.

A third factor in the decline of the Chicago School was the growth of other centers of sociology and of resentment toward Chicago's preeminent place in sociology and dominance of both the American Sociological Society and *The American Journal of Sociology*. The growth of sociology in various departments in the East was especially notable, and the Eastern Sociological Society was founded in 1930. Eastern sociologists grew increasingly vocal about the dominance of the discipline by the Midwest in general and by Chicago in particular (Wiley, 1979:63). By 1935 the revolt against Chicago had led to a non-Chicagoan secretary of the ASS. More important, a new official journal of the ASS, *The American Sociological Review*, was founded and the hegemony of *The American Journal of Sociology* was broken (Lengermann, 1979). To this day these two journals vie for preeminence in American sociology. However, while it is still in existence and of great importance and is still based at the University of Chicago, *The American Journal of Sociology* no longer reflects the orientation of the Chicago School as it has been described here. The sociology department at the University of Chicago today is a very different setting with little or no resemblance to its predecessor.

With the events of the mid-1930s, the Chicago School began a descent from its lofty heights. Wiley (1979:63) argues that "the Chicago school had fallen like a mighty oak," but that is an overstatement. As we will see in Chapter 6, Everett Hughes did not return to Chicago as a professor until 1938 (he had gotten his Ph.D. from Chicago in 1928), and it was from that point on that he virtually single-handedly created the subfield known as the sociology of work. Other leading sociologists remained at Chicago and carried on the school's tradition. Most notable was Herbert Blumer (1900–1987), who continued and even extended the Chicago School's theoretical and methodological traditions (Blumer, 1969). In fact, it was Blumer who coined the term *symbolic interactionism* in 1937. Blumer's essays continued to extol the virtues of the Chicago approach. Blumer also occupied leadership positions in Chicago's department, the ASS (he was elected president in 1956), and *The American Journal of Sociology*, which he edited between 1941 and 1952. Furthermore, other sociologists of note, especially Erving Goffman (whose ideas on dramaturgy were mentioned in Chapter 1), emerged from Chicago's sociology department and taught in it. Finally, as is discussed in the exhibit in this chapter, an argument can be made that a Second Chicago School of sociology emerged after World War II, one that included people such as Hughes, Blumer, and Goffman.

WOMEN IN THE EARLY YEARS AT THE UNIVERSITY OF CHICAGO

Up to this point in this chapter, indeed in the entire book, I have been discussing the work of *male* sociologists. But what about the women? Weren't women active in the beginning of sociology in general and more specifically in the beginning of the Chicago School? These questions are especially pertinent since today there are large numbers of women in sociology, many of them occupying leadership positions. Some light has been cast on the issue of the role of women in the Chicago School by the historian Ellen Fitzpatrick in *Endless Crusade* (1990).

Fitzpatrick looks at four women—Sophonisba Breckinridge, Edith Abott, Katharine Bement Davis, and Francis Kellor—all of whom were graduate students at the University of Chicago during its initial decade, 1892–1902. Of the four, only Kellor was trained in sociology (although Davis minored in sociology and worked with Small, Thomas, and George Vincent), but the other three were students in the closely allied, and in those days difficult to differentiate, field of political economy. More generally, between 1893 and 1899 ten women were offered fellowships by the departments of sociology, political economy, and political science; about a quarter of the graduate students in those fields were women. Interestingly, the department of sociology was not as receptive to women as the other departments were. Between 1894 and 1900, seventeen fellowships were awarded to men but only *one* to a woman (Fitzgerald, 1990:80). While its women students were comparatively few in number, the University of Chicago was taking the lead in recruiting female graduate students and offering them economic support.

What happened to these four outstanding women? Interestingly, *none* became professors in their chosen fields. Thus, in the main they made relatively few intellectual contributions to their fields and were not in a position to train the next generation of students, especially female students. The sociologist, Francis Kellor, did not even complete the work for her Ph.D. Despite this, she published four articles in *The American Journal of Sociology* and in 1901 published a book entitled *Experimental Sociology.*

The fact was that while women such as these could gain entry into Chicago's progressive graduate program, they had a far more difficult time breaking down the barriers for women who wanted to hold academic posts in colleges and universities throughout the United States. During the University of Chicago's first fifteen years, nine women obtained doctorates in sociology, political science, and political economy but not one was able to obtain a regular teaching position at a coeducational college or university. In contrast, two-thirds of their male classmates were able to obtain such positions (Fitzgerald, 1990:72). However, these women had been drawn originally by the University of Chicago's reform orientation and interest in social problems and their solutions. Thus, faced with barriers to academic careers, and with an interest in reforming society, these four women tended to drift into nonacademic positions.

Katharine Bement Davis received her Ph.D., cum laude, in 1900. Instead of an academic job, Davis became the superintendent of the new women's reformatory at Bedford Hills, New York. Kellor left the university without a degree in 1902 and got involved in community work. Breckinridge received a doctorate in 1901 and said: "'Although I was given the PhD degree magna cum laude . . . no position in political science or in Economics was offered me. The men in the two departments . . . went off to positions in College and University Faculties'" (cited in Fitzgerald, 1990:82). Instead of obtaining such a position, Breckinridge entered law school at Chicago and obtained a law degree in 1904. Still unable to find a position in the social sciences, she was finally able to find an instructorship in Chicago's newly created department of household administration. It was acceptable for a woman to hold an academic position in such a sex-segregated department. Abbott was able to obtain a faculty position after she received her degree (magna cum laude) in 1905, but her position was at Wellesley, a women's college. After a year she returned to Chicago, but not to the university, in a research capacity related to social welfare. All four of these women, denied access to a normal academic career, opted for careers that brought their training to bear on social problems and social reform.

The interesting thing about all four women is that although they were unable to follow a normal academic career, they all had a far larger impact on American society than did their colleagues who moved easily into academic positions. Although several of them published important books and articles, their major contributions lay in the public arena. Davis made her mark as a prison superintendent and was eventually named commissioner of corrections in New York City. Davis took that position in 1914 and was the first woman to hold a cabinet-level position in the New York City government. Kellor eventually became chief of the New York State Bureau of Industries and Immigration. More important, she became a leading figure in Progressive party politics and was a close adviser to Theodore Roosevelt in the election of 1912. Abbott and Breckinridge were founders of the School of Social Service Administration at the University of Chicago, where they became associate professors. This school was the forerunner of modern schools of social work.

Thus, what happened to women in the early years of the Chicago School? Denied traditional academic careers, they made important contributions to the larger society. In many ways their contributions were greater and more long-lasting than those of their male colleagues who were able to follow normal academic careers. Thus, in an odd twist of fate, American society benefited from the sexism that impeded the careers of these women. It seems certain that if it were not for this kind of sexism, this chapter, as well as many others in this book, would have much more to say about the contributions of women to various sociological beginnings.

CONCLUSION

In this chapter I have focused on the beginnings of the Chicago School and its central role in the beginnings of sociology in the United States. This school developed a coherent orientation to the social world, and around that orientation there developed a cluster of academics and students. This group of sociologists was central not only to the development of sociology in the United States but also to the growth and spread of the distinctive Chicago approach to social issues. In Chapter 5 I continue this story with a discussion of the evolution of Chicago's distinctive methodological and theoretical contributions to the beginnings of sociology.

CHAPTER 5

Methodological and Theoretical Beginnings: The Chicago School, Participant Observation, and Symbolic Interactionism

In this chapter I pick up the story of the Chicago School, this time focusing on its two best known and most distinctive contributions to sociology. These contributions involved two of the discipline's most important aspects: methods and theories. *Methods* are the tools used by sociologists to collect data that are of importance to them. Sociological *theories* are systems of ideas that are used to make sense out of those data. Thus, there is, or at least there should be, a close relationship between sociological methods and theories. That relationship is made even closer by the fact that while theories may be derived from various sources, they often emerge from empirical research. Thus, the methods chosen by sociologists affect the kinds of data they collect, and those data in turn affect the nature of the sociological theories derived from them.

There are many methods in sociology, including participant observation, questionnaires, interviews, and experiments in the laboratory or the social world. Similarly, there are many sociological theories, including symbolic interactionism, structural functionalism, conflict theory, exchange theory, and ethnomethodology. Each of these methods and theories has its own beginnings, and each of those origins could be traced in this chapter. I have chosen to focus on participant observation and symbolic interactionism because they were, respectively, the most important methodological and theoretical innovations of the Chicago School. Thus, a discussion of their origins fits in nicely with the historical story that I began in Chapter 4 on the Chicago School and will continue in Chapter

6. That is, both participant observation and symbolic interactionism had their origins in the Chicago School and were important to early Chicago sociologists interested in the study of work.

I focus on this specific method and this particular theory for several other reasons. First, because of the similar historical origins and parallel development of participant observation and symbolic interactionism, there is a coherent story to be told here rather than the discrete stories that would have to be recounted in the case of other methods and theories. Second, as was pointed out above, both participant observation and symbolic interactionism continue to be important in contemporary sociology, whereas some other methods and theories that were of importance in the 1920s and 1930s have ceased to be important. Finally, it is possible to describe participant observation and symbolic interactionism in terms that a beginning sociology student can understand, whereas other methods and theories are often too complex and technical for a newcomer to the field. This is not to imply that participant observation and symbolic interactionism do not have their own complexities. What makes participant observation and symbolic interactionism more easily understood is the fact that they have strong affinities to things that people, including readers of this book, do in their everyday lives.

I should reiterate that while the origin of these orientations in the Chicago School is of historical interest, they also remain significant in contemporary sociology. Thus, in reading about these historical beginnings, the student is also learning about theoretical and methodological aspects of contemporary sociology.

One other introductory point needs to be made: While participant observation and symbolic interactionism had their origins at the University of Chicago, primarily in the 1920s and 1930s, neither existed in an explicit and formal sense until late in this period. The early Chicago sociologists employed this method and utilized this theory, but not in a self-conscious manner. Furthermore, they did not have the labels we now apply to them. As was pointed out previously, the term *symbolic interactionism* was first coined by Herbert Blumer in 1937. Similarly, the term *participant observation* can be traced to the publication of Paul Cressey's *The Taxi Dance Hall* in 1932 (Madge, 1962:117). Although they may not have had the labels we now possess, the early Chicago sociologists were practicing the theories and methods those labels describe.

PARTICIPANT OBSERVATION

A variety of observation techniques are used in sociology. While all are related to participant observation, only one can be seen as "pure" participant observation. *Exploratory observation* is the most informal and subjective of the observation techniques and is therefore closest to the kind of observation in which we all engage. This technique is employed by sociologists before they begin a research project. They use exploratory observation techniques to uncover the issues or questions they will study when they actually undertake the planned research. Exploratory observation helps define the proposed research project. It is not really a research tool but a preresearch tool and will concern us no further here.

The remaining four types *are* research tools, and this categorization is based on the way in which sociologists participate in the groups being studied (Gold, 1969). The first type and the one of greatest concern here is (pure) *participant observation.* There is nothing mysterious about participant observation; its name describes the method very well. That is, the sociologist becomes a participant in the group or community that is being studied and then observes, usually over months or even years, what takes place in that setting. Researchers become members of the group or community, but they always retain their identities as researchers. In other words, they cannot become so involved in the group or community that they lose their objectivity or forget their research agenda. While the researcher becomes a member of the group being studied, he or she does *not* inform the group members that a research project is being undertaken. The researcher may purposely mislead the subjects or simply fail to mention that in addition to belonging to the group, he or she is doing research. After the research has been completed, the observations are written up in order to describe and better understand key aspects of the social setting being studied.

The second observation technique is called *participant as observer.* The major difference between this method and "pure" participant observation lies in the fact that subjects *are* informed that they are being studied. In fact, this technique has come to be used more frequently than pure participant observation because it avoids most of the ethical questions that arise when researchers disguise their identity. Ethical purity is gained at the expense of lost information because the researcher's intent and identity are known to group members. Subjects are less likely to be completely honest with known researchers than with people they believe to be fellow members of the group. However, devotees of this approach reply that the participants quickly forget that a researcher is in their midst and behave as they would under normal circumstances.

The third technique associated with this genre is *observer as participant.* This method is differentiated from participant as observer by the fact that it is most frequently used in studies requiring a single visit to a community or stay in a group and does not require multiple visits or lengthy stays. A researcher using this technique may spend an hour or a day observing subjects rather than the weeks, months, or even years required in the first two types. Because of these time limitations, this technique must be more structured than those two methods. Researchers must have a fairly clear idea of what they are looking for and must focus their observations on those issues. This is a more efficient method, but it is also restrictive. As a result of time constraints and a more rigid format, the observer as participant is less likely to make unexpected discoveries. This is a serious problem because in many ways the great strength of observation techniques lies in the ability to make such discoveries.

While there is, as we have seen, a "pure" form of participant observation, the term is almost always used to describe all three of the types discussed above. I will follow that precedent in this chapter. The fact is that in all three types the researcher is an observer and a participant.

The fourth technique is the *complete observer*. This is the only one of the four types in which the researcher does not in any sense become a participant in the group or community being studied. Thus, in a strict sense this type falls outside the domain of participant observation. In this case, the researcher is a total outsider and the group members are completely unaware that they are being observed and studied. The researcher simply observes what occurs in the group and records what he or she sees without becoming part of the group. The researcher may use disguises, subterfuges, or even a one-way mirror to observe the group without being detected. This kind of observation can be carried on for short or long periods, although the longer the research project, the more likely it is that the researcher will be uncovered. It has the asset of most observation techniques of allowing for the discovery of unforeseen social phenomena. It can be either highly structured or highly unstructured. Its major drawback lies in the fact that as an outsider, the researcher is not privy to the kinds of information that can be obtained by a researcher who is also considered an insider by the group. In other words, it lacks the advantages of the other three methods, all of which involve the researcher in the group.

Although I will focus on participant observation in this section, we will see that the Chicago researchers also often used a variety of other methods. Chicago sociologists engaged in what is now known as multimethod research (Brewer and Hunter, 1989), that is, the use of a number of different methods to study the same research question (see the exhibit on quantitative methods). Nevertheless, it was participant observation for which they were best known.

Everyone is an observer of the social world. More specifically, we all at times have been participant observers. That is, we all have participated in certain groups and communities with or without letting the members know that our intention was to observe. What, then, differentiates the

Quantitative Methods in the First and Second Chicago Schools

While I am focusing on the Chicago School's qualitative methods, especially participant observation, the researchers associated with that school used many different methods. Although the school was associated with qualitative methods, the fact is that there was also a significant concern with quantitative methods. This was true of both the first (Bulmer, 1984) and second (Platt, forthcoming) schools.

One of the ironies of the association of the First Chicago School with qualitative methods is that inscribed on the Social Science Research Building which housed the department is a quotation from Lord Kelvin: "When you cannot measure/your knowledge is/meager/and/unsatisfactory" (cited in Bulmer, 1984:151). Qualitative research, especially participant observation, is long on description and short on measurement. However, there was a far stronger emphasis on quantitative measurement in the First Chicago School than is often assumed.

Bulmer demonstrates that quantitative work occurred in the early years of the First Chicago School, but the key development came later with the hiring of William Fielding Ogburn in 1927. Ogburn had been a professor at Columbia University. The sociology department at Columbia was known for its quantitative emphasis, and Ogburn was one of its leading practitioners. The following is an excerpt from a recruiting letter sent to Ogburn in 1926: "'We are weak in statistical work and you would have full charge of as much of that as you cared to cultivate'" (cited in Bulmer, 1984:170). In a letter to the vice president at Chicago, the case for Ogburn was made in terms of the growing importance of quantitative work: "'The statistical aspect of sociology is obviously of the highest importance. The development of statistics in all fields has been very rapid and our work here needs such a man imperatively'" (cited in Bulmer, 1984:171). When Ogburn accepted the position, his appointment was described in the following way: "'Professor Ogburn's chief interest in research is in the quantitative aspects of sociology. He plans to develop the statistical approach in a way not hitherto done at the university'" (cited in Bulmer, 1984:171). Thus, in recruiting Ogburn, the Chicago School was clearly admitting its relative weakness in quantitative studies and the need to strengthen itself in that area.

Once on the scene, Ogburn began teaching courses on methods and statistics. In fact, his arrival in the sociology department marked the beginning of serious quantitative work that was to have a long-term impact on the development of sociology. Eventually, many of Ogburn's students, most notably Samuel Stouffer, became notable quantitative researchers. There was an interdisciplinary emphasis on quantitative methods at Chicago, and especially notable from this point of view is the fact that the noted Chicago psychologist L. L. Thurstone had considerable influence on the quantitative sociologists at Chicago. As a result of these factors and many others, Chicago's sociology department rapidly became a major center of quantitative research. The work of people such as Ogburn, Thurstone, and Stouffer had a profound effect on the development of quantitative sociology.

However, given the qualitative core of the Chicago School, it should come as no surprise that there was considerable conflict between quantitative and qualitative sociologists. For example, one member of the school recalled that departmental softball games of that period tended to pit a team of qualitative sociologists against one made up of their quantitatively oriented peers. Thus, a struggle was being fought out on a softball diamond that was also being waged in the discipline as a whole. No matter which group most often emerged victorious on the diamond, in the field as a whole the future belonged to the quantitative researchers.

Just as the First Chicago School was more diverse methodologically than is often assumed, so too was the Second Chicago School (Platt, forthcoming). Looking at the postwar Chicago sociologists, Platt finds considerable diversity among the faculty members, with those who were interested in highly quantifiable areas such as demography-ecology being as numerous as those associated with qualitative methods. Similarly, in looking at theses and dissertations, Platt finds that while many used qualitative methods, this was *not* the dominant methodology. Platt also compared published articles by Chicago and non-Chicago scholars and found that the Chicago sociologists were only slightly more likely to use qualitative methods than were others. In spite of the lack of strong findings on the qualitative (participant observation, fieldwork) orientation at Chicago, Platt (forthcoming:26) concludes that "even if fieldworkers were never dominant at Chicago, there was a noticeable cluster there when there was no equivalent at other leading schools; their presence could, thus, reasonably be seen as a distinguishing feature of the department." In short, the Second (or, for that matter, the First) Chicago School may not have been predominantly qualitative, but it was far more qualitative than other comparable programs.

---

sociologist as participant observer from the layperson who uses the same technique?

First, the layperson is usually very casual in making observations, while the sociologist makes observations systematically and rigorously. Second, years of training and experience in doing this kind of research have led to lots of guidelines and dos and don'ts for professional sociologists who engage in participant observation. The researcher is provided with all this knowledge before going out into the field, while the layperson is left to learn on his or her own in the field. Third, when sociological researchers venture into the field, they are often looking for specific aspects of the social world and are therefore more likely than lay observers to discover them and learn many things about them. However, it should be clear that a sociologist using this method must be open to unforeseen but nonetheless significant aspects of the social world. Fourth, sociologists, unlike laypeople, systematically record what they do as well as the results obtained. A layperson, by contrast, is unlikely to pass on information obtained or methodological lessons learned in a systematic way.

Thus, sociologists, unlike laypeople, are able to develop a body of knowledge based on participant observation research. Since the methods used have been recorded, later researchers can replicate the research project to see whether similar results can be obtained. Furthermore, we can be more certain of the results obtained by sociologists compared with lay observation because sociologists publish their results, which are then subjected to critical review by their peers in the field. In this way, erroneous conclusions tend to be weeded out while "correct" findings tend be supported by additional research.

All in all, while participant observation is generally considered to be a "soft"—that is, not highly scientific—method, it is clearly "harder"—that is, more rigorous—than lay observation. Furthermore, the Chicago sociologists, contrary to received wisdom in sociology, tended to see themselves as "scientists" and participant observation as a scientific methodology. However, participant observation *is* softer than many other sociological methods. For example, findings are filtered through the eyes and ears of the researcher. Thus, the question arises, How much of what is reported is biased by the perceptions and orientations of the researcher? Practitioners of harder methods such as experiments and questionnaires also attack participant observation studies for their inability to provide a body of cumulative knowledge. Observational studies are typically aimed at adding seemingly random bits of information to the existing body of knowledge rather than building a cumulative body of knowledge. Such researchers are likely to gather data in a previously unexamined group or community. The collection of additional discrete pieces of information is characteristic of this type of research. Furthermore, the data collected by participant observers are usually qualitative in character, and it is far more difficult to develop cumulative knowledge from such data than from the quantifiable data obtained through research methods such as questionnaires and interviews. The basis for the accumulation of knowledge in a strict scientific sense—that is, the testing and refining of hypotheses with the ultimate objective of developing a general theory involving a set of such hypotheses—is generally absent in observation research.

For their part, participant observers have taken a strong stand against the kind of *scientism* practiced by the supporters of harder methods. In this context, it is important to examine the thoughts of Herbert Blumer, who, as we have seen, was one of the leading figures in the Second Chicago School (see the exhibit in Chapter 4). Blumer is particularly important here because he is notable not only for his thoughts on participant observation as a method but also for symbolic interactionism as a theory. In other words, he represents the key linkage between the two concerns of this chapter.

Blumer attacked the harder methods associated with a more scientistic approach to sociology and defended participant observation by leveling several attacks on scientism. First, he argued that scientific sociologists were trying to be fashionable in "seeking to emulate the advanced procedures of physical sciences" (Blumer, 1969:34). While it may be faddish to be scientistic, that does not mean that this is the best approach for issues of concern to sociologists. Second and more specifically, Blumer asserted that such sociologists were trying to use certain aspects of the scientific model that were inappropriate to sociology. Among these aspects, Blumer attacked the tendency to wholeheartedly embrace mathematical schemes and statistical approaches, develop increasingly precise quantitative techniques, and insist that sociologists follow the canons of research designs that are more appropriate to the natural sciences. Third, scientific sociologists start with and give priority to a theoretical model and then test hypotheses derived from it. The emphasis is on the model and on the scientific techniques needed to use it to study the social world. This stands in contrast to the approach preferred by Blumer and implicit in participant observation:

> To begin with, most research inquiry (certainly research inquiry modeled in terms of current methodology) is not designed to develop a close and reasonably full familiarity with the area of life under study. There is no demand for the research scholar to do a lot of free exploration in the area, getting close to the people involved in it, seeing it in a variety of situations they meet, noting their problems and observing how they handle them, being party to their conversations, and watching their life as it flows along (Blumer, 1969:37).

Implied in the latter part of this quotation is a preference for participant observation: free exploration, observing, being involved in conversations, watching life as it proceeds along.

This leads to Blumer's fourth critique, the substitution of scientific procedure for firsthand knowledge of the social world:

> I merely wish to reassert here that current designs of "proper" research procedure do not encourage or provide for the development of firsthand acquaintance with the sphere of life under study. Moreover, the scholar who lacks the firsthand familiarity is highly unlikely to recognize that he is missing anything. . . . In this way, the established protocol of scientific inquiry becomes the unwitting substitute for a direct examination of the empirical social world. The questions that are asked, the problems that are set, the leads that are followed, the kinds of data that are sought, the relations that are envisioned, and the kinds of interpretations that are striven towards—all of these stem from the scheme of research inquiry instead of familiarity with the empirical area under study (Blumer, 1969:37–38).

Finally, scientistic techniques do not, in Blumer's view, permit the researcher to get close enough to the social world to uncover that which is hidden from view. According to Blumer,

> the empirical social world consists of ongoing group life and one has to get close to this life to know what is going on in it. . . .
>
> The metaphor that I like is that of lifting the veils that obscure or hide what is going on. The task of scientific study is to lift the veils that cover the area of social life that one proposes to study. The veils are not lifted by substituting, in whatever degree, preformed images for firsthand knowledge. The veils are lifted by getting close to the area and by digging deep into it through careful study. Schemes of methodology that do not encourage or allow this betray the cardinal principle of respecting the nature of one's empirical world (Blumer, 1969:38–39).

In addition to attacking hard methods, Blumer makes the case for what are usually considered soft methods such as participant observation. Indeed, Blumer rejects the idea that participant observation *is* a soft methodology:

> How does one get close to the empirical social world and dig deeply into it? This is not a simple matter of just approaching a given area and looking at it. It is a tough job requiring a high order of careful and honest probing, creative yet disciplined imagination, resourcefulness and flexibility in study, pondering over what one is finding, and a constant readiness to test and recast one's views and images of the area. . . . It is not "soft" study merely because it does not use quantitative procedure or follow a premapped scientific protocol (Blumer, 1969:39–40).

If we all informally do participant observation on a regular basis, how did this method come to be associated with the Chicago School? The key figure in this development was Robert Park. Several aspects of Park's background and orientation led him in the direction of using various techniques, including those which ultimately came to be grouped under the heading of participant observation. Park in turn led many of his students and colleagues into the field to do research that was primarily reliant on this methodology.

First, I must remind the reader of Park's background as a newspaper reporter between 1891 and 1898. For one thing, this led Park, once he became a sociologist, to focus on the city. For another, it led him to the belief that sociologists were to use the same methods as reporters, largely the gathering of firsthand information on what was taking place in the social world. Park was quite explicit about the relationship between his background as a reporter and his research orientation, stating that

> it was . . . while I was a city editor and a reporter that I began my sociological studies. . . . In the article I wrote about the city (1915) I leaned rather heavily on the information I had acquired as a reporter regarding the city. Later on, as it fell my lot to direct the research work of an increasing number of graduate students, I found that my experience as a city editor in directing a reportorial staff had stood me in good stead. Sociology, after all, is concerned with problems in regard to which newspapermen get a good deal of firsthand knowledge. Besides that, sociology deals with just those aspects of social life which ordinarily find their most obvious expression in the news and in historical and human documents generally. One might fairly say that a sociologist is merely a more accurate, responsible, and scientific reporter (Park, cited in Blumer, 1984:91).

A second influence on Park was anthropology and its methods. Park had become familiar with anthropology through his contacts with W. I. Thomas and while he was working as Booker T. Washington's secretary. The observational methods of anthropology fit in nicely with Park's predilections given his background as a reporter:

> Urban life and culture are more varied, subtle, and complicated [than primitive life and culture], but the fundamental motives are in both instances the same. The same patient methods which anthropologists . . . have expended on the life and manners of the North American Indian might be even more fruitfully employed in the investigation of the customs, beliefs, social practices, and general conceptions of life prevalent in Little Italy on the lower North Side of Chicago, or in recording the more sophisticated folkways of the inhabitants of Greenwich Village (Park, cited in Blumer, 1984:91–92).

Third, these conceptions led Park to the idea of using the city as a "social laboratory" in which to study social life. However, he considered it to be a laboratory very different from the artificially created laboratories used by psychologists to study their subjects. Park believed that it was necessary for sociologists to go out and study people in their natural environment. To get at people in that environment, it was clear that at least one major research method had to be participant observation.

Fourth, Park's training in philosophy led him to an understanding of the importance of getting at the subjective point of view of the subjects being studied. As Park put it, "what sociologists most need to know is what goes on behind the faces of men, what it is that makes life for each of us either dull or thrilling" (Park, cited in Blumer, 1984:93). Thus, Park sought to go beyond the detached and often cynical approach taken by reporters. Instead, sociologists were to be involved with the people they were studying, *to be participants* in the groups under analysis. Furthermore, their observations were to involve an effort to see the world as the members of the group did. This meant an emphasis not only on observation but also on the use of personal documents [for example, the personal letters and diaries used by Thomas and Znaniecki (1918–1920) in *The Polish Peasant*] that reflect the viewpoint of the actors involved.

In fact, although I am focusing on participant observation here, it would be wrong to assume that Park and his students relied solely on that single method. As pointed out earlier, Chicago researchers used a variety of methods, almost all of them relying on the subjective viewpoints of the subjects being studied. Thus, the use of letters and diaries, like participant observation, was based on such points of view.

With these perspectives, Park, along with his colleague and sometime coauthor Ernest W. Burgess, played a key role in sending students out into the field to study social life on a firsthand basis, utilizing participant observation as one of the preferred methods. Here is what Park told his students:

> You have been told to go grubbing in the library, thereby accumulating a mass of notes and a liberal coating of grime. You have been told to choose problems wherever you find musty stacks of routine records based on trivial schedules prepared by tired bureaucrats and filled out by reluctant applicants for aid or fussy do-gooders or indifferent clerks. This is called "getting your hands dirty in social research." Those who counsel you are wise and honorable; the reasons they offer are of great value. But one more thing is needful: first-hand observation. Go and sit in the lounges of the luxury hotels and on the doorsteps of the flophouses; sit on the Gold Coast settees and on the slum shakedowns; sit in the Orchestra Hall and in the Star and Garter Burlesk. In short, gentlemen,

> go get the seat of your pants dirty in real research (Park, cited in Blumer, 1984:97).

It was this call that led many graduate students at the University of Chicago to go out in the field and study social life on a firsthand basis, and it was those studies that played a key role in defining the research produced by the Chicago School of sociology. Let us look at one of those studies and the ways in which it reflected the Chicago approach in general and participant observation in particular.

The study of concern here is Nels Anderson's *The Hobo* (1923/1961). Anderson (1975), in fact, had been a hobo; indeed, he was in the process of leaving that world through his graduate work at the University of Chicago:

> I did not descend into the pit, assume a role there, and later ascend to brush off the dust. I was in the process of moving out of the hobo world. To use a hobo expression, preparing the book was a way of "getting by," earning a living while the exit was under way. The role was familiar before the research began (Anderson, cited in Blumer, 1984:98).

Anderson did his research and spent most of his time in the Madison–Halstead Street area of Chicago, the center of what was known as "Hobohemia." In fact, Anderson (1983:403) took a room in what he described as a "workingman's hotel" in that area, where he slept and worked for more than a year. He recalled that the only advice he ever received from Park (although Burgess was his adviser) was "Write down only what you see, hear, and know, like a newspaper reporter" (Anderson, cited in Blumer, 1984:98).

In reporting what he saw and heard, Anderson was operating as a participant observer. The following are some of his descriptions based on spending a night at a flophouse, "Hogan's Flop":

> The air was stuffy, the light dim. I walked around the place looking for a place to lie down. Dozens of men were sleeping on the floor with their heads to the wall. Some were lying on paper, others on the bare floor. Some were partly covered by their overcoats; some had no overcoats. . . .
>
> I found a vacant place on the floor where I could have about two feet between myself and my nearest neighbor so I spread my papers and lay down. . . . I asked the man nearest me if the bugs bothered him much . . . . Another man chimed in. He said they were better organized than the German army. How well organized they were I can't say but I was not long in learning that they were enterprising. . . .
>
> After an hour or so I felt something on my hand. I crushed it. There were others to be seen on the white papers. I lay down to try to sleep again. A second attack brought me to my feet. . . .

> A man jumped to his feet and hastened out. He was cursing the bugs and saying that he knew an engine room that had this "place beat all hollow." I felt better. Someone else had weakened first. I got up and started home (Anderson, 1923/1961:32–33).

This quotation makes clear the great strength of participant observation: its ability to offer a vivid sense of the world being studied.

While it is best known for its use of participant observation, *The Hobo,* like most other Chicago studies, involved the use of other methods as well. For example, Anderson conducted nearly 400 interviews. He describes his informal interviewing technique (a technique that formally involved the interview method but that we would today associate with participant observation) as follows:

> Wisely or not, I began with informal interviews, sitting with a man on the curb, sitting in the lobby of a hotel or a flop house, going with someone for a cup of coffee with doughnut or rolls. I had to develop some system for these interviews, as I had to devise some system in writing them down. . . .
>
> I discovered that one sitting next to someone else can effectively start conversation by thinking out loud. It invites attention and one needs but to come out of his reveries, tell of the thought in mind. One must avoid causing those approached to feel that he is after something; the price of a beer, a cup of coffee or a meal. One must expect to do some spending but must keep at the level of frugal spending (Anderson, 1975:165–166).

In many ways *The Hobo* was *not* pure, classical participant observation. First, a participant observer is ordinarily first and foremost a sociologist. However, as Anderson makes clear, he was still primarily a hobo, albeit one who was struggling to escape from that position through his social research. He seemed to be more at home with hoboes than with researchers. Anderson identified himself psychologically more as a hobo than as a researcher. Second, Anderson seemed to be very casual in his observation and interviewing techniques: He did not use the somewhat more formal approach that came to define later researchers. This may be because *The Hobo* was the first of the major studies produced by graduate students at Chicago. It was also the case because neither Park nor Burgess was very directive in guiding graduate students, including Anderson. Finally, *The Hobo* involved the use of a variety of different methods, not just participant observation. Nonetheless, as Anderson (1975:170) points out, it became known for its use of participant observation: "the book made me known among sociologists, thousands and thousands of students were required to read it as an example of 'participant observer' sociological research, a term which did not get into the sociological vocabulary until long after the study had been done."

Anderson was followed by a number of other Chicago graduate students [for example, Landesco's (1929) study of organized crime and Cressey's (1932) study of the taxi-dance hall] whose works, while characteristically employing a variety of methods, are best known for their use of participant observation.

SYMBOLIC INTERACTIONISM

Symbolic interactionism developed as a theoretical perspective at the University of Chicago during the same period when participant observation was evolving as a method. The major figure in the development of this theory was, as was pointed out earlier, George Herbert Mead. Although Mead was a professor in the philosophy department, his courses were popular with graduate students in sociology.

Symbolic interactionism is difficult to define succinctly. In fact, one analyst has said that it has a "deliberately constructed vagueness" and a "resistance to systematisation" (Rock, 1979:18–19). Nevertheless, a few basic ideas can give the reader a sense of symbolic interactionism. First, it assumes that human beings, unlike lower animals, are endowed with the capacity to think. While this is an innate ability, it is shaped by our interaction with others, such as parents and teachers. Through interaction, people also learn meanings and symbols that allow them to exercise their distinctively human capacity for thought. Symbols are social objects that stand for whatever people agree they should stand for. Symbols can be words ("fire!"), physical artifacts (a crucifix), or physical actions (a clenched fist). Especially important to the capacity to think are words as symbols, or more generally what we mean by language. To a symbolic interactionist, thinking is essentially an internal conversation that we carry on with ourselves using words. These meanings and symbols not only allow people to interact with themselves (think) but also allow them to interact with others. Finally, it is the patterns of these human actions and interactions that make up groups and societies. To put it more succinctly, it is through interaction that people learn symbols and it is through those symbols that people are able to interact with themselves and others and produce what symbolic interactionists consider to be society.

Thus, symbolic interactionism is concerned with people's ability to think and looks at society as a series of actions and interactions. These two characteristics set it apart from two other broad theoretical perspectives that were competing for dominance in sociology in the 1920s and

1930s and are competing even to this day. On the one hand, there is "behaviorism," a perspective which rejects the importance and sometimes even the idea of people's thoughts. On the other hand, there is "sociologism," which focuses on large-scale social phenomena such as Durkheim's social facts and sees people's thoughts and actions as being determined by those phenomena (Tiryakian, 1962). Furthermore, sociologism contends that what people think and do is determined by these large-scale social phenomena.

We can learn a great deal about symbolic interactionism by examining how its supporters sought to differentiate themselves from those who accepted behaviorism and sociologism. Once again we return to the work of Herbert Blumer.

In line with the general position articulated above, Blumer clearly saw symbolic interactionism as being embattled on two fronts. On the one side were the behaviorists, who saw human behavior as caused by external stimuli. On the other side were those who adopted a sociologistic perspective and saw behavior as caused by the larger culture and the structures of society. Blumer was troubled by both perspectives largely because they saw action as mechanistically caused by external factors rather than as being created by people. In Blumer's view, what is important in the social world is the fact that people are endowed with the conscious ability to create their social actions and interactions and do so on a regular basis.

Blumer regarded behaviorists as psychological reductionists and rejected them on that basis. That is, behaviorists reduced all social phenomena to automatic responses to stimuli. An external stimulus is applied, and the person is seen as reacting automatically much as a cat reacts to putting a paw on a hot stove. Behaviorists ignore both the mental and social processes involved in human action. These processes allow people to create and construct their responses to situations rather than merely having responses forced upon them by external stimuli.

Blumer rejected other perspectives for much the same reason. For example, he criticized sociologists and psychologists who relied on the conventional notion of "attitude" to explain human actions (Blumer, 1969:94). In his view, most social scientists think of an attitude as an "already organized tendency" that exists within the actor's consciousness. Thus, actions are seen as being impelled by attitudes. This is another example of mechanistic thinking. To Blumer, what is important is not attitude as an internalized tendency "but the defining process through which the actor comes to forge his act" (Blumer, 1969:97). Again, the imagery is of actors constructing ("forging") their acts rather than having them impelled by the operation of internal forces.

Blumer was also critical of reductionistic theories that saw action as impelled by either conscious or unconscious motives over which people have no control. Reductionists see people as being impelled by these motives rather than adopting the view, accepted by Blumer, that people are in control of their motives. A good example of what Blumer was critiquing is Freudian theory, which sees people as being obliged to act in the way they do because of the coercive impact of psychological forces such as the id and the ego. In short, Blumer was opposed to any psychologistic theory that ignores the processes by which people construct their actions as well as their social worlds.

On the other side, Blumer was opposed to sociologistic theories that view human actions as being impelled by large-scale external forces. He had in mind theories that focused on phenomena such as the social system, social structure, culture, roles, norms, and values. In Blumer's view, it is people who define what it is that they do, not these larger forces. Furthermore, there was a tendency among symbolic interactionists to reject the whole idea of such large-scale social phenomena. What existed and mattered were people and their thoughts, actions, and interactions. In general, the view that was adopted by symbolic interactionists contended that society was nothing more than the sum total of those thoughts, actions, and interactions.

Thus, to Blumer society is not made up of large-scale social structures. The essence of society is to be found in actors and action: "Human society is to be seen as consisting of acting people, and the life of the society is to be seen as consisting of their actions" (Blumer, 1969:84). Human society is action; group life is a "complex of ongoing activity." However, Blumer does not go so far as to suggest that society is nothing more than isolated human acts. There is also collective action in which individuals fit "their lines of action to one another" (Blumer, 1969:85). However, the key here is that it is what people do that matters; it is people, busily involved in fitting their lines of action together, who make up the collective life of society. These actors are actively involved in creating collective life; they are not passively constrained by it.

However, Blumer, at least at times, does have a sense of what sociologists call "emergence," or the fact that large-scale social phenomena grow out of—"emerge from"—human action and interaction. Blumer called these large-scale phenomena *joint action,* a term that clearly suggests that the roots of these phenomena lie in human action. Each joint action is formed anew by social actors. However, Blumer recognizes that these joint actions are likely to take on well-established and repetitive forms. In the end, Blumer was prepared to give even these large-scale phenomena only a very limited role in his sociological view of the world. For example, he most often thought of these large-scale phenomena as little more than "frameworks" within which the really important aspects of social life—

action and interaction—take place. Large-scale structures set the conditions and place limitations on human action, but they do not determine it.

Even when he recognized preestablished patterns of action, Blumer hastened to underscore the equal or greater importance of unprescribed action. Not only are there many unprescribed areas of the social world, even in prescribed areas joint action has to be consistently created and recreated.

Overall, Blumer and later symbolic interactionists rejected any perspective, psychologistic or sociologistic, in which "human actors who are acting are either bypassed or swallowed up" (Blumer, 1969:3). Instead of being swallowed up by other forces, human actors are the center of their sociology.

THE IDEAS OF ERVING GOFFMAN

To give this discussion more depth, I want to return to the ideas of Erving Goffman (1959), especially his thoughts on the way in which people use dramaturgy to manipulate social situations. In terms of the previously discussed front stage–back stage distinction, the focus here is on what people do in the front stage.

Generally, people try to present an idealized image of themselves in the front stage. They want to present themselves in the best possible light to those with whom they are interacting. Doing this requires that through the use of various dramaturgical techniques they conceal things about themselves that would serve to destroy the idealized image they are seeking to present. First, they may want to conceal secret pleasures engaged in before the performance. For example, your life insurance agent might have been drinking before coming to your house to sell you a new policy. Aware that you would be less likely to buy insurance from someone who appears to be drunk, the agent might have gulped several cups of coffee before visiting and may suck on mints during the appointment to hide the odor of alcohol. Similarly, people may want to conceal things about their past lives. For example, the hypothetical life insurance agent would not want you to know that he or she served time in prison for embezzlement.

Second, people seek to conceal the errors they made in preparing for a performance as well as steps they might have taken to correct those errors. The life insurance agent might have made some errors in calculating the rates you need to pay and then hurriedly done some new calculations immediately before his or her visit. Since you are likely to lose confidence in an agent who makes such errors, the agent would try to conceal this from you.

To take another example, people may seek to conceal the "dirty work" (a concept, as you will see in Chapter 6, that Goffman borrowed from Everett Hughes) involved in preparing the end product to be presented during the performance. In the case of the life insurance agent, the end product is the proposal for new insurance. What the agent would not want you to know is that he or she is dealing with a shady underwriter and that the insurance policy is therefore valueless. (To see how other Chicago sociologists describe and theorize about deviance, see the exhibit Labeling Theory and the Second Chicago School in this chapter.)

In addition to concealing various things in performances, people engage in more positive dramaturgical actions. For example, the performer often wants to foster the impression that he or she is closer to the audience than is actually the case. A real estate agent wants you to believe that he or she is interested in you and what is best for you. Furthermore, the agent wants you to believe that the performance that is being put on for you is unique and that there is a special relationship between you and the agent.

While at times the actor may pretend that he or she is very close to the audience, at other times the actor may want to convey the impression that he or she is quite distant from the audience. For example, a surgeon often tries to convey the impression of being removed from (dispassionate about) a patient's problems. This dramaturgical device is used to give the patient greater confidence in the ability of the surgeon to perform the operation. Presumably, patients would worry about the capabilities of an overly emotional surgeon.

What Goffman is describing is what he called *impression management*, the things we do to manage the impressions we make on others. This idea was the subject of a study of university students and the way they manage impressions after having examinations returned and receiving their grades (Albas and Albas, 1988). The authors differentiate among three types of students: "Aces" (those who received high grades), "Middle of the Roaders" (average grades), and "Bombers" (poor grades). The focus of the study was on the Aces and the impression management strategies they design to allow themselves to reveal their high grades to others without appearing to be immodest and on the Bombers and the strategies they use to conceal their poor grades.

While the norm of immodesty prevents the Aces from overtly expressing their joy over their high grades, they often employ an impression management strategy of "repressed bubbling," through which their satisfaction is made to appear as though it were seeping through against

Labeling Theory and the Second Chicago School

Paul Colomy and J. David Brown (forthcoming) argue that one of the many products of the Second Chicago School was what has come to be called the *labeling theory* of deviance. One of the leading figures in the creation of labeling theory was Howard S. Becker, a sociologist whose work we will encounter again in Chapter 6 in terms of his contributions to a product of both the First and Second Chicago Schools: the sociology of work. In fact, Becker fashioned his labeling theory by drawing on his training in and knowledge of the sociology of work.

Becker (1963, 1964) drew on the work of both predecessors (Lemert, 1951) and contemporaries (Erikson, 1961; Kitsuse, 1962) in formulating his approach to labeling theory. More generally and more importantly in the context of this chapter, labeling theory was in line with and heavily influenced by symbolic interactionism.

Labeling theory focuses on the social process by which some individuals label others as deviant. Also of interest is the way individuals change, especially in terms of self-image, when they have been successfully labeled as deviant. This process is consistent with symbolic interactionism for three reasons. First, it focuses on interaction, or the labeling of one person by another. Second, it deals with changes in the self and the self-image. Third, the deviant label itself is seen as highly symbolic, with powerful implications for the way in which society views the person being labeled.

The process of becoming deviant usually begins when people perform acts that are disapproved of by certain members of society. Some people rape, steal, or become mentally ill. These behaviors may result from various social causes (for example, poor home life or community), but the labeling theorist focuses not on these underlying causes but on the labels that are created and applied to these people. From a labeling perspective, a deviant is simply someone to whom a deviant label has been successfully applied (Becker, 1963:9). Thus, it is not necessary for someone to commit a "deviant" act in order to be so labeled. For behavior to be considered deviant, it simply must be labeled as such because

> social groups create deviance by making rules whose infraction constitutes deviance and by applying these rules to particular people and labeling them as outsiders. From this point of view, deviance is not a consequence of the act the person commits, but rather a consequence of the application of rules and sanctions to an "offender" (Becker, 1963:9).

In other words, no specific behavior is inherently deviant; behavior becomes deviant only when others define and label it as such. Later Becker (1964:2) says, very much in line with symbolic interactionism, that deviance is "always and everywhere a process of interaction between at least two kinds of people: those who commit (or are said to have committed) a deviant act and the rest of society, perhaps divided into several groups itself."

In order to have deviance we must have not only someone who is seen to have committed deviance but *social control agents* who are in a position to create and enforce social rules. In other words, there are two types of social control agents: *rule creators* who devise rules (and norms and laws) and *rule enforcers* who enforce those rules. From the point of view of labeling theory, deviants and social control agents need each other to exist. There would be no deviants without rules, and there would be no social control agents without deviance. While we usually think of formal agencies as rule creators (for example, Congress) and rule enforcers (for example, the police), we all act on occasion as both. For example, your parents undoubtedly created rules for you when you were a child and then acted to enforce them, for example, by "grounding" you if you violated a rule. If you continually violated those rules, your parents were likely to have labeled you as a deviant, perhaps more specifically as a "problem child."

One of Becker's distinctive contributions, as was pointed out above, was to bring the sociology of work, as derived from the Chicago School, to bear on the issue of deviance. Among other things, this led him (1963) to think in terms of "deviant careers," and as we will see in Chapter 6, the study of careers is central to the Chicago approach to the sociology of work. To Becker, the end result of the labeling process was that at least for some individuals, deviance becomes a career. They come to organize their self-concepts around the deviant label. Labeled as deviant, they are less and less able to associate with "straight" members of society. At the same time, they are more likely to associate with others with the same deviant label. Ultimately, a subgroup of deviants is formed, and as a result, the deviance that society sought to control through the labeling process becomes more, rather than less, likely to occur. The group develops and passes on to its members ever-improved ways of practicing the deviant behavior.

While labeling theory has critics such as Rodgers and Buffalo (1974), it remains an important theoretical approach to the study of deviance. As such, it is a direct legacy of the Second Chicago School and a more indirect inheritance from the original Chicago School in general and symbolic interactionism in particular.

their will. Thus, a slight grin, quickly wiped away, makes it obvious to others that the Ace has done well on the exam. A more overt strategy involves Aces "accidentally" allowing others to see their high grades. Similarly, Aces may ask others how they did on the exam with the expectation that they will respond by asking the Aces how they did, thus allowing the Aces to reveal their high grades.

While Aces try to reveal their grades, Bombers use impression management to conceal their performance. For example, anticipating poor grades, Bombers may not attend the class in which the exam is to be returned or may leave at the first possible moment after the exam has been returned. Bombers may also remain but make it absolutely clear that they do not want to talk about the exam. Or they may simply lie and tell others how well they did.

Goffman (1961) also developed the concept of *role distance,* an idea that helps us further understand the impression management techniques of Bombers. Role distance involves the fact that people often try to separate, or distance, themselves from the roles they are in. A Bomber may express role distance by appearing to be uninvolved in the student role. More specifically, Bombers may act as if they were unconcerned about their grades and may appear nonchalant when exams are returned.

One of Goffman's most interesting works is *Stigma* (1963). A *stigma* may be said to exist when there is a gap between what people ought to be and what they are actually like. Anyone with such a gap may be said to be stigmatized. Goffman differentiates between two types of stigma and the fact that the two types present different dramaturgical problems. The first type involves a *discredited* stigma, that is, a stigma which is obvious to the audience. An example would be a person who is a paraplegic or has lost a limb. The second involves a *discreditable* stigma, one which is not known by the audience or perceivable by it. Examples would include someone who has had a colostomy and a homosexual passing as straight. For someone with a discredited stigma, the basic impression management problem is to handle the tension associated with having people know about one's problems. For someone with a discreditable stigma, the problem is managing information so that the problem remains unknown to the audience. However, in both cases the key point is that people must engage in impression management.

Most of *Stigma* is devoted to people with obvious, often grotesque stigmas, for instance, the loss of a nose. However, as the book unfolds, the reader realizes that Goffman is really saying that we are *all* stigmatized at one time or another or in one setting or another. That is, all of us on occasion, if not regularly, must deal with a gap between what we are supposed to be and what we actually are. His examples include Jews passing in a Christian community, a fat person in a group of people with normal weight, and an individual who has lied about his past and must constantly make sure that the audience does not learn this. When looked at from this point of view, *all* of us have been stigmatized at one time or another in our lives, and thus as human actors we have had to engage in impression management to reduce tension (if the stigma was discredited) or manage information (if the stigma was discreditable).

By according human actors center stage, we can begin to see why symbolic interactionism (and Goffman in particular) and participant observation grew up together at the University of Chicago and fit so well together. While the symbolic interactionist urged that we focus theoretically on the human actor, the participant observer focused attention in social research on the actions of human beings. In short, both the theory and the method have the same focus.

CONCLUSION

In this chapter I have continued the story of the Chicago School, focusing on the beginnings of its important methodological (participant observation) and theoretical (symbolic interactionism) perspectives. It is necessary to remember that both of these aspects can also be seen as important ideas that played a key role in the later development of sociology. In addition, they were ideas that led to the development of bodies of research and theorizing that were themselves productive of many other ideas.

I turn in Chapter 6 to one final aspect of the Chicago School (First and Second): its role in the creation of a key substantive concern in contemporary sociology, the sociology of work.

CHAPTER 6

The Emergence of a Sociological Specialty: The Case of the Sociology of Work

In this chapter I continue to discuss the Chicago School of sociology, this time focusing on the emergence within that context of one of sociology's substantive specialties: the sociology of work (Ritzer and Walczak, 1986; Abbott, forthcoming). Sociologists have a wide range of specialties, including medical sociology (Wolinsky, 1988), the sociology of deviance (Simon and Eitzen, 1992), the sociology of race and ethnic relations (Feagin and Feagin, 1993), and even the sociology of sport (Vogler and Schwartz, 1993). There are as many specialties in sociology as there are areas of social life [see any conventional textbook in introductory sociology for a discussion of many of these specialties, for example, Kammeyer, Ritzer, and Yetman (1992)]. There are stories to be told about the beginnings of all these specialties. I have opted to focus on the sociology of work because it fits in nicely with the previous discussions of the Chicago School and because it is one of my areas of specialization. One of the reasons it fits so nicely is that sociologists of work, at least in the early years of the field, tended to use participant observation as their method and symbolic interactionism as their theoretical orientation.

The key figure in the history of the sociology of work is Everett C. Hughes (Becker et al., 1968). Hughes received a Ph.D. from the University of Chicago in 1928. After a stint as a professor at McGill University in Canada, he returned to Chicago in 1938, a time when the First Chicago School had already passed its prime and was in the early stages of its descent. Hughes remained in the department until 1961 and played a major role in it from 1938 on (he was chairman of the department for a time), especially in the Second Chicago School. More specifically, Hughes succeeded in institutionalizing the sociology of work and giving it a highly distinctive orientation in spite of the fact that the distinctive departmental orientation was being gradually but inexorably transformed. Nevertheless, Hughes was highly influenced by the methodological emphasis at Chicago on participant observation and the distinctive theoretical orientation toward symbolic interactionism.

While I will focus on the role played by Hughes and his students and disciples, it would be a mistake to assume that there was no sociology of work before Hughes and the Chicago School. For one thing, Hughes's influence on the sociology of work was not restricted to his years at Chicago; he also had an impact in his pre-Chicago days at McGill (Solomon, 1968:4–5). He continued to influence the field and newcomers to it in his postretirement years as a professor emeritus at Brandeis University and Boston College.

Sociologists had studied work before Hughes arrived on the scene; in fact, most of the leading sociologists in the history of the discipline had devoted some attention to work, and in some notable cases it lay at the center of their studies.

PREDECESSORS IN THE SOCIOLOGICAL STUDY OF WORK

Clearly, Karl Marx (1867/1967) was, among other things, a sociologist of work. Many of his writings were oriented to the study and critique of the nature of work in capitalist society. Marx started with the view that people obtained meaning, in fact even fulfilled themselves as human beings, in their work. To be human, people had to produce things, and it was in the act of production that people fulfilled their human nature. However, all known societies had served to *alienate,* or separate, people from their work—from the production process and from the finished product (Marx, 1932/1964). As a result, people were not able to affirm their human nature in their work.

It was Marx's view that alienation reached its peak in the capitalist system. In that system, the owners (capitalists) controlled the production process and owned the finished products. Instead of working for themselves to fulfill their human nature, workers (the proletariat) were laboring for capitalists in order to make the capitalists wealthy. The capitalists imposed work on their employees, and it was often so repetitive and simplistic that proletarians found it impossible to express their creative energies in their work. Further, the products that emerged from the work process belonged not to the proletariat, as Marx thought they should, but to the capitalists. Thus, the workers were alienated from both process and products and, more generally, from their work.

Marx described and criticized the alienation of the worker under capitalism in great detail. More important, he urged the creation of a communist society in which workers would not be alienated (Marx and Engels, 1848/1948). They would not be alienated because they would not be separated from the production process and from the final products. That is, the workers, taken collectively, would "own" both that process and the products that emanated from it. Clearly, Marx was a sociologist of work, and his ideas, especially the idea of alienation, have had a profound influence on that field (Blauner, 1964). To this day sociological studies of work continue to be done from a Marxian perspective (Abbott, forthcoming).

Work was almost as central to the writings and research of Max Weber (1921/1968) as it was to the work of Karl Marx. For one thing, Weber accepted Marx's ideas on alienation and even extended them. That is, Weber argued that people were alienated not only in the work world but in other settings as well. Specifically, Weber described the alienation of people in bureaucratic systems and in the military. In other words, it is not just production workers in the factory who are alienated but also office workers, soldiers, and many other types of workers. The extension of the idea of alienation into the office and to white-collar workers is especially important today because the work world has come to be dominated by such employees. The manual, blue-collar workers who were of concern to Marx are of less and less importance in the work world, at least in the United States.

Weber's (1904–1905/1958) major ideas on work are embedded in his thoughts on the rise of capitalism in the West and the barriers to the creation of such an economic system in other societies. In his focus on capitalism, Weber, unlike Marx, was not focally concerned with the issue of the exploitation of the worker. As we saw in Chapter 3, his main concern was with how capitalism created an environment and an atmosphere in which entrepreneurs were motivated to maximize their profitability. That environment and atmosphere were created by the Protestant ethic, which led to the spirit of capitalism, which in turn led to the capitalist economic system. It was this process that interested Weber the most, although he did recognize the Marxian view that in maximizing their profits, capitalists were also driven to exploit their employees.

Weber's greater significance in the sociology of work, as was pointed out above, was to shift attention from the manual worker to the office worker. This shift in focus resulted not only from Weber's concern with alienation but, more generally and importantly, from his interest in the increasing importance of the bureaucracy and the bureaucrat in modern Western society. Weber described the nature of bureaucratic positions as well as the character of the work of bureaucrats. While he felt the bureaucracy was indispensable, he was, as was pointed out before, concerned about the alienation confronting these white-collar workers. He also worried that these workers were being "harnessed" into these bureaucratic systems and had little or no possibility of escape. Weber's interest in this kind of work is of increasing significance today as fewer and fewer workers work in factories and more and more have white-collar bureaucratic jobs.

The third great figure in the history of sociology, Émile Durkheim, also concerned himself with the nature of work. In Durkheim's (1893/1964) writings this took the form of a concern with the division of labor in modern society. Durkheim saw the world changing historically from one with relatively little division of labor to a modern society in which there is an enormous division of labor. Thus, while in more primitive societies people tended to be jacks-of-all-trades, in the modern world there is a high degree of specialization. Instead of each of us doing all kinds of work ourselves, we specialize in a particular occupation (secretary, manager, college professor, and so on). Society is held together by the fact that we no longer can survive on our own but require the results of the work of many people in many occupations.

Another aspect of Durkheim's contribution to the sociology of work is related to his focal concern with the problem of *anomie*, or the sense of normlessness or rootlessness that characterizes people in modern society. In Chapter 1 we encountered Durkheim's application of this idea to suicide; here I discuss the way he applied it to the work world. (Like alienation, anomie has proved to be a key idea in sociology, one that has lain at the base of much work in the field.) In earlier societies, with their modest division of labor, people were essentially alike. They were held together by a strong, shared morality. Thus, people were united by what they believed in strongly and collectively, and this common morality gave them a strong sense of their roots in society. As a result, there was little or no need for formally instituted constraints such as laws.

However, that common morality has eroded in the modern world with its elaborate and growing division of labor. Because people are so different and are involved in so many varied activities, there is little of a shared morality to hold them together. Thus, in Durkheim's view, they tend to have a far greater sense of rootlessness, a far higher level of anomie, than do people in simpler societies. One of Durkheim's solutions to this problem was to form occupational associations which were to bring together all the people in all the different occupations in a given industry. These associations were to create, in a more limited way, the strong common morality that characterized earlier societies and thus could reduce the problem of anomie.

Thus, the sociology of work had its beginnings long before the accomplishments of Everett Hughes at the University of Chicago. In fact, many other sociologists did sociological analyses of the work world before Hughes's involvement in the field. However, in most cases, especially in the case of such far-ranging theorists as Marx, Weber, and Durkheim, the concern for work was subordinated to a larger set of issues and concerns. With Hughes as well as many sociologists who came after, work became *a,* if not *the,* focal concern. Hughes gave a focus to the sociology of work, and as a result mainly of his efforts, it was able to coalesce as a distinctive subfield of sociology around his contributions, those of his students, and the way he defined the nature of the field. Thus, while there were many predecessors, the sociology of work as a distinctive subfield began with the contributions of Everett Hughes.

Hughes was not only a student of Robert Park but also his close friend. As Hughes makes clear, Park and his sociological perspective played a key role in the development of his interest in occupations:

> Since I belonged to no interesting minority and had no special cause on my mind when I went to graduate school, no thesis topic was built into my system. I was what one might call a footloose soul. Robert Park and the sociological view of the world rescued me. I wrote a paper on policemen in [Ernest] Burgess' course on crime. In Park's course on the newspaper and public opinion . . . I had great fun learning about the press agent. . . . It was the press agent as a budding profession that interested me. I got interested in the marvelous propaganda which real estate men made for the "good guys" in real estate—about how they were truly experts on land values and brokers: in short, professionals, not businessmen. Since I had already read and heard a great deal about cities as the places where many services and occupations took on an abstract, disinterested professional quality, I was soon taken with the thought that here was a wonderful case where the professional attitude was fostered by some in the same market (for land and houses) . . . (Hughes, 1970).

In this statement about his early development as a sociologist, we already have an expression of Hughes's interest in various occupations—police officers, press agents, realtors—as well as the more general question of what made an occupation a profession, or the issue of professionalization. *Professionalization* is the process by which an occupation comes to achieve the prestigious, powerful, and high-paying position of a profession (Ritzer and Walczak, 1986).

Under Park's direction in 1928, Hughes wrote his dissertation on the real estate board in Chicago. He was interested in both the board as a form of organization and real estate as an occupation. As Hughes put it, at the time when he completed his dissertation, there was "really no occupational sociology." It was left to Hughes to create over the next several decades the sociology of work or, as it is sometimes called, the sociology of occupations. (Most of those studies focused on male workers, but as the exhibit in this chapter demonstrates there has recently been a boom in the study of the position of women in the work world.)

While Hughes (1958) almost single-handedly created the field of the sociology of work, he recognized that others before him had made contributions to this area, including some of the classic sociologists mentioned above:

> Of course, people have always, in the western world at any rate, been interested in work. With the coming of the industrial revolution there began to be writings on the relations of workers to their work. The assumption was that since the worker no longer owned his own tools [an allusion to Marx's theory of alienation] his work would go down. The main trouble with that is there is no evidence that it ever was up. At any rate, there was a good deal of writing on the subject moving toward the later work on alienation. Marx had already started along this line; a Belgian, LeMan, continued, Max Weber had already before 1910, done a monograph on industrial work, and Sombart had done some similar work in his book on capitalism. Both of them talk of the great change of habit and attitude required to turn the handworker into a clockbound machine worker (Hughes, 1970).

Hughes went on to also recognize that people in other fields, such as F. W. Taylor in scientific management, Thorstein Veblen in economics, and Elton Mayo in human relations, had also done significant work that was relevant to the development of the sociology of work.

As a result of these influences as well as others, especially the teaching and work of Robert Park, Everett Hughes began teaching courses in this area: "Around 1938 or 1939 I gave a course at the University of Chicago on the professions and later broadened the title and simplified it . . . to the sociology of work" (Hughes, 1970). It is rare to be able to trace the origin of a field to a specific time and place, but one can trace the origins of the sociology of work to that course at Chicago in the late 1930s.

THE CONTRIBUTIONS OF EVERETT HUGHES

Hughes started with an interest in the issue of professionalization, which involved in the main the highest-status professions in our society, such as physicians and lawyers. However, eventually Hughes came to focus on, and had his students concentrate on, low-status occupations. Like much else in Hughes's work, this interest is traceable to the work of Robert Park, particularly Park's concern with low-status occupations in the city. Here is the way Park (1925:14) expressed that interest:

> The effects of the division of labor as a discipline, e.g., as a means of molding character, may therefore best be studied in the vocational types it has produced. Among the types which it would be interesting to study are: the shopgirl, the policeman, the peddlar, the cab-man, the night-watchman, the clairvoyant, the vaudeville performer, the labor agitator, the quack doctor, the bartender, the ward boss, the strikebreaker, the school teacher, the reporter, the stockbroker, the pawnbroker: all of these are characteristic products of the conditions of life; each, with its own special experience, insight, and point of view, determines for each vocational group and for the city as a whole its individuality.

Taking his lead from this quotation and his considerable exposure to Park's ideas, Hughes argued that the best place to study the dynamics of occupational life was in low-status occupations, or what we now would call "semiskilled and unskilled occupations" (Ritzer and Walczak, 1986: Chapters 11 and 12). He believed that they offered an excellent laboratory for the study of occupational life because there is less distortion of what really takes place in them than is the case in high-status occupations. In all types of jobs people strive to make their work more tolerable to themselves and more important in the eyes of others. Hughes contends that there is less of an effort to disguise the true nature of this process, as well the nature of the work itself, in low-status occupations. Furthermore, those who labor in such occupations have less of an ability to conceal reality than do those in high-status occupations. Because it is easier to see the essential processes (for example, striving for higher status, conflict with competing occupations, conflict with customers or clients) of work in them, Hughes urged his students to begin with low-status occupations. He argued that when one studies low-status occupations, insights are gained "about work in any and all occupations" (Hughes, 1958:49). Behind this contention is the basic premise that "the essential problems of men at work are the same whether they do their work in some famous laboratory or in the messiest vat room of a pickle factory" (Hughes, 1958:48). This idea, created by Hughes, was of critical importance to the development of the sociology of work.

Not only did Hughes urge his students to study low-status occupations, he urged them to do so using the defining method of the Chicago school, participant observation. Donald Roy, one of Hughes's students who himself became an important occupational sociologist and whose work I will discuss below, says of Hughes: "Many years ago, in a course on methods of field research, he taught us that it was fun to sally forth with pencil and notebook, like newspaper reporters, to observe and to question'' (Roy, 1968:49). As a result of Hughes's efforts and directives, the products of the Second Chicago School as well as those of many others who followed in their footsteps produced an enormous variety and quantity of highly insightful participant observation studies of various, mainly low-status occupations.

However, the Chicago sociologists ventured even farther down the occupational hierarchy to the study of deviant occupations. To be considered deviant, an occupation must be illegal and/or its activities must be seen as being in violation of society's norms and values and/or its lifestyle or culture must be viewed as being involved in rule-violating behavior (Ritzer and Walczak, 1986:374). Thus, drug dealing would be considered a deviant occupation because it is illegal (Adler and Adler, 1983). Although their work is legal, strippers are seen as participating in a deviant occupation because their activities (taking off one's clothes in public, dancing in a lewd and lascivious manner) violate society's norms and values (Boles and Garbin, 1974). Finally, the heavy metal rock musician would be viewed as a deviant occupation because it is thought that the lifestyle and culture associated with it generate rule-violating behavior such as violence and drug use (Weinstein, 1992).

In fact, many of the early classics of the Chicago School inspired by Park were studies of deviant occupations such as Anderson's (1923/1961) study, *The Hobo* (Chapter 5); Paul G. Cressey's (1932) work, *The Taxi Dance Hall*, especially in regard to the women who worked there as dancers (Hong and Duff, 1977); and Sutherland's *The Professional Thief* (1937). Hughes, as a disciple of Park, continued this interest in deviant occupations. Furthermore, he was also interested in deviance in otherwise ''straight'' (that is, nondeviant) occupations. More generally, Hughes expressed an interest in both ''dirty work'' and ''mistakes at work.'' Dirty work involves unpleasant work-related tasks shunned by most people. For example, coroners and funeral directors (Pine, 1975) who work with corpses are generally seen as performing dirty work. Mistakes at work involve errors and oversights on the job. For example, physicians have often been accused of making mistakes at work (such as botching an operation) and of not doing a good job of punishing those who make such egregious mistakes (Freidson, 1975). These ideas reflect Hughes's interest in studying what may be termed the underside of the work world.

Hughes's interest in deviant occupations was animated by the same orientation that led him to focus on low-status straight occupations. That is, one could study occupational processes better in these occupations; people in deviant occupations ordinarily have even less of an ability to conceal what really goes on in them than do those in low-status straight occupations. Hughes's orientation here, as was the case with low-status work, led to a flowering of research into deviant occupations as well as deviance, dirty work, and mistakes in straight occupations.

Interestingly, despite his preference for the study of low-status and deviant occupations, Hughes made important contributions to our understanding of high-status professional occupations. In 1928 Hughes made one of the first attempts to develop what is now the widely accepted idea of an *occupational continuum,* or the full range of occupations ranging from high-status professionals on one end to low-status deviant occupations on the other. The ability of an occupation to move toward the professional end of the continuum depended on a number things, most notably the standing of the occupation "in the eyes of the community" (Hughes, 1958:32). To be a profession, an occupation must wage a kind of public relations campaign, and even if successful, that occupation must keep waging that campaign if it is to maintain its position atop the occupational continuum. Such a view serves, among other things, to demystify the professions. They are professions not because there is something inherently different or special about them but because of their successful efforts to convince the public of their distinctiveness. This is demystifying in another sense since such public relations activities seem more than a little demeaning if not outright reprehensible. There is the faint sense here that professionals are engaged in little more than a confidence game.

Another aspect of Hughes's approach to the professions is to give them a dynamic or processual quality. Professions are not in this conceptualization static structures. Rather, the focus is on the process by which occupations struggle to climb up the hierarchy to professional status. There is also the sense that a profession is not a static structure but rather a system involving a series of internal processes. As we will see, these ideas, like Hughes's notion of a professional continuum, were picked up by later occupational sociologists, especially his students.

This concern for dynamics and process is reflected in another of Hughes's concerns and another important area of interest in the sociology of work: the study of *occupational careers or career patterns* (Ritzer and Walczak, 1986: Chapters 6 and 7). This involves the steps or stages involved in one's tenure in a given occupation. Wilensky (1960:554) defines a career pattern as "a succession of related jobs, arranged in hierarchy of prestige, through which persons move in an orderly, predictable sequence." For example, as was mentioned earlier, professors have a career pattern usually involving three major steps: assistant professor, associate professor, and full professor. To take another example, a large law firm may have a career hierarchy involving the following steps: beginning associate, middle-level associate, senior associate, permanent associate, and finally partner. Many occupations, especially higher-status professional and managerial occupations, have similar career patterns.

It was Hughes's belief that the study of careers could yield insights into the nature of the occupation, the individual, and the larger society. At the occupational level, as we have seen, higher-status occupations tend to have career patterns involving many steps, whereas careers in low-status occupations tend to involve few if any career steps. For example, once one becomes a taxi driver, one has achieved the one and only step in that career; there are no higher positions to which to aspire. (It is possible that a taxi driver could come to own his or her own fleet of cabs. However, the person would then have moved on to another occupation—owner—and would no longer be a taxi driver.) Thus, the nature of its career pattern tells us much about the status of an occupation.

On the individual level, Hughes sees the career pattern as "the moving perspective in which the person sees his life as a whole and interprets the meaning of his various attributes, actions, and the things which happen to him" (Hughes, 1958:63). Thus, people tend to see themselves from the vantage point of their careers. If they have moved up the career ladder and moved up it quickly (see the later discussion of timetables), they are likely to have a positive view of themselves, but if they languish at the bottom of the career hierarchy for much if not all of their work lives, they are likely to suffer from low self-esteem.

Hughes also tells us that the study of careers yields great insights into the structure of the larger society. For example, in an extremely rigid society career patterns consist "of a series [of] . . . clearly defined offices" (Hughes, 1958:63). In contrast, in more open societies career patterns are more highly variable. By studying careers, one is able to "throw light on the nature of our institutions" and "reveal the nature and the 'working constitution' of a society" (Hughes, 1958:67).

HUGHES AND HIS STUDENTS

Hughes was significant in the sociology of work because of his own scholarly work and the work of his students. According to Hughes, "Oswald Hall, Howard S. Becker, Harvey Smith, Edward Gross and Julius Roth would certainly consider themselves my students" (Hughes, 1970). Other occupational sociologists who were influenced by Hughes while students at Chicago include Donald Roy, Harold Wilensky, William Kornhauser, Nelson Foote, Anselm Strauss, and Kirson Weinberg. These students and many others, taken together, represent a "Who's Who" of

The Emergence of a Subspecialty: Women and Work

As with most specialties in sociology, the sociology of work was dominated by men (as is clear in this chapter) and focused primarily on men at work and on predominantly male occupations. To put it another way, there was little work done on the issue of women and work. This is reflected in a study of articles in the sociology of occupations that were published between 1953 and 1959 (Smigel et al., 1963). Ten major topics (for example, careers, occupational status, and mobility) were reflected in studies done during this period, but women and work was *not* one of them. In fact, there was so little work done on, and even consciousness of, women and work that as was mentioned in the body of this chapter, the first edition of my text in this field was entitled *Man and His Work* (Ritzer, 1972). However, I should add that in each chapter in my text on a major occupational category a section was devoted to the issue of women in that occupation. Nevertheless, the book came under attack by feminists, and the second edition was retitled *Working: Conflict and Change* (Ritzer, 1977). In a more recent study of the field, Hall (1983) found an increase in interest in the study of women and work. Most recently Abbott (forthcoming) found that the issue of gender and work has emerged as *the* most important topic in the field.

The question is, Why this dramatic increase in the degree of concern with women and work? First, of course, this issue was greatly underrepresented in early work in the field, and the recent spate of work has simply redressed the historical imbalance. Second, relatively few women were in the field and studying women and work in its early years. However, in recent years large numbers of women have become sociologists of work, and many of them have focused on gender-related issues. Third, the sociology of gender has emerged as a major topic in sociology, and the relationship between gender and work is an important concern in that subfield. Finally, the resurgence of feminism in general, and feminist theory in particular, has played a key role in the growth in interest in this topic.

The new scholarship on women and work has taken several different forms. A good deal of literature has been devoted to the issue of various problems confronting women at work. Let me enumerate a few of these problems:

- *Occupational sex segregation.* Many studies have shown that occupations are segregated by sex (Resnick and Roos, 1989; Jacobs, 1992). That is, men tend to be found in certain occupations, and women in others. Furthermore, men tend to be in high-paying, high-status occupations (for example, physicians and lawyers) while women tend to be in far lower-paying and lower-status occupations (for example, nurses and elementary school teachers).

- *The earnings gap.* Another common problem in research on gender and work is the fact that women earn less than similarly employed men. For many years studies indicated that on average women earned about 60 percent of what men earned in comparable occupations. In recent years the gap has narrowed to 70 percent. However, it is clear that women continue to earn substantially less than men in comparable occupations (England, 1992).
- *Sexism.* The fact that the work world is segregated by sex and that women earn considerably less than men indicates that it is dominated by sexism. That sexism can take the form of negative attitudes and discriminatory behavior toward women in the workplace. More important, it can take the form of *institutional sexism,* in which the day-to-day operations of the work world operate to the detriment of women. For example, because women continue to bear the major responsibility for child raising, the absence of adequate child care facilities at most workplaces makes it difficult for women to work full-time or to continue on a career path without interruption.
- *Sexual harassment.* Sexual harassment on the job involves such things as unwelcome sexual advances, requests for sexual favors, and unwelcome verbal or physical conduct of a physical nature. While sexual harassment has long been a problem in the work world, it has received increasing public attention in recent years, most notably in the 1991 hearings on Clarence Thomas's appointment to the Supreme Court. During those hearings Thomas was accused of various types of sexual harassment on the job by Anita Hill.

In addition to a concern for problems, there is a growing interest in the study of women in specific occupational categories. In fact, many recent major studies of occupations have focused on women. Among the most notable of these studies are those on the way flight attendants and those in many other occupations sell their emotions and then are forced to control them in the face of hostile passengers (Hochschild, 1983), studies of women in direct sales organizations such as Mary Kay Cosmetics (Biggart, 1989), studies of the plight of women in male-dominated professions in general (Witz, 1992) and engineering in particular (McIlwee and Robinson, 1992), and studies of domestic workers (Romero, 1992). It is through such studies that we are learning more not only about occupations in general but about the role of women in specific occupations and in the work world in general.

scholars responsible for the major early contributions to the sociology of work, and their students in turn have made additional contributions to the field. I will have occasion to discuss the contributions of some of them below.

I should add that Hughes also had a powerful effect on many other occupational sociologists who had no affiliation with the University of Chicago. For example, although I was not trained at Chicago and met Hughes only a few times, my orientation to the sociology of occupations was heavily influenced by his perspectives on work. In homage to Hughes, I entitled the first edition of my text in the sociology of work, *Man and His Work* (Ritzer, 1972), after Hughes's collection of essays *Men and Their Work* (1958).

Thus, I have traced briefly the roots of the beginnings of the sociology of work to Everett Hughes and his writings as well as his courses on the topic, which were first offered in the late 1930s. However, to represent a beginning, Hughes's ideas on the sociology of work had to be picked up and used by others. In the rest of this chapter I look at the way in which many of Hughes's students and other direct and indirect inheritors of the Chicago tradition followed up on those ideas and elaborated them in research on the work world, especially in the 1950s and 1960s.

As was noted above, Hughes urged his students to go out and study low-status occupations, utilizing participant observation as the preferred methodology. No one did this better than Donald Roy. In a series of studies Roy detailed the ways in which low-status factory workers dealt with boring and alienating work and with managers who were often regarded as enemies. What was uncovered in the process of this research was the *informal organization* of industry, that is, the way in which things were really structured in the workplace. The actual organization of work—its informal organization—stood in contrast to the *formal organization,* or the way things were supposed to function. Organizational leaders design and implement the formal organization in an effort to define what is to take place within the organization. However, over time the workers develop their own informal organization. Sociologists of work have long argued that a true understanding of the work world requires a comprehension of this informal organization. Such knowledge tells us much more about organizational life than does an understanding of formal organization.

In one study of this informal organization, Roy took a job in a machine shop. As a participant observer, Roy (1954:257) noted the informal organization of the machine shop: "We machine operators did 'figure the angles,' we developed an impressive repertoire of angles to play and devoted ourselves to crossing the expectations of formal organization with perseverance, artistry, and organizing ability of our own." In other words, what seemed to be random or irrational behavior on the part of the workers was in fact rational and highly organized. Roy's study also underscores the point that the informal organization is often set up to run in opposition to the formal organization created by management. In a later study, Runcie (1980:108) reported similar behavior among drivers who moved completed cars from one part of an automobile factory to another: "Although three of us were assigned to the task . . . we worked out a schedule so that two of us were available at any one time, with the third hiding out of sight, reading a newspaper, napping, or eating lunch."

A good example of this was uncovered by Roy when management attempted to set piecework rates for the workers. This means that managers were timing how long it took the workers to do specific tasks so that they could determine how much to pay the employees for each object produced. Piecework workers are paid for each item ("piece") they produce and not, as is normally the case, by the hour or the week.

It was clearly in the interest of the workers studied by Roy to slow down production when their work was being timed. In that way, they could earn more when they returned to their normal rate of work and were able to produce far more "pieces" than managers expected. Thus, during the timing of the work, the workers would run the machines at slower speeds or utilize extra movements such as "little reachings, liftings, adjustings, dustings and other special attentions of conscientious machine operation and good housekeeping that could be dropped instantly with the departure of the time-study man" (Roy, 1954:257). Of course, it was important that all members of the group work in this manner when the work was being timed. If even one member of the group worked at full speed, the time-study experts would see that the rest of them were working at a reduced speed. Thus, the group had to be tightly organized and its members had to work together to get the work timed the way they wanted.

Once the workers were successful in getting the work timed to their satisfaction and the desired piece rate was set, they were free to return to the normal work pace. In this way, they were able to produce more pieces in a given time period than management anticipated and thus earn larger sums of money than they would have if management had been allowed to time their work at the regular pace.

In another participant observation study of machine operators Roy (1959–1960) turned his attention to the question of how members of a work group made what was otherwise a boring job more meaningful. As Roy put it, he was interested in how machine operators prevented themselves from "going nuts." The work involved was not only repetitious but simple and mindless, requiring long hours and a six-day week. This is Roy's description of the work he and his coworkers performed:

> Standing all day in one spot beside three old codgers in a dingy room looking out through barred windows at the bare walls of a brick warehouse, leg movements largely restricted to the shifting of body weight from one foot to the other, hand and arm movements confined, for the most part, to a simple repetitive sequence of place the die—punch the clicker—place the die—punch the clicker, and intellectual activity reduced to computing the hours to quitting time (Roy, 1959–1960:160).

The research issue for Roy in this study was the devices these workers employed to find meaning in this otherwise meaningless occupation. First, he found that they often tried to give a little variety to their work by changing the colors of materials or the die shapes or by breaking the monotony by occasionally engaging in maintenance work on the machinery. More important, the workers created a variety of events that helped the day pass more quickly and interestingly. During the morning "peach time" was announced, at which point one worker took out two peaches and divided them among the four workers in the group. Then there was "banana time." The same man who brought the peaches also brought one banana that was supposed to be for his own consumption. However, regularly each morning, just as he was about to eat the banana, one of the other workers would steal it and consume it gleefully while running around the shop floor shouting "Banana time!" The worker who had brought the banana would just as routinely protest and would be admonished on every occasion by his fellow workers for protesting so vociferously. As the workday progressed there were other "exciting" events such as "window time," "lunch time," "pickup time," "fish time," and "Coke time." I will leave it to the reader to imagine what took place during each of those times. Suffice it to say that it was through these pathetic devices that workers in an essentially meaningless job struggled to make their work lives more meaningful and bearable. While these games represent signs of the indomitable spirit of workers, they are sad because it is clear that they do nothing to change the work situation that is the cause of the workers' problems.

In still another study Roy (1974) pointed to yet another game designed to cope with alienation among machine operators: sex play! He found that sexual relations among coworkers and various kinds of games with sexual overtones helped workers deal with the undesirable aspects of their jobs. Here is an example of such a game that will give the reader the flavor of this type of activity and its significance in the work world:

> I [Donald Roy] recall a factory job in my early work experience in which the massive boredom of performing simple repetitive operations as a

> member of a cooky-machine crew was alleviated by the lewd antics of a moronic operative. . . . This mentally but not sexually defective fellow would rescue the rest of us from our pit of painful boredom at intervals by flashing an erection and whirling back and forth with it, to and from the oven, quite gracefully in fact, and by responding to the cheers, laughter, and obscene suggestions of his workmates by imbecilic grinning (Roy, 1974:45).

While the workers, to say nothing of the readers of this book, might find such activities amusing, once again it should be noted that sex play of this type does nothing to alter the structural conditions that compel workers to find meaning through such activities.

It should be noted that while workers in low-status occupations today still struggle to find meaning in their work, many have to deal with the far greater problem of unemployment stemming from the recent decline of American industry. As symbolic interaction theory would suggest, unemployment has a negative effect on self-esteem. Said one unemployed worker not too long ago: "*On a bad day . . . I'll take it personally. Those are the days I feel incompetent, very unsure of myself*" (Burman, 1988:200).

Hughes, as we have seen, also urged his students to go out and study deviant occupations, and the classic example of that type of research is Howard Becker's (1963) study of jazz musicians. (Incidently, Becker is an accomplished jazz musician who to this day performs at sociology meetings.) As a student at the University of Chicago, Becker had done fieldwork on a tavern, and he gave Everett Hughes the notes from that research to read:

> Everett read them and when I came back to see him he treated me royally. It was great. . . . It turned out that he had had a lot of students who had studied various professions, medicine and law in particular, but he found it very difficult to get people to study lowly kinds of occupations. Here was somebody doing it without being urged (cited in Rock, 1979:6).

This initial work led, among other things, to Becker's research on the "lowly" occupation of jazz musician.

While today the jazz musician would not be considered a deviant occupation, a few decades ago it was in the sense that it was not considered by the majority of members of society to be a "proper" occupation. The jazz musician is a kind of deviant "service" occupation in which the service provided to the client/consumer is the music. In pointing out the similarity between the jazz musician and straight service occupations, Becker is following through on Hughes's idea that the problems of the work world are the same throughout its structure but can be studied more easily in deviant and low-status occupations. Here is the way Becker puts the issue:

> He [the jazz musician] is a member of a service occupation and the culture he participates in gets its character from the problems common to service occupations. The service occupations are, in general, distinguished by the fact that the worker in them comes into more or less direct contact and personal contact with the ultimate consumer of the product of his work, the client for whom he performs the service. Consequently, the client is able to direct or attempt to direct the worker at his task and to apply sanctions of various kinds, ranging from informal pressure to the withdrawal of his patronage and the conferring of it on some others of the many people who perform the service (Becker, 1963:82).

There is a built-in conflict between jazz musicians and the audience, just as there is in the relationship between individuals in *every* service occupation and the consumers of their services. For example, conflict is built into the relationship between car salesperson and potential buyer (Miller, 1964), waiter and diner (Butler and Snizek, 1976), and airline attendant and passenger (Hochschild, 1983). As is generally the case in service occupations, the power in this relationship lies with the clients/customers, in this case, the audience.

Jazz musicians are usually deeply committed to their work and feel that the audience, whose members they generally label as "square," is incapable of assessing the quality of their performance yet is in a position to exercise control over it. This is especially threatening since the "square is thought of as an ignorant, intolerant person who is to be feared, since he produces the pressures forcing the musician to play inartistically" (Becker, 1963:89). This situation is almost intolerable because the squares have the ultimate power; if the jazz musicians do not play what the audience wants to hear, the audience will not pay to hear it.

Some jazz musicians relent and "go commercial," playing the more popular tunes preferred by the audience. Others do not conform and employ a variety of devices to mitigate the threat from the audience, which the musician views as essentially hostile. Among other things, musicians set themselves up on a stage and physically separate themselves from the audience and its demands. They also try in other ways to avoid physical contact with the audience, and this even goes as far as efforts to avoid eye contact. All this is aimed at preventing the audience from forcing the musicians to play the kind of music that violates their artistic sensibilities.

One of Becker's fellow students in courses with Everett Hughes was Eliot Freidson. While Becker focused on low-status and deviant occupations, Freidson concentrated on the high-status professions. In fact, Freidson became the leading sociological student of the professions. However, one of Freidson's (1960) early studies of the medical profession illustrates the similarity in processes in high-status and low-status occupations.

We do not often think of patients as having power over physicians; we usually think that the reverse is the case and that physicians exercise inordinate power over patients. While physicians do have considerable power, we must not ignore the power that patients exercise over physicians; they do this in much the same way that the audience exercises control over jazz musicians.

For example, physicians do not have the power to define patients as ill, in need of medical attention, and in need of a specific physician's medical services. All this power lies with patients, and physicians can do little more than wait for patients to come to these definitions and take the steps needed to obtain their services.

Physicians also must, at least to some degree, please the patient culture if they are to stay in practice. It is by pleasing patients that physicians obtain and retain patients. Physicians, then, take a variety of actions to satisfy the patient culture. At a minimum they must demonstrate a sufficiently pleasant "bedside manner," but sometimes they must go much further. For example, they may not prescribe unpopular drugs even though they think that those drugs are best for the condition in question. In cases where patients demand drugs even though the condition does not warrant it, physicians may prescribe placebos just to keep them satisfied (Freidson, 1960).

The problem confronting physicians is especially acute with new patients. Many patients visit physicians on a "tryout" basis. The patient assesses the physician's performance and may compare it to that of other physicians. Only if the assessment is positive will the patient return to that doctor. Referrals of friends to the physician are also dependent on a favorable evaluation and continued positive reactions. Although we often think of the physician as a professional who is free of client control, it is clear that patients exert control over physicians, just as the audience exercises control over jazz musicians. Thus, the work of two of Hughes's students, Becker on jazz musicians and Freidson on physicians, illustrates the utility of Hughes's argument for the need for a comparative analysis of the highest- and lowest-status occupations.

Freidson also points out that the amount of client control over physicians varies among medical specialities. Clients exert the greatest control over general practitioners. However, the situation is different for specialists, who usually receive their patients on referral from other doctors, often general practitioners. Thus, the specialist has a greater need to satisfy other physicians than to satisfy the client culture. Furthermore, by the time patients make their way to a specialist, they are likely to be quite ill or at least afraid that they are seriously ill and therefore more willing to surrender authority in the relationship with the physician.

In discussing physicians, we are obviously in the realm of the professions, and this brings us back to Hughes's ideas on the occupational continuum and the process of professionalization. As a result of Hughes's work, occupational sociologists became concerned with the steps or stages in the process of becoming a profession. A good example of this kind of concern is found in the work of another product of the Chicago School, Harold Wilensky (1964).

In Wilensky's view, professionalization involves a series of steps. Occupations which successfully negotiate those steps become professions; that is, they move up the occupational continuum to its professional endpoint. First, an occupation must become a full-time undertaking. Many occupations begin as part-time work, and part-time occupations have no chance of becoming professions. Thus, becoming a full-time undertaking is a prerequisite to professionalization. Once it has become full-time, the occupation needs to set up a training school, preferably at the undergraduate, or even better the graduate, level. This will allow its members to acquire the needed knowledge base and receive the requisite educational credentials. Third, it is necessary to establish a national association akin to the American Medical Association to represent the occupation's interests and fight for professional recognition. Fourth, the national association must lead the fight to achieve legal recognition of the occupation as a profession deserving of a variety of special rights and privileges. Fifth, the association also needs to take the lead in creating a code of ethics so that it can make sure that all individuals in the occupation behave in a professional manner. An occupation that has moved through all five steps is a profession.

This image of the professionalization process leaves one with the impression that many occupations, perhaps every occupation, can take the steps necessary to achieve professional recognition. In fact, another Chicago product and student of Hughes's, Nelson Foote (1953), argued that even blue-collar laborers were becoming professionalized. Clearly, if one could conceive of comparatively low-status blue-collar workers becoming professionalized, it was possible for virtually any occupation to achieve professionalization. In a response to Foote's argument, Wilensky (1964) labeled this the "professionalization of everyone" and countered that "this notion of the professionalization of everyone is a bit of sociological romance." Clearly, only a limited number of occupations have the characteristics and resources to achieve professional recognition, yet it is important to recognize that professional status is something that is achieved by occupations and is not the result of their inherent qualities.

One of the biases of the Chicago approach on this issue is its concern for professionalization, or the steps needed to move *up* the occupational hierarchy. However, occupations can also move *down* the occupational hierarchy; they can lose professional status. A good example of this is the decline in professional status of the clergy in recent decades as society has grown increasingly secularized. Thus, later researchers (Haug, 1975; Toren, 1975; Ritzer and Walczak, 1988) recognized this bias and developed the idea of *deprofessionalization* to complement the notion of professionalization.

The dynamic sense of professionalization held by the Chicago sociologists leads one to be quite critical of and cynical about professions. They are seen not as unique occupations with highly laudable characteristics but as occupations whose main distinction has been their ability to move up the occupational hierarchy by convincing others, often falsely, of their distinctiveness. One of the earliest critics of the professions and our tendency to place them on an occupational pedestal was yet another of Hughes's students, Julius Roth (1974).

Roth rejected the idea that there is something distinctive about the knowledge base of the professions. In his view, professions, like other occupations, possess knowledge that has great gaps, numerous inconsistencies, and even grave fundamental differences that lead to controversies over the most basic matters. While there is no qualitative difference between the knowledge of professions and that of other occupations, the professions labor mightily to create the illusion that there is such a difference. Roth was also critical of the idea that the professions are distinguished by codes of ethics that are in place to protect the public:

> The evidence we do have about realtors, lawyers, psychologists, insurance agents, physicians, and other occupational groups with codes of ethics shows overwhelmingly that, although these codes sometimes curb competition among colleagues, they have almost no protective value for the clientele or the public. Indeed, the existence of such codes is used as a device to turn aside public criticism and interference (Roth, 1974:10).

Thus, the Chicago approach leads one to be critical of the professions' codes of ethics and to see them as self-serving devices rather than mechanisms to protect the public. Another criticism by Roth (1974:10–11) is that contrary to their desired image, the professions do not provide service to all: "There is a mass of evidence already publicly available on the bias of professional workers and their service organizations against deviant youth, the aged, women, the poor, ethnic minorities, and people they just didn't like the looks of." Finally, Roth argues that contrary to what the professions would like them to believe, clients have considerable power over professionals.

The critical attitude of the Chicago School toward the professions helped lead to a transformation in the way sociologists look at the professions. This transformation was spearheaded by Eliot Freidson (1970), who took the lead in arguing that the most distinguishing feature of the medical profession—indeed, of all professions—is their *power*. That is, what it really takes to become a profession, to professionalize, to move up the professional continuum, is power. Raw power is the main distinguishing feature of professions. Professions exercise this power over clients, other occupations, and even the state. For example, the medical profession seeks to control its patients, subordinate other occupations (for example, nurses and chiropractors), and determine government actions that relate to medicine (for example, the long-running effort of the American Medical Association to prevent "socialized medicine"). This came to be known as the "power approach to the professions" (Klegon, 1978), and while it was not created by Hughes, it was derived from his theoretical orientation to the professions and was pioneered by his students, most notably Freidson and Roth.

At another level, Hughes's orientation toward the professions was transformed into an interest in the processes internal to professions. Here the work of two other Chicago products, Rue Bucher and Anselm Strauss (Bucher and Strauss, 1961; Bucher, 1962), is important. Bucher and Strauss refused to look at professions as structures but instead saw them as being defined by internal processes. These internal processes are shaped by the fact that professions are composed of a number of *segments*. This leads to the view of professions as "loose amalgamations of segments pursuing different objectives in different manners and . . . delicately held together" (Bucher and Strauss, 1961:326). Such a view of professions gives us a better understanding of the internal conflict and change that are characteristic of professions. That is, professional segments are often in conflict, and their shifting fortunes and allegiances often lead to change in the professions. We thus have the kind of dynamic view of the professions that was urged by Hughes in his early work in this area.

Bucher (1962) gave some specificity to this orientation in a study of segments within the profession of pathology. She argues that there are two major segments within pathology. One is oriented to scientific research and the advancement of knowledge; the other is interested in providing services to physicians by aiding them in the diagnostic process. The older segment consists of the scientific pathologists, but it is being threatened by the rise of the practitioner segment. These two segments battle for control of the profession, and each tries to have its definition imposed on the profession as a whole. They also struggle over new recruits to the profession, with each trying to attract as many newcomers as possible to its side and cause. This conflict between segments is having a dramatic effect on pathology and leading to dramatic changes in this profession. More generally, all professions are segmented and therefore laden with conflict and likely to change as a result of these internal processes and tensions.

Another of Hughes's processual concerns within the work world was the study of occupational careers and career patterns. Here we encounter, once again, the work of Julius Roth (1963). Roth's contribution is to emphasize the importance of time in a person's career. More specifically, as was mentioned earlier in this chapter, he argues that there are *timetables* associated with most careers. This means that there are a variety of career steps and that there is a sense that people ought to be able to reach each step in a certain amount of time. If one meets the timetable or achieves the various steps early, that is a sign that one is doing well. One is likely to feel good about one's career progress, and others are likely to approve of one's career advancement. By contrast, if one is late in reaching various career steps, one is likely to worry about one's career steps and be disapproved of by others.

Let me illustrate this in terms of the academic career. In general, it takes about five years of postgraduate study to obtain a Ph.D. Those who do it in five years or less are likely to be seen as future "stars," whereas those who take more time are likely to be regarded negatively. After receiving a Ph.D., it generally takes seven years to receive tenure and be promoted from assistant professor to associate professor; then it is likely to take another seven years to be promoted to full professor. Those who make these steps in less time are likely to be perceived, and to perceive themselves, as doing well in their careers. The opposite is true of those who are slow to move up the career ladder or never achieve a certain career step. Thus, there are professors who never move beyond being assistant professors and many others who retire as associate professors.

While some occupations have clear timetables like the one for professors, others have less clear, even ambiguous timetables. Roth argues that in those cases workers are uncomfortable with the absence of markers to indicate how they are doing in their careers. They often try to set up timetables for themselves in order to be able to assess how they are faring. Thus, a worker in such a position may choose a given set of coworkers as a reference group and constantly compare his or her progress to that of the members of the reference group. If one is moving faster than the reference group, that is an indication of career success; failure is perceived when one is moving more slowly than one's peers. If a person continually falls behind the peer group, that person may try to find another reference group in which individuals are moving as slowly as or even more slowly than he or she is. Thus, the idea of a career timetable is a powerful addition to our understanding of the dynamics of occupational careers.

CONCLUSION

The sociology of work has progressed far beyond the work of Hughes and his students. Nevertheless, Hughes and his followers left an indelible mark on the field. The comparative study of occupations, an interest in the full range of occupations from professions to low-status and deviant occupations, professionalization, professional processes (for example, among segments), careers, and many other issues continue to lie at the heart of the sociology of work. Beyond that, a wide range of ideas were created by Hughes and expanded upon by his students, who in turn developed a range of interesting ideas of their own. The number of those ideas continues to grow as the sociology of work progresses.

CHAPTER 7

The Beginnings of a Sociological Idea: McDonaldization

In the preceding chapters I dealt with the ideas of other sociologists. Although those ideas continue to be important today, they had their beginnings decades, and in some cases centuries, ago. In this chapter and Chapter 8 I turn the spotlight on two of my own new sociological ideas: McDonaldization and hyperrationality. My objective is to discuss in a very personal way the beginnings of these two new ideas. In addition to discussing their origins, I will of course outline their nature and significance.

At one level, the roots of both ideas lie in the sociological theories of Max Weber, especially his ideas on rationality and the rationalization of society. Equally important, they also lie in my personal experiences in and analyses of the social world.

I begin in this chapter with the idea of McDonaldization because it came first in my own work and played a role in the later development of the idea that will be discussed in Chapter 8: hyperrationality.

HOW I BECAME INTERESTED IN MCDONALDIZATION

The place to begin is with some of my early background. My thinking about McDonaldization was shaped by the fact that I grew up before the fast-food restaurant was developed and was raised in a city, New York, which was in many ways during those years the antithesis of a society dominated by the fast-food restaurant and its principles and mentality.

I was born in 1940; Ray Kroc did not found the first McDonald's franchise until 1955. Furthermore, the early McDonald's fast-food restaurants were primarily medium-sized town and suburban phenomena; they did not make their way into the big cities until much later. The first time I saw a McDonald's occurred when I was a college freshman in 1958 and was visiting a friend in Massachusetts. For some reason the sight of those "golden arches" had a profound effect on me, and I remember it to this day. I had by that time heard of McDonald's, but I had not actually seen one firsthand. I had lunch there that day, but being a New Yorker with a sophisticated palate, I was not impressed with the cuisine. Nonetheless, I sensed that this was something new and important, although I did not at that point know why it was an important development. It was only later, with training in sociology in general and in Max Weber's theory of rationalization in particular, that I was able to better understand the meaning of the growth of McDonald's and, more generally, of fast-food restaurants.

Thus, I was an adult before I ever saw a McDonald's, and that gives me a perspective different from that of the vast majority of students reading this book, who were born into a society already dominated by McDonald's and its clones not only in the fast-food business but in other businesses as well (for example, AAMCO Transmissions and H & R Block). Unlike most of you, I am able to remember a world without McDonald's. By virtue of my age, I lived through the revolution wrought by the fast-food restaurant and saw the changes it brought about in society. This gives me a longer-term perspective with which to look at the phenomenon of McDonaldization.

In addition to time, the issue of place is important: It is important to understand the nature of New York City when I was growing up in the 1940s and 1950s. Even more then than now, New York was an ethnic city with well-defined ethnic neighborhoods, each with its own shops and restaurants. Virtually every one of those shops and restaurants was a small, individually run enterprise. They often had a homey quality and usually served homemade food. Quality was kept high by the intense competition for the New Yorker's food dollars. Even the nonethnic shops and restaurants had similar qualities and delivered high-quality goods and services. In addition, especially in one's own neighborhood, one often got very personalized service, and it was not unusual to be on a first-name basis with shopkeepers, restaurant owners, waiters, and waitresses.

Given that kind of background, now all but gone from the American scene, especially in the big cities (and even to some extent in New York), the reader can better understand why the fast-food restaurant and its many clones came as such a shock to me. Gone were the high quality, the personalized first-name basis services, the homey atmosphere, the homemade food, and everything else that characterized the shops and restaurants of that era. In their place, at least from my viewpoint, were mediocre or poor-quality goods and services, impersonal treatment, an institutional atmosphere, and food that bore little resemblance to home cooking.

In contrast to my experiences as a youth in New York City in the 1940s and 1950s, most of you have known only times and places dominated by McDonaldized restaurants and shops. Thus, in many cases they are all you know; there is little for you to compare them to. Lacking a comparison, it is difficult to be critical of McDonaldization, conceive of alternatives to it, or imagine a society organized in a different way.

From the late 1950s on I was certainly conscious of McDonald's and its clones and their expansion throughout society. While I was observing what was occurring, I don't remember feeling alarmed by it. Then, in 1975, I lived in Europe for the first time. While I lived in the Netherlands, I was able to travel around most of Western Europe and a bit of Eastern Europe as well. I particularly remember an extended visit to Vienna and the feeling that it reminded me of what New York had been like when I was growing up in the 1940s. While one could find a fast-food restaurant here and there in Europe in 1975, by and large that continent had not yet undergone the process of McDonaldization. The contrast between Europe and the rampant McDonaldization taking place in the United States made me acutely aware of what was happening back home. While I was living in the United States, the change was so gradual that I was largely oblivious to it. However, from the vantage point of a Europe without McDonaldization, the dramatic changes taking place in the United States were clear. Also clear was the fact that this change was not all to the good. Many European restaurants still had the qualities I remembered from my youth in New York City, and I realized even more acutely that those qualities were disappearing from the American scene.

Over the years I have had a number of occasions to return to Europe to visit and live. Those intermittent trips have allowed me to see clearly the McDonaldization of European society. While a rare sight in 1975, McDonald's is now a very visible presence throughout Europe, often in the most notable locations, such as the Champs Elysée in Paris. Not only are these restaurants very visible, they are also very popular and are almost always crowded. Furthermore, they have been joined by many other American chains. Thus, Burger King now also has an outlet on the Champs Elysée. Even more striking is the fact that the American chains and franchises have now been joined by similar enterprises indigenous to various European countries. Thus, in Paris fast-food croissanteries are the rage; Parisians can now get croissants on the run. The success of the fast-food croissanterie is particularly surprising given the French love affair with fine cooking, particularly with their cherished croissants.

In 1992 I spent some time in Moscow and was struck again by the spread and significance of McDonaldization. There, in the heart of an otherwise depressing and decaying city, stood the new McDonald's. It had been the world's largest and busiest until 1992, when an even larger and busier McDonald's was opened in the center of Beijing. Despite its being supplanted in its exalted position by the newer outlet in China, this restaurant still attracted droves of Muscovites. Many things drew them to it, not the least of which was that it was the symbol of the rationalization of America and its coveted market economy. The rationality of McDonald's stands in stark contrast to the irrationalities of the remnants of communism. Long lines and long waits (so much for fast food) are common, but on a sunny Saturday in May the line stretched as far as the eye could see. In fact, teenagers were offering, in exchange for a few rubles, to get you a "Beeg Mek" in no more than ten or fifteen minutes. Russians are in a headlong rush toward McDonaldization (over twenty additional McDonald's outlets are planned for Russia, and Moscow already has a Pizza Hut, a Baskin-Robbins, and a Benetton), seemingly oblivious to the potential problems that are of such great concern to me.

Awareness of what was going in Europe opened my eyes even farther to the spread of McDonaldization throughout American society. I was attuned to the opening of each new fast-food restaurant. I was stunned as one began to find McDonald's in increasingly surprising places: in airports, on highways, on college campuses, on airplanes, and so on. I was shocked as one business after another adopted the principles pioneered by McDonald's. Everywhere I turned, it seemed, there was evidence of the expansion of McDonaldization. Even more surprising, almost everyone seemed to be thrilled by this development. Virtually everyone seemed to love McDonald's and to welcome every new incursion of McDonaldization into yet another sector of our lives. Not only did most people not seem to question it, they seemed to welcome it; the more the McDonaldization, the better as far as they were concerned. I was growing increasingly concerned, but I seemed to be all but alone in this.

These personal experiences are part of the background for my concerns with and about McDonaldization, but there is also an academic backdrop. After I started teaching sociology at the university level in 1968, I devoted more and more attention to reading and teaching sociological theory. One of the theorists who appealed to me most was Max Weber, especially his theory of rationalization (Chapter 3). As you recall, Weber was interested in the rationalization process in the West. More generally, he was interested in why the West had rationalized while the rest of the world had failed to do so. Weber was ambivalent about the rationalization process taking place in the West. While he recognized the many advantages flowing from rationalization, he was very much aware of the negative aspects and consequences. Most generally, he was afraid of the possibility of what he called the "iron cage of rationality." His fear was that when all aspects of modern society were rationalized to a high degree, there would be no way for us to escape and no place to which we could flee.

While Weber analyzed many aspects of rationalization in the West, his model case was the bureaucracy. To Weber, the bureaucracy was the epitome of rationalization. The bureaucracy represented a kind of iron cage, and those who worked in a bureaucracy were locked into it. Furthermore, as more and more sectors of society were bureaucratized, the cage would grow larger, enclosing more and more people. Weber was writing in turn-of-the century Germany, where the modern bureaucracy was a relatively new and expanding phenomenon. However, in today's society, while still an important example of rationalization and still posing the dangers suggested by Weber, the bureaucracy no longer seemed to me to be the model of rationalization. From my vantage point, the fast-food restaurant had replaced it as the model.

Thus, my interest in and orientation to the fast-food restaurant was shaped by both my personal experiences and my theoretical interests. The two coalesced increasingly, and by 1983 I had written an article entitled the "McDonaldization of Society" (Ritzer, 1983). In that essay I described the process of McDonaldization, outlined its basic elements, and warned about some of its dangers. With that off my chest, I moved on to other things, although I often thought and lectured about rationalization. Then, in 1990, I was giving a talk about some of my recent work on the theory of rationalization, mainly dealing with the newer idea of hyperrationality, which will be discussed in Chapter 8. To my surprise, when it came time for questions from the audience, virtually everyone wanted to talk about McDonaldization. That idea had clearly touched a raw nerve in the audience, and I sensed enormous interest in and concern with the process. I resolved to drop my other work and write a book on McDonaldization. That book was published in 1993. What astounded me during the research for and the writing of that book was the degree to which McDonaldization had spread in the decade since I had first written about it. I was surprised by how much more dangerous it had become.

This narrative represents some reflections on how I first grew interested in and concerned about McDonaldization, how I created the idea of McDonaldization. McDonaldization is *"the process by which the principles of the fast-food restaurant are coming to dominate more and more sectors of American society as well as the rest of the world"* (Ritzer, 1993:1). Let me turn now to some of the arguments I make in *The McDonaldization of Society* about the state of McDonaldization in the 1990s.

THE SPREADING TENTACLES OF MCDONALDIZATION

The most obvious and perhaps least important extension of McDonaldization is the fact that fast-food restaurants have grown and expanded. The McDonald's chain, which began operation in 1955, opened its twelve thousandth branch in 1991; the leading 100 restaurant chains operate over 110,000 outlets in the United States alone (Ramirez, 1990). No longer restricted to the good old American hamburger, fast-food chains now traffic in pizza and Italian, Mexican, Chinese, and Cajun food, among other types. Nor are fast-food chains limited any longer to low-priced restaurants; now there are "upscale" chains such as Sizzler (steaks), Red Lobster (seafood), and Fuddruckers (gourmet burgers) as well as trendy saloons such as Bennigan's and TGIFridays. Then there is the geographic expansion of American fast-food restaurants throughout the world (about one-quarter of McDonald's outlets are now overseas). In addition to the expansion of American chains, many other countries are developing their own, most notably the fast-food croissanteries of Paris that were discussed above.

Another area of expansion consists of the locales in which one finds fast-food chains. As was mentioned above, McDonald's began in suburbs and medium-sized towns. In more recent years it has moved into the big cities, even the most desirable (at least from a business point of view) areas, such as Times Square. Fast-food restaurants have also migrated into even smaller towns that people thought could not support them (L. Shapiro, 1990). They have expanded in other ways as well. Instead of being content to surround college campuses, fast-food restaurants are increasingly found *on* campus. We are even beginning to see more involvement by the chains in the food served at high schools and grade schools (Farhi, 1990). Once characterized by an odd and unpredictable mix of restaurants, interstate highways are coming to be increasingly populated by fast-food chains. A similar thing is happening at the nation's airports, and one wonders whether the food served on airplanes can be far behind. In fact, after the preceding was written, United Airlines announced that it would begin serving McDonald's meals to children on flights to Orlando, Florida. The military has been forced to serve fast food at its bases and on its ships. Fast-food outlets are turning up increasingly *in* hospitals in spite of innumerable attacks on the nutritional value of the food. The latest, but undoubtedly not the last, incursion of the fast-food chains is into the nation's baseball parks and other sports venues.

Still another element of the expansion of fast-food restaurants involves the degree to which a wide array of other kinds of businesses are coming to be operated in accordance with the principles (see below for a discussion of the principles of efficiency, calculability, predictability, and increased control through the substitution of nonhuman for human technology) pioneered by fast-food chains. For example, the vice chairman of one of those businesses, Toys R Us, said: "We want to be thought of as a sort of McDonald's of toys" (Egan, 1990:29). Other chains with a similar model and similar ambitions include Jiffy-Lube, AAMCO Transmissions, Midas Muffler, Hair Plus, H & R Block, Pearle Vision Centers, Kampgrounds of America (KOA), Kinder Care (dubbed "Kentucky Fried Children"), Nutri/System, and Jenny Craig.

The influence of McDonald's is also felt in the number of social phenomena that have come to be prefaced by "Mc." Examples include McDentists, McDoctors, McChild Care Centers, McStables (for the nationwide racehorse training operation of Wayne Lucas), and McPaper (Prichard, 1987) (for *USA Today,* whose short news articles are sometimes called "News McNuggets"). When *USA Today* began a television program modeled after the newspaper, it was immediately dubbed "News McRather" (Zoglin, 1988).

With these kinds of extensions, I get to the real core of the expansion of McDonaldization and my real reason for examining the process. In the 1980s and early 1990s McDonaldization has extended its reach into more and more regions of society, and those areas are increasingly remote from the heart of the process in the fast-food business. As the examples in the last paragraph make clear, dentistry, medicine, child care, the training of racehorses, newspapers, and television news have come to be organized along the lines of the fast-food restaurant.

The derivatives of McDonald's are in turn having their own influence. For example, the success of *USA Today* ("McPaper") has led to changes (for example, shorter stories, color weather maps) in many newspapers across the nation. As one *USA Today* editor put it: "'The same newspaper editors who call us McPaper have been stealing our McNuggets'" (Prichard, 1987:32–33). The influence of *USA Today* is manifested most blatantly in the *Boca Raton News,* a Knight-Ridder newspaper. This newspaper is described as "a sort of smorgasbord of snippets, a newspaper that slices and dices the news into even smaller portions than does *USA TODAY,* spicing it with color graphics and fun facts and cute features like 'Today's Hero' and 'Critter Watch'" (H. Kurtz, 1991). As in *USA Today,* stories in the *Boca Raton News* do not "jump" from one page to another; they start and finish on the same page. To meet this need, long and complex stories often have to be reduced to a few paragraphs. Much of a story's context and much of what the principals have to say are severely cut back or omitted entirely. The main function of the newspaper seems to be to entertain with its emphasis on light and celebrity news and its color maps and graphics.

The objective of the remainder of this chapter is to get at the full reach of the influence of McDonaldization throughout society. I will do this by breaking McDonaldization down into its key elements and then demonstrating how each element is being manifested in more and more sectors of society.

Efficiency

The first element of McDonaldization is *efficiency,* or the choice of the optimum means to an end. Many aspects of the fast-food restaurant illustrate efficiency (drive-through windows, for example), especially from the viewpoint of the restaurant, but none illustrates it better than the degree to which the customer is turned into an unpaid laborer. For example, customers are expected to stand in line and order their own food rather than having a waiter do it and to "bus" their own paper, plastic, and Styrofoam rather than having it done by a busperson.

Fast-food restaurants have also pioneered the movement toward handing the consumer little more than the basics of a meal. The consumer is expected to take the naked burger to the "fixin' bar" and there turn it into the desired sandwich by adding such things as lettuce, tomatoes, and onions. We all therefore are expected to a log a few minutes a week as sandwich makers. In a more recent innovation, we are now handed an empty cup and expected to go the fountain and fill our glasses with ice and a soft drink, spending a few moments as what used to be called a soda jerk. In some ultramodern fast-food restaurants people are met by a computer screen when they enter and must punch in their own orders. In these and other ways, the fast-food restaurant has grown more efficient, often by imposing inefficiencies on the consumer.

The salad bar, also popularized if not pioneered by the fast-food restaurant, is a classic example of putting the consumer to work. The customer buys an empty plate and then loads up on the array of vegetables and other foods available that day. Quickly seeing the merit in all this, many supermarkets have instituted their own salad bars with a more elaborate array of foods. The salad lover can now work as a salad chef at lunch hour in the fast-food restaurant and then do it all over again in the evening at the supermarket. All this is very efficient from the perspective of the fast-food restaurant and the supermarket since only a very small number of employees are needed to keep the various compartments well stocked.

Of course, the fast-food restaurant did not create the idea of imposing work on the consumer, getting the consumer to be in effect an unpaid employee, but it institutionalized and expedited this development. There are many other examples of this process of imposing work on the consumer. Old-time grocery stores where the grocer retrieved the needed items have been replaced by supermarkets where the shopper may put in several hours a week "working" as a grocery clerk seeking out wanted items during lengthy treks down seemingly interminable aisles. Having obtained the groceries, the shopper then unloads the food at the checkout counter and in some cases even bags the groceries. This is all efficient from the point of view of the supermarket, but it is clearly inefficient from the perspective of the shopper.

Virtually gone are gas station attendants who filled gas tanks, checked oil, and cleaned windows. At self-service stations we all now put in a few minutes a week as unpaid attendants pumping gas, checking oil, and cleaning windows. Furthermore, instead of having a readily available attendant to pay for our gasoline, we must trek into the station to pay. Indeed, in many stations we must pay first, return to pump the gas, and, if we haven't pumped as much gas as we expected, trek back to the kiosk to get our change. In the latest "advance" in this realm, customers put a credit card in a slot and pump the gas, the credit-card account is automatically charged the correct (we hope) amount for the gas pumped, and finally the receipt and the card are retrieved with no contact with or work done by anyone employed in the gas station. (For an analysis of the origin and use of credit cards, see the exhibit in this chapter.)

This development was pioneered in the banking industry with the advent of the cash machine, which allows us all to work for a few moments as unpaid tellers. The phone companies now make us put in a few minutes a day as operators. Instead of asking a long-distance operator to make our calls, we are urged to dial such calls ourselves, requiring us to keep lengthy lists of phone numbers and area codes. A similar effort by the phone companies involves having us look up numbers in the phone book rather than calling an operator for information. For those who still use the operator to get such information, there is now a fairly hefty charge for the service. In some doctors' offices we are now being asked to weigh ourselves and take our own temperatures. Instead of being interviewed by a government census taker, we are now likely to receive a questionnaire in the mail that we are expected to fill out on our own.

When we call many businesses these days, instead of dealing with a human operator who makes the connection for us, we must deal with "voice mail" and follow a series of instructions from a computer voice by pushing a bewildering array of numbers and codes before we get to the desired extension (Barron, 1989). The post office has us do some of its work by pressing us to know and utilize increasingly lengthy ZIP codes. The post office is also relying on more and more automated technologies to sort mail. However, the technology breaks down when an address is

The Beginnings of a Sociological Idea: Creditcardization

While the golden arches seem to be visible almost everywhere we turn, the credit card is much more pervasive (Mandell, 1990). In fact, given the many forms that credit cards take—bank cards (VISA), "universal" cards (American Express), department store cards, gasoline company cards, and many others—it is probably impossible to determine how many credit cards exist in the United States and the rest of the world. However, it seems safe to guess in the billions of cards, and the number is growing by leaps and bounds.

While forerunners of the credit card can be traced to the early twentieth century, the modern credit card was born with the creation of Diner's Club in 1949 and the entrance of American Express into the business in 1958 (Friedman and Mehan, 1992). The first bank cards appeared in the early 1950s; the forerunner of VISA came on the scene in 1958. Thus, the credit card came into existence at about the same time as the fast-food restaurant (Ray Kroc's first restaurant was opened in 1955) and for many of the same reasons (see exhibit in Chapter 8). Meteoric expansion has characterized the credit-card business, especially in recent years. There has been growth in the number of people who have credit cards, the average number of credit cards held by each person, the amount of consumer debt attributable to credit-card purchases, the number of facilities accepting credit cards, the number of banks issuing cards, and the internationalization of the credit-card business. In some senses the credit card has invaded our lives far more deeply and insidiously than has the fast-food restaurant. After all, we drive in and out of fast-food restaurants on occasion, but it is likely that several credit cards are with us at all times in our wallets.

In the analysis of McDonald's (as well as the discussion of hyperrationality in Chapter 8), I have relied for my inspiration on the works of Max Weber. In this discussion of creditcardization I build not only on Weber's work but also on the ideas of one of Weber's contemporaries, Georg Simmel. While there were obviously no credit cards in Simmel's day (although some primitive "charga-plates" were used by American retailers as early as 1914), Simmel is *the* classic sociological theorist who had the most to say about and the greatest insights into the immediate precursor—money—of the credit card (Simmel, 1907/1978). Many of Simmel's insights into the nature of money are applicable or can be extended to the nature of the credit card.

While Simmel did not anticipate the credit card, he did deal with the general issue of credit, which he regarded as an "intensification of capital" (Kintzele, 1986–1987). Following this logic, the credit card leads to an intensification in the use of money. That is, people can spend more than they actually have in money or resources and can spend more frequently. Many people have come to rely on the credit card to permit them to purchase more things and to live a lifestyle that they otherwise could not afford.

The economy has also come to depend on the wide-scale use of the credit card. No longer is it enough for people to spend all their available money, they must go into debt via credit-card use (as well as other types of credit, such as auto, home equity, and personal loans) to keep the economy humming. In fact, the lingering recession of the early 1990s can be attributed in part to the fact that many consumers have approached, if not reached or exceeded, the upper limits of their credit-card indebtedness. Many people find it necessary and/or desirable to draw down their credit-card indebtedness before incurring new debts. Since seemingly ever-expanding credit-card indebtedness helped fuel the boom in the American economy, that boom has been deflated as a result, at least in part, of the current unwillingness of consumers to incur new credit-card debt.

The invention and expansion of the credit card are of course far from the end of the process of the intensification of capital. Hendrickson (1972), for example, sees this as only the beginning of the emergence of a cashless society. Many believe that debit cards and electronic funds transfer (EFT) will eventually supplant credit cards. Through the use of debit cards, funds are transferred directly from one account (say, that of a purchaser) to another (say, that of a department store). We already see the forerunner of a large-scale debit card and EFT system in the ATM systems now used by many banks. The next step—the development of so-called point-of-sale (POS) (for example, in supermarkets) terminals using debit cards—has been slowed by the fact that consumers prefer the short-term credit offered by credit cards to the immediate debiting of their bank accounts. However, the elimination of "free" short-term credit is precisely the reason that will lead banks and other creditors to push for the wider use of debit-card systems.

Thus, in analyzing the credit card, I am examining not the endpoint of a process but simply another stage in a historical process which began with barter, moved on to money, and has now come to be dominated by the use of the credit card in many types of transactions, such as the payment of department store purchases, the purchase of airline tickets, and the payment of hotel bills.

Given this general introduction, in the exhibit in Chapter 8 I will compare and contrast creditcardization and McDonaldization.

---

not clearly written on the envelope. Thus, the post office is now asking people not only to write clearly but to type addresses on envelopes (National Public Radio, 1990).

Efficiency has been extended to the booming diet industry, which encompasses diet drugs, diet books, exercise videotapes, diet meals, diet drinks, weight-loss clinics and "fat farms" (Kleinfeld, 1986). Diet books promising all sorts of efficient shortcuts to weight loss are often at the top of the best-seller lists. Losing weight is normally difficult and time-consuming; this explains the lure of diet books that promise to make weight loss easier and quicker, that is, more efficient.

For those on a diet, and many people are on more or less perpetual diets, the preparation of low-calorie food has been made more efficient. Instead of cooking from scratch, we can use an array of prepared diet foods in frozen or microwavable form. For those who do not wish to go through the inefficient process of eating these diet meals, there are diet shakes that can be mixed and consumed in a matter of seconds.

A fairly recent development is the growth of diet centers such as Nutri/System and Jenny Craig (*Washington Post Health,* 1989). Dieters at Nutri/System are provided (at substantial cost) with prepackaged freeze-dried food. All the dieter needs to do is add water when it is time for the next meal. Freeze-dried foods are efficient not only for the dieter but also for Nutri/System because they can be efficiently packaged, transported, and stored. Furthermore, the dieter's periodic visits to a Nutri/System center are efficiently organized. A counselor is allotted ten minutes with each client. During that brief period weight, blood pressure, and measurements are taken; routine questions are asked; a chart is filled out; and some time is devoted to "problem solving." If the session extends beyond the allotted ten minutes and other clients are waiting, the receptionist will buzz the room. Counselors learn their techniques at Nutri/System University, where after a week of training (no inefficient years of matriculation here) they earn certification and an NSU diploma.[1]

Calculability

The second dimension of McDonaldization is *calculability.* McDonaldization involves an emphasis on things that can be calculated, counted, quantified. Quantification refers to a tendency to emphasize quantity rather than quality. This leads to a sense that quality is equal to certain, usually (but not always) large quantities of things.

As in many other aspects of its operation, the emphasis on quantity at McDonald's (for example, the Big Mac) is mirrored by other fast-food

[1] I would like to thank Dora Giemza for these and other insights into Nutri/System.

restaurants. The most notable is Burger King, which stresses the quantity of the meat in its hamburger called the "Whopper" and of the fish in its sandwich called the "Whaler." At Wendy's we are offered a variety of "Biggies." Similarly, 7-Eleven offers its customers a hot dog called the "Big Bite," a large soft drink called the "Big Gulp," and the even larger "Super Big Gulp." This emphasis on quantity in a McDonaldized society is not restricted to fast-food restaurants. For example, United Airlines boasts that it serves more cities than does any other airline.

What is particularly interesting about this emphasis on quantity is the seeming absence of interest in communicating anything about quality. Thus, United Airlines does not tell us anything about the quality (for example, passenger comfort) of its numerous flights. The result is a growing concern about the decline or even absence of quality not only in the fast-food business but in society as a whole (Tuchman, 1980). If fast-food restaurants were interested in emphasizing quality, they might give their products names such as the "Delicious Mac," the "Mac with Prime Beef," and the "All-Beef Frankfurter," but the fact is that typical McDonald's customers know they are *not* getting the highest-quality food.

One observer has argued that we do not go to McDonald's for a delicious, pleasurable meal but to "refuel" as rapidly as possible (Berger, 1983:126). McDonald's is a place to which we go when we need to fill our stomachs with calories and carbohydrates so that we are able to move on to the next rationally organized activity. It is far more efficient to think of eating as refueling rather than as a dining experience.

As with efficiency, calculability has been extended from fast-food restaurants to many other settings, including dieting. Given its nature, the diet industry is obsessed with things that can be quantified. Weight, weight loss or gain, and time periods are measured precisely. Food intake is carefully measured and monitored. Diet foods detail the number of ounces of food, the number of calories, and many other things.

Organizations such as Weight Watchers and Nutri/System are obsessed with calculability. Thus, their efforts to carefully measure caloric intake per day, number of calories in each food product, and weight lost per week are not surprising. What is striking is their increasing desire to provide foods that can be prepared in a short time. For example, Nutri/System boasts that most of its freeze-dried "dinner entrees can be ready in under five minutes. So you don't have to spend a lot of time in the kitchen." However, in its endless search to further reduce the amount of time devoted to food preparation, Nutri/System is now "offering an increasing number of microwavable entrees that can be on your plate, ready to eat, 90 seconds after you take them from your cupboard."[2]

[2] These quotations are from official Nutri/System publications.

An interesting extension of the emphasis on quantity rather than quality is found in *USA Today.* This newspaper is noted for its "junk-food journalism," or the lack of substance in its stories (Prichard, 1987:8). Instead of offering detailed stories, *USA Today* offers a large number of short, easily and quickly read stories. It is the kind of newspaper that can be read in about the time it takes one to consume a meal at a fast-food restaurant. Said one executive: "USA TODAY must sell news/info at a fast, hard pace" (Prichard, 1987:113). One observer underscored the newspaper's corresponding lack of concern for quality and relationship to the fast-food restaurant: "'Like parents who take their children to a different fast-food joint every night and keep the refrigerator stocked with ice cream, USA TODAY gives its readers only what they want. No spinach, no bran, no liver'" (Prichard, 1987:196).

There is growing emphasis on the number of credentials one possesses. For example, people in various occupations are increasingly using long lists of initials (for example, my B.A., M.B.A., and Ph.D. are supposed to persuade the reader that I am competent to write this book) after their names to convince prospective clients of their competence. Said one insurance appraiser with ASA, FSVA, FAS, CRA, and CRE after his name: "'The more [initials] you tend to put after your name, the more impressed they [potential clients] become" (Gervasi, 1990:D5). However, the sheer number of credentials tells us little about the competence of the person sporting them. Furthermore, this emphasis on the quantity of credentials has led people to simply concoct letters to put after their names. For example, one camp director put the letters ABD after his name to impress the parents of prospective campers. While these letters may appear impressive to a layperson, academics know that this is an informal and largely negative label—all but dissertation—for people who have completed their graduate courses and exams but have not written a dissertation. Also to be noted here is the development of organizations whose sole reason for existence is to supply meaningless credentials, often through the mail.

The emphasis on the quantity rather than quality of publications among academics has led to an announcement by the president of Stanford University, Donald Kennedy, that there would be a change in that university's emphasis on the quantity of publications in the decision to hire, promote, or grant tenure to faculty members. He was disturbed by a report that indicated "that nearly half of faculty members believe that their scholarly writings are merely counted—and not evaluated—when personnel decisions are made" (Cooper, 1991:A12). Said Kennedy:

> "First, I hope we can agree that the quantitative use of research output as a criterion for appointment or promotion is a bankrupt idea. . . . The overproduction of routine scholarship is one of the most egregious as-

> pects of contemporary academic life: It tends to conceal really important work by sheer volume; it wastes time and valuable resources" (Cooper, 1991:A12).

To deal with this problem, Kennedy proposed to limit the number of publications used in making personnel decisions. He hoped that the proposed limits would "'reverse the appalling belief that counting and weighing are the important means of evaluating faculty research'" (Cooper, 1991:A12). It remains to be seen whether Stanford, to say nothing of the rest of American academia, will be able to limit the emphasis on quantity rather than quality.

Predictability

Rationalization involves an increasing effort to ensure *predictability* from one time or place to another. In a rational society people want to know what to expect in all settings and at all times. They neither want nor expect surprises. They want to know that when they order a Big Mac today, it is going to be identical to the one they ate yesterday and the one they will eat tomorrow.

The movie industry is increasingly characterized by predictability. One manifestation of this is the growing reliance on sequels to successful movies rather than the production of completely new movies based on new concepts, ideas, and characters. The Hitchcock classic, *Psycho,* for example, was followed by several sequels (of course, not made by Hitchcock), as have less artistically successful horror films such as *Halloween* and *Nightmare on Elm Street.* Outside the horror movies genre, a range of other movies have been succeeded by one or more sequels, including *Star Wars, The Godfather, Back to the Future,* and *Terminator.*

The routine use of sequels is a relatively new phenomenon in Hollywood. Its development parallels and is part of the McDonaldization of society. The attraction of sequels lies in their predictability. From the point of view of the studios, the same characters, actors, and basic plot lines can be used over and over. Furthermore, there seems to be a greater likelihood that sequels will be successful at the box office than is the case with completely original movies; profit levels are more predictable. From the viewers' perspective, there is great comfort in knowing that they will once again encounter favorite characters played by familiar actors who find themselves in accustomed settings. Thus, in a series of *Vacation* movies Chevy Chase plays the same character. The only thing that varies is the vacation setting in which he practices his familiar antics. Moviegoers seem to be more willing to shell out money for a safe and familiar movie than for a movie that is completely new to them. Like a McDonald's meal, sequels are typically not of as high quality as the originals, but at least the consumers know what they are getting. In fact, it is almost always the case that the first sequel is not as good as the original movie and that each succeeding sequel is worse than its predecessor.

One of the early manifestations of predictability, the TV dinner, has now been joined and in some cases superseded by even more rational meals eaten at home. The microwavable dinner may not be any more predictable than the TV dinner was, but it is more efficient to store (in the closet rather than the freezer) and cook (a few minutes in the microwave rather than a half hour in the oven). But make no mistake about it: microwavable foods do offer considerable predictability. To this list of advances we can now add the freeze-dried foods that blossom into predictable dishes merely through the addition of water.

A similar process can be seen in camping. While some people still "rough it," many others have sought to eliminate most if not all of the unpredictability from camping. Said the owner of a campground: "'All they wanted [in the past] was a space in the woods and an outhouse. . . . But nowadays people aren't exactly roughing it'" (D. Johnson, 1986:B1). We have witnessed the development of "country-club campgrounds" spearheaded by franchises such as Kampgrounds of America (KOA) (*Newsweek,* 1984). Instead of using simple tents, modern campers may venture forth in a recreational vehicle (RV) or with a trailer with an elaborate pop-up tent to protect themselves from unexpected thunderstorms, tick bites, and snakes. Of course, "camping" in an RV also tends to reduce the likelihood of catching sight of wandering deer or bear. Furthermore, the RV frequently carries within it all the predictable elements that one has at home: refrigerator, stove, television, video recorder, stereo, and so on. Said one camper relaxing in his air-conditioned thirty-two-foot trailer: "'We've got everything right here. . . . It doesn't matter how hard it rains or how the wind blows'" (D. Johnson, 1986:B1).

Much of the attraction of the shopping mall is traceable to its predictability. For example, the unpredictability of weather is eliminated: "'One kid who works here told me why he likes the mall. . . . It's because no matter what the weather is outside, it's always the same in here. He likes that. He doesn't want to know it's raining—it would depress him'" (Kowinski, 1985:27). This quotation points to another predictable aspect of shopping malls: They are always upbeat and rosy. Malls, like fast-food restaurants, are also virtually the same from one place or time to another: One finds the same chains represented in malls throughout the country. Finally, those who spend their days wandering through malls are relatively free from the unpredictabilities of crime that beset them when they wander through city streets.

An interesting example of predictability in a previously highly unpredictable area is the rationalization of the training of racehorses. The leader here is the trainer Wayne Lukas, who has set up a string of stables around the United States that have been labeled, as was mentioned previously, "McStables" (Beyer, 1990). In the past, training stables were independent operations specific to a given track. Thus, there has been great variation from one racetrack to another and from one stable to another in the way in which training is done. Lukas has set up a set of uniform stables throughout the racetracks of the United States:

> Lukas has thrived by establishing and supervising far-flung divisions of his stable. "I think the absolute key to doing this is quality control," he said. "You cannot ever see a deviation of quality from one division to the other. The barns are the same. The feeding program is the same. . . .
>
> "This is what makes it easy to ship horses around the country. Most horses, when they ship, have to adjust. There's never an adjustment necessary in our divisions. *It's the McDonald's principle.* We'll give you a franchise, and that franchise is going to be the same wherever you go" (italics added; Beyer, 1990:F8).

Part of the success of *USA Today* is traceable to its predictability. Since it is a national newspaper, travelers are reassured by the fact that the familiar masthead and contents will be available wherever they go. Also quite predictable is the vending machine (which, by the way, looks reassuringly like a television set), which is identical from one place to another. As one executive put it: "'A business traveler in Washington, D.C., can pick up a copy on Monday and have an identical rack smiling at him in Los Angeles on Tuesday'" (Prichard, 1987:102). The structure and makeup of the newspaper are highly predictable from one day to the next. The stories are all predictably short and easily digestible. There are as few surprises in one's daily *USA Today* as there are in one's nightly Big Mac; in fact, they are best consumed together.

I close this discussion of predictability in a McDonaldized society with the example of modern suburban housing. Many of Steven Spielberg's movies take place in these rationalized and highly predictable suburbs. Spielberg's strategy is to lure the viewer into this highly predictable world and then have a highly unpredictable event occur. For example, in *E.T.—The Extra-Terrestrial,* the extraterrestrial wanders into a suburban development of tract houses and is discovered by a child who lives in one of those houses and who up to that point has lived a highly predictable suburban existence. The unpredictable ET eventually disrupts not only the lives of the child and his family but also that of the entire community. Similarly, *Poltergeist* takes place in a suburban household, and the evil spirits ultimately disrupt its predictable tranquillity. (The spirits first manifest themselves through that key element of a McDonaldized society: the television set.) The great success of Spielberg's movies may be traceable to our longing for some unpredictability, even if it is frightening and menacing, in our increasingly predictable lives.

Control through the Substitution of Nonhuman for Human Technology

I now combine the discussion of two elements of McDonaldization: *increased control* and *the replacement of human by nonhuman technology*. The reason for the combination is that these two elements are closely linked. Specifically, replacement of human by nonhuman technology is often oriented toward greater control. The great sources of uncertainty and unpredictability in a rationalizing system are people—either the people who work within those systems or the people who are served by them. McDonald's seeks to exert increasing control over both its employees and its customers. It is most likely to do this by steadily replacing people with nonhuman technologies. After all, technologies such as robots and computers are far easier to control than are humans (except, perhaps, for fictional computers like HAL in *2001: A Space Odyssey*). In addition to the elimination of some people and their replacement by technologies, those who continue to labor within McDonald's are better controlled by the new technologies. These nonhuman technologies also exert increasing control over the people served by the system.

As in the production and consumption of food in the fast-food restaurant, the production of some of the raw materials required by such restaurants—bread, fish, meat, and eggs—has come to be characterized by increasing control through the substitution of nonhuman for human technology. For example, in the case of the raising of animals for food, relatively small, humanized family-run farms are being rapidly replaced by "factory farms" where people and animals are controlled by nonhuman technologies (Singer, 1975). One of the first animals to find its way into the factory farm was the chicken. Here is a description of a chicken "factory":

> A broiler producer today gets a load of 10,000, 50,000, or even more day-old chicks from the hatcheries, and puts them straight into a long, windowless shed. . . . Inside the shed, every aspect of the birds' environment is controlled to make them grow faster on less feed. Food and water are fed automatically from hoppers suspended from the roof. The lighting is adjusted . . . for instance, there may be bright light twenty-four hours a day for the first week or two, to encourage the chicks to gain [weight] quickly. . . .
>
> Toward the end of the eight- or nine-week life of the chicken, there may be as little as half a square foot of space per chicken—or less than the area of a sheet of quarto paper for a three-and-one-half-pound bird. (Singer, 1975:96–97).

Among their other advantages, such farms allow one person to manage over 50,000 chickens. Raising chickens in this way involves a series of highly predictable steps. Furthermore, the chickens will be far more predictable in size and weight than are free-ranging chickens. It is also obviously far more efficient to "harvest" chickens confined in this manner than it is to catch chickens that are free to roam over large areas.

However, confining chickens in such crowded quarters creates unpredictabilities such as violence and even cannibalism. These irrational "vices," which are caused by the unnaturally crowded conditions in which the chickens are forced to live, are dealt with in a variety of ways, such as dimming the light as the chickens approach full size and "debeaking" chickens so that they cannot harm one another.

Hens have another use: producing eggs. In the modern world of factory farming, hens are viewed as little more than "converting machines," transforming raw material (feed) into a finished product (eggs). Here is a description of the technology employed to rationalize egg production:

> The cages are stacked in tiers, with food and water troughs running along the rows, filled automatically from a central supply. They have sloping wire floors. The slope . . . makes it more difficult for the birds to stand comfortably, but it causes the eggs to roll to the front of the cage where they can easily be collected . . . in the more modern plants, carried by conveyor belt to a packing plant. . . . The excrement drops through [the wire floor] and can be allowed to pile up for many months until it is all removed in a single operation (Singer, 1975:105–106).

This is obviously a very efficient way to produce eggs, but it also leads to a more predictable supply and more uniform quality in the eggs.

The replacement of human by nonhuman technology and the consequent increase in control are found not only in food production and the fast-food restaurant but also in home cooking. Technologies such as the microwave oven or the conventional oven with a temperature probe "decide" when food is done rather than leaving that judgment to the cook. Ovens, coffee makers, and other appliances now turn themselves on and off. The instructions on all kinds of packaged foods dictate precisely how the food is to be prepared and cooked. Premixed products such as Mrs. Dash combine an array of seasonings, eliminating the need for the cook to come up with creative combinations of seasonings. Even the now old-fashioned cookbook was designed to take creativity away from the cook who was inclined to flavor to taste and put it in the hands of the rigid guidelines laid down by the cookbook.

One of the latest advances in this realm is Nissin Foods' new "Super Boil" soup, the soup that cooks itself. A turn of a key starts a chemical reaction in a special compartment at the bottom of the can that eventually boils the soup in the top compartment. While it is available only in Japan at the moment, it seems only a matter of time until Super Boil soup will be available in the United States (*Scholastic News*, 1991).

A very similar development has taken place in supermarkets. In the past, prices were marked on food products and the supermarket checker had to read the price and enter it into the cash register. As with all human activities, there was a chance for human error. To counter this problem, many supermarkets have installed optical scanners. Instead of the human checker reading the price, the mechanical scanner "reads" the code, and the price for a given code number has been entered into the computer that is the heart of the modern cash register. This nonhuman technology has eliminated some of the human uncertainty from the job of supermarket checker. It has also reduced the number and level of sophistication of tasks performed by the checker. The checker no longer needs to read the amount and enter it in the cash register. Less skilled tasks such as scanning the food and bagging it are all that is left. In other words, the supermarket checker has undergone "deskilling," a decline in the amount of skill required on the job.

The next step in this development is to have the customer do the scanning, eliminating the need for a checkout person. In fact, a nearby Safeway has instituted such a system. To make things easier, Safeway is providing its customers with a brochure entitled "Checkout for Yourself Just How Easy It Is" (of course, one might ask, Easy for whom?). Here are three "easy" steps as described in the brochure:

1. Pass the item's bar code over the scanner. Wait for beep. Place item on conveyor belt.
2. When you are finished scanning all items, touch END ORDER button on screen.
3. Pick up receipt at the end of the lane. Proceed to the pay station.

Such militarylike orders exert great control over the customer and allow for the elimination of the checkout person. Self-checkout is also part of the process, discussed above, of passing more work on to the customer. Indeed, after they are done scanning, customers must then bag their own groceries. The developer of one of these systems predicted that "within five years, self-service grocery technology could be as pervasive as the automatic cash machines used by bank customers" (E. Shapiro, 1990:D1). One customer, obviously a strong believer in McDonaldization, said of the system: "'It's quick, easy and efficient. . . . You get in and out in a hurry'" (E. Shapiro, 1990:D8). The next "advance" will be a technology that permits the insertion of the customer's credit or debit card in the scanning system, avoiding the need to move on to a human cashier and pay for the food.

Supermarket scanners allow other kinds of control over customers.

Before the scanner, customers could examine their purchases and see how much each one cost; they could also check to make sure that they were not being overcharged at the cash register. With the advent of the scanner, prices no longer appear on goods, only bar codes. This change has given the supermarket greater control over customers: It is almost impossible now for the consumer to keep tabs on the checkers. When the scanners were instituted at my local market, the management announced that it was issuing markers to customers who were interested in writing the price on each item. This is consistent with the trend toward getting the consumer to do work historically done by others, in this case by grocery clerks who worked deep into the night to mark each item. In any case, the supermarkets did not keep the markers very long since few hurried shoppers had the desire to put in several additional minutes a day as grocery clerks.

Telemarketing is ubiquitous in our modern society. Many of us are called several times a day in an effort to get us to buy something. Those who work in these telemarketing "factories" are rigidly controlled. They often have scripts that they follow mindlessly. Furthermore, there are a range of alternative scripts designed to handle most foreseeable contingencies. Those doing the phoning are often listened in on by supervisors to make sure the correct procedures are followed. There are rigid standards for numbers of calls and sales required in a given period. If employees fail to meet the quotas, they are summarily fired.

The people who receive such calls and do not hang up immediately are dealing with human robots who mindlessly follow their scripts. Again, following the usual progression, instead of having people solicit us over the phone, some companies are now using computer calls. Computer voices are far more predictable than even the most rigidly controlled human operator.

Not only do we have computer calls, we now have computers that respond to the human voice, or have voice recognition systems. A person receiving a long-distance collect call may be asked whether he or she will accept the charges. The computer voice demands: "Say yes or no" or "Press one for no, zero for yes." While efficient and cost-saving, such a system is anonymous and dehumanizing: "The person senses that he cannot use free-flowing speech. He's being constrained. The computer is controlling him. It can be simply frustrating. . . . People adapt to it, but only by filing it away subconsciously as another annoyance of living in our technological world" (Lander, 1990:H3).

An even more extreme version of this is found in the educational variant of the fast-food restaurant, Kinder-Care. Kinder-Care tends to hire short-term employees with little or no training in education. What these employees do in the "classroom" is determined by a uniform "instruction book" that includes a preset, ready-made curriculum. All that is required is that the staff member open up the manual to the appropriate place, where all activities are spelled out in detail on a day-by-day basis. Clearly, a skilled, experienced, and creative teacher is not the kind of person McChild Care Centers seek to hire. Rather, relatively untrained employees are more easily controlled by the nonhuman technology of the omnipresent instruction book.

Another example of this is the franchised Sylvan Learning Center, which has been labeled the "McDonald's of Education," while its founder has been called "the Colonel Sanders of teaching" (*Newsweek*, 1985:61). Sylvan Learning Centers are after-school centers for remedial education. The corporation "trains staff and tailors a McDonald's type uniformity, down to the U-shaped tables at which instructors work with their charges" (*Newsweek*, 1985:61).

The modern, computerized airplane, such as Boeing's 757 and 767, represents an interesting case of substituting nonhuman for human control. Instead of flying "by the seat of the pants" or using old-fashioned autopilots for simple maneuvers, modern pilots "can push a few buttons and lean back while the plane flies to its destination and lands on a predetermined runway" (Lavin, 1989:1). Said one FAA official, "We're taking more and more of these functions out of human control and giving them to machines" (Lavin, 1989:6).

The new automated airplanes are in many ways safer and more reliable than older, less technologically advanced models. However, there is a fear that pilots, having become dependent on these technologies, will lose the ability to find creative ways of handling emergency situations. Said an airline manager, "If we have human operators subordinated to technology, then we're going to lose that creativity. I don't have computers that will do that [be creative]; I just don't" (Lavin, 1989:6).

Irrationality of Rationality

Great gains in increasing rationalization have resulted from increases in efficiency, predictability, calculability, and control through the substitution of nonhuman for human technology. The economic columnist Robert Samuelson (1989) confesses that he "openly worship[s] McDonald's" and thinks of it as "the greatest restaurant chain in history." [However, Samuelson does recognize that there are those who "can't stand the food and regard McDonald's as the embodiment of all that is vulgar in American mass culture" (1989:A25)]. Let me enumerate some of the advantages of the fast-food restaurant and, more generally, of other elements of a McDonaldized society.[3]

[3] I would like to thank my colleague Stan Presser for suggesting that I enumerate some of these advantages.

The fast-food restaurant has expanded the alternatives available to consumers: More people now have ready access to Italian, Mexican, Chinese, and Cajun foods; the salad bar enables people to make salads exactly the way they want them; and microwave ovens and microwavable foods allow us to have dinner in minutes or even seconds. For those with a wide range of shopping needs, supermarkets and shopping malls are very efficient sites and home shopping networks allow us to shop more efficiently without leaving home. Today's high-tech for-profit hospitals are likely to provide higher-quality medical care than did their predecessors, and we can get almost instantaneous medical attention at the local drive-in McDoctors. Computerized phone systems allow people to do things, such as getting a bank balance in the middle of the night, that were impossible before, and automated bank teller machines allow people to obtain money any time of the day or night. Package tours permit large numbers of people to visit countries they would otherwise be unable to see; diet centers such as Nutri/System allow people to lose weight in a carefully regulated and controlled system; the twenty-four-second clock in professional basketball has enabled outstanding athletes such as Michael Jordan to more fully demonstrate their extraordinary talents; RVs let the modern camper avoid excessive heat, rain, and insects; and suburban tract houses have permitted large numbers of people to afford single-family homes.

Rational systems also allow us to avoid the problems created by nonrational systems in other societies. Here is a description of a recent visit to a pizzeria in Havana, Cuba:

> The pizza's not much to rave about—they scrimp on tomato sauce, and the dough is mushy. . . .
>
> It was about 7:30 p.m., and as usual the place was standing-room-only, with people two deep jostling for a stool to come open and a waiting line spilling out onto the sidewalk. . . .
>
> The menu is similarly Spartan. . . . To drink, there is tap water. That's it—no toppings, no soda, no beer, no coffee, no salt, no pepper. And no special orders. . . .
>
> A very few people are eating. Most are waiting. . . . Fingers are drumming, flies are buzzing, the clock is ticking. The waiter wears a watch around his belt loop, but he hardly needs it; time is evidently not his chief concern. After a while, tempers begin to fray. . . .
>
> But right now, it's 8:45 p.m. at the pizzeria, I've been waiting an hour and a quarter for two small pies . . . (Hockstader, 1991:A12).

Few would prefer such irrational systems to the rationalized elements of our society.

However, while there are many advantages to a McDonaldized society, there are also great costs which can be dealt with largely under the heading of *the irrationality of rationality*. In other words, it is my thesis, following Weber, that rational systems inevitably spawn a series of irrationalities that limit, ultimately compromise, and perhaps even defeat their rationality.

We can conceive of the irrationality of rationality in several ways. At the most general level, it is simply an overarching label for all the negative aspects and effects of McDonaldization. More specifically, it can be seen as the opposite of rationality and its several dimensions. That is, McDonaldization can be viewed as leading to inefficiency, unpredictability, incalculability, and loss of control. Most specifically, irrationality means that rational systems are *unreasonable* systems. By that I mean that they deny the basic humanity, the human reason, of the people who work within or are served by them. In other words, rational systems are dehumanizing systems. Thus, while in other contexts rationality and reason are often used interchangeably, here they are employed to refer to antithetical phenomena.

The most obvious manifestations of the inefficiency of the fast-food restaurant are the long lines of people that are often found at the counters and the long lines of cars that snake by the drive-through windows. What is purported to be an efficient way of obtaining a meal turns out to be quite inefficient. (Recall the long lines at the McDonald's in Moscow described earlier in this chapter.) The fast-food restaurant is far from the only aspect of our McDonaldized society that operates inefficiently. Here is the way columnist Richard Cohen describes the inefficiencies of automated teller machines (ATMs) and in the process deals with a point raised earlier in this chapter—the tendency in a rational society to utilize the consumer as an unpaid worker:

> Oh Lord, with each advance of the computer age, I was told I would benefit. But with each "benefit," I wind up doing more work. This is the ATM rule of life. . . . I was told—nay promised—that I could avoid lines at the bank and make deposits or withdrawals any time of the day. Now, there are lines at the ATMs, the bank seems to take a percentage of whatever I withdraw or deposit, and, of course, I'm doing what tellers (remember them?) used to do. Probably, with the new phone, I'll have to climb telephone poles in the suburbs during ice storms (Cohen, 1990:5).

At least three different irrationalities are underscored in this quotation: Rational systems are not less expensive, they force us to do a range of unpaid work, and most important from the point of view of this discussion, they are often inefficient. The fact is that a rationalized system is often not the most efficient means to an end. It may be more efficient to deal with a human teller, either in the bank or at a drive-through window, than to wait on line at an ATM machine, perhaps on a cold, snowy night. For many people it would be far more efficient to prepare a meal at home than to load the family in the car, drive to McDonald's, fill up on food, and then drive home again. This may not be true of some meals cooked at home from scratch, but it is certainly true of TV dinners, microwave meals, and full-course meals brought in from the supermarket. Yet many people persist in the belief, fueled by endless propaganda from fast-food chains, that it is more efficient to eat there than to eat at home.

The main reason why I think of McDonaldization as irrational and ultimately unreasonable is that it tends to be a dehumanizing system that may become antihuman or even destructive of human beings. There are a number of ways in which the health and perhaps the lives of people have been threatened by progressive rationalization (Spencer, 1983). One example is the high caloric, fat, cholesterol, salt, and sugar content of the food served in fast-food restaurants. Such meals are the last things the vast majority of Americans need. Many Americans suffer from being overweight and have high cholesterol levels, high blood pressure, and perhaps diabetes. The kinds of meals typically served at fast-food restaurants make these health problems much worse. Even more worrisome, they help create eating habits in children that contribute to the development of these and other health problems later in life. It can be argued that with their appeal to children, fast-food restaurants are creating not only lifelong devotees of fast food but also people who will grow addicted to diets high in salt, sugar, and fat.

The fast-food industry has run afoul not only of nutritionists but also of environmentalists. It produces an enormous amount of trash, some of which is nonbiodegradable. Many people have been critical of the eyesores created by litter from innumerable fast-food meals strewn across the countryside. Almost two decades ago, before much of its enormous expansion, it was estimated that it took 315 square miles of forest to provide the paper needed for a year by McDonald's (Boas and Chain, 1976). That figure must be far greater today even though some paper containers have been replaced by Styrofoam and other products. Even greater criticism has been leveled at the widespread use by the fast-food industry of virtually indestructible plastics. Styrofoam debris piles up in landfills, creating mountains of waste that will remain there for years, if not forever.

McDonaldized institutions have a negative effect not only on our health and the environment but also on some of our most cherished institutions, most notably the family. For example, a key technology in the destruction of the family meal has been the microwave oven and the vast array of microwavable foods it has helped generate (Visser, 1989). It is striking to learn that over 70 percent of American households have a microwave oven. The *Wall Street Journal* indicated that Americans consider the microwave their favorite household product (*Wall Street Journal,* 1989). In fact, the microwave in a McDonaldizing society is seen as an advance over the fast-food restaurant. Said one consumer researcher: "It has made even fast-food restaurants not seem fast because at home you don't have to wait in line" (*Wall Street Journal*, 1989:B1). Consumers are demanding meals that take no more than ten minutes to microwave, whereas in the late 1970s people were willing to spend about a half hour cooking dinner and in the early 1970s were willing to spend an hour. This emphasis on speed has of course brought with it poorer taste and lower quality, but people do not seem to mind this loss: "'We're just not as critical of food as we used to be'" (*Wall Street Journal*, 1989:B1).

The speed of microwave cooking, along with the wide variety of foods available in that form, makes it possible for family members to eat at different times and places. To give even children independence, companies are marketing products such as Kid's Kitchen, Kid Cuisine, and My Own Meals. As a result, "those qualities of the family meal, the ones that imparted feelings of security and well-being, might be lost forever where food is 'zapped' or 'nuked' instead of cooked" (Visser, 1989:40).

The advances in microwave cooking continue. There are already plastic strips on some foods that turn blue when the food is done. The industry is promising strips that communicate cooking information directly to the microwave oven:

> With cooking reduced to pushing a button, the kitchen may wind up as a sort of filling station. Family members will pull in, push a few buttons, fill up and leave. To clean up, all we need do is throw away plastic plates (Visser, 1989:42).

What is lost, of course, is the family meal, and we need to decide whether we can afford the loss:

> The communal meal is our primary ritual for encouraging the family to gather together every day. If it is lost to us, we shall have to invent new ways to be a family. It is worth considering whether the shared joy that food can provide is worth giving up (Visser, 1989:42).[4]

Thus, we see that contrary to McDonald's propaganda and the widespread belief in it, fast-food restaurants and other McDonaldized institutions are *not* truly reasonable systems. They spawn all sorts of problems for the health of their customers and the well-being of the environment, tend to be dehumanizing and therefore unreasonable in various ways, and often lead to the opposite of what they are supposed to create (for example, they lead to inefficiency rather than increased efficiency). All this is not to deny the many advantages of McDonald's that were mentioned above, but it points to the fact that counterbalancing and perhaps even overwhelming problems are associated with a fast-food society. These problems, these irrationalities, need to be understood by a popu-

[4] Quotations by Margaret Visser reprinted with permission from Psychology Today Magazine. Copyright © 1989 (Sussex Publishers, Inc.).

lation which has been exposed to little more than an unrelenting set of superlatives created by McDonaldized institutions to describe themselves.

Perhaps the ultimate irrationality of McDonaldization is the possibility that we could come to lose control over the system while it could come to control us. Already, many aspects of the lives of most people are controlled by these rational systems, although it at least appears that these systems are ultimately controlled by people. However, these rational systems can spin beyond the control of even the people who occupy the highest positions within them. This is one of the senses in which we can, following Weber, talk of an "iron cage of McDonaldization." It can become a system that comes to control all of us.

There is another fear here, and that is that these interlocking rational systems can fall into the hands of a small number of leaders who will then be able to exercise control over all of society. Thus, there are authoritarian and totalitarian possibilities associated with the process of McDonaldization. We may come to be increasingly controlled by the rational systems themselves or by a few leaders who master those systems.

This kind of fear has animated many science fiction writers and is manifested in futuristic classics such as *1984, Brave New World,* and *Fahrenheit 451*. The problem is that these novels described a feared and fearsome future world, while McDonaldization is with us now, has been with us for a while, and is extending its reach throughout society.

CONCLUSION

This, then, is my concept of McDonaldization. As I indicated at the beginning of this chapter, the idea had its roots in the time and place in which I grew up as well as in my exposure to the theories of Max Weber, from which the idea of McDonaldization is derived.

This theory is at its beginning. At one level, in the near future McDonaldization is likely to continue to expand in many different ways. There will be more fast-food restaurants, there will be many more institutions that adopt their principles, and more societies will be penetrated to an increasing degree by McDonaldization. At another level, it is hoped that other thinkers and researchers in sociology will pick up the idea of McDonaldization and develop it further in their work. That work may take the form of critiques, theoretical extensions, or empirical studies. If sociologists in fact do further work on this idea, what we now know about the process of McDonaldization will pale in comparison to what we will know in the coming years.

In Chapter 8 I turn to the roots of a second idea derived from my personal experiences and the theories of Max Weber: hyperrationality.

CHAPTER 8

The Beginnings of Another Sociological Idea: Hyperrationality

Hyperrationality, like the idea of McDonaldization, is derived from Weber's theory of rationality. While the two ideas stem from the same intellectual roots, their beginnings in my personal life were quite different.

HOW I BECAME INTERESTED IN HYPERRATIONALITY

Before I became a sociologist, I had an earlier life in the field of personnel administration (now called human resource management). I received a master's degree in business administration, with a specialty in personnel management, from the University of Michigan in 1964. Soon afterward I began work in the personnel department at the Ford Motor Company. I spent only a year at Ford before returning to graduate school at Cornell University to get a Ph.D. However, that year opened my eyes to the problems of the highly rationalized (or, in the terms used in Chapter 7, McDonaldized) systems developed by Ford, every other American automobile manufacturer, and most large American organizations. The two most rationalized systems at Ford were the white-collar bureaucracy in which I labored and the blue-collar assembly line that I often had occasion to visit. What struck me about both were the innumerable problems associated with their excessive rationalization.

Interestingly, the bureaucracy and the assembly line are generally thought of as two of the main sources of the problems that have had a negative effect on the American automobile industry in general and the Ford Motor Company in particular over the last two decades. Problems associated with the assembly line, especially poor product quality and high labor costs, have made it increasingly difficult for American automobile companies to compete with their Japanese counterparts. Similarly, the bureaucracies that characterized American automobile companies, with their large numbers of workers who contribute little or nothing to the value of the car, have also caused competitive disadvantages. In fact, in recent years American automobile companies have undertaken major programs to improve the quality of production and reduce labor costs on the assembly line and to slim down the bureaucracy by reducing the number of white-collar workers.

But I am getting ahead of the story. Let me return to my experiences at Ford and the beginnings of my thinking on hyperrationality as it applies to the automobile industry: I start with the bureaucracy. Although I did not have such theoretical tools in those days, the following discussion is informed by my knowledge of Weberian theory.

Ford in the 1960s resembled Weber's classic model of a bureaucratic system. The Ford bureaucracy was a huge pyramid culminating in the position of the president of the company and its board of directors. The people who occupied every position in that hierarchy performed a series of set tasks and fulfilled specific functions, and all were rigidly bound by endless rules that seemed to cover every contingency. The office carried with it the authority for its incumbents to perform those functions and gave them the power to require people to carry out their dictates within each office holder's specified area of competence. Each position in the bureaucratic hierarchy required specialized skills; therefore, to fill them, incumbents needed specialized training. What Marx called the means of production—the material (typewriters, desks, tools) required to carry out a position's tasks—were owned by Ford, not the employee. The employee did not control the position; the organization controlled the position. Finally, virtually everything that went on in a given position and in the organization as a whole was spelled out and documented in writing, especially the seemingly unending number of volumes of the Ford manual.

On a more general level, as the paradigm case, or model, of formal rationality, Weber saw the bureaucracy, like the one at Ford, as manifesting the four elements of formal rationality (Chapter 3), or what I have called McDonaldization. In discussing the Ford bureaucracy in these terms, I return to those elements—efficiency, predictability, calculability, and the replacement of human with nonhuman technology—as they were employed in Chapter 7. To broaden this discussion and further illustrate these elements, I will use not only the example of the Ford bureaucracy but also that of two other well-known bureaucracies: the federal government's Internal Revenue Service (IRS) and the Social Security Administration.

The bureaucracy is the most *efficient* structure for handling large numbers of tasks requiring a great deal of paperwork. No other structure can handle a massive quantity of work as efficiently as a bureaucracy can. For example, no other structure could handle the millions of tax returns as well as the highly bureaucratized Internal Revenue Service does. The efficient management of forms is the raison d'être of any personnel department. As a member of the personnel department at Ford, I can attest not only to the efficient handling of massive quantities of paper but also to playing a central role in creating the innumerable forms and demands for reports that were crucial to the generation of all that paper.

Because of their well-entrenched rules and regulations, bureaucracies operate in a highly *predictable* manner. The occupants of a given office know with great assurance how the incumbents in other offices will behave. They know what they will be provided with and when they will receive it. Outsiders who receive the services that a bureaucracy dispenses know with a high degree of confidence what they will receive and when they will receive it. Thus, the millions of recipients of checks from the Social Security Administration know precisely when they will get their checks and exactly how much money they will receive. The same could be said of the wages and salaries dispensed by the personnel department at Ford. In fact, the predictability of my work was one of the key factors in my eventual decision to leave the Ford Motor Company. It seemed to me that there was a Ford way of doing virtually every task, and many of those steps were spelled out in great detail. Everyone was supposed to do virtually the identical thing in a given circumstance. Ford strove to make managerial work, indeed *all* work, highly predictable. I did not want to be a highly predictable employee doing the expected thing on each and every occasion.

Bureaucracies seek to *quantify* as many things as possible. The performance of the incumbents in a bureaucracy is reduced to a series of quantifiable factors. Thus, an IRS agent may be expected to process a certain number of tax returns each day. Satisfactory performance is thought to consist of the actual handling of the required number of cases. Handling less than that number is seen as unsatisfactory performance, and handling more is viewed as excelling at one's work. Similarly, in one of my work assignments at Ford I was in charge of hiring blue-collar workers. Each week I was told how many workers to hire, and I was expected to complete the task in as short a time as possible. If I failed to hire the desired number of people or took too long doing the hiring, I was likely to be admonished by my superiors.

Of course, the problem here is the difficulty with all systems that focus exclusively on quantity and regard high quality as the handling of large numbers of things: There is little or no concern for the actual quality of the handling of each case. The idea is to finish the task, and little attention is paid to how well the job is handled. Thus, an IRS agent who manages large numbers of cases and as a result is positively evaluated by his or her superiors may actually handle the cases quite poorly, costing the government thousands or even millions of dollars in uncollected revenue. Even though, or perhaps because, cases are handled quickly, taxpayers may be angered by the way in which they are treated by IRS agents. Similarly, given the need to hire large numbers of people, Ford personnel officers paid relatively little attention to how well those people would perform their work over the long term.

In my own case, under great pressure to hire lots of people in a short period of time, I was little concerned with how they would work out over the long haul. Instead, I was almost exclusively preoccupied with fulfilling my "quota" of hirings for the week. As a result, many of those employees did not work out in the long run and had to be let go. This turnover was costly to the organization, as was the need to hire other people to take their places. Sadly, a number of the new employees, hired under the same pressures, were likely to experience the same fate as did many of their predecessors.

Bureaucracies emphasize *control over people through the replacement of human with nonhuman technology*. Indeed, the bureaucracy itself, including the Ford bureaucracy, may be seen as one huge nonhuman technology. The nearly automatic functioning of the Ford bureaucracy can be viewed as an effort to replace the human judgment of an employee with the dictates of rules, regulations, and structures. I was also controlled by the division of labor, which allocated to my position a limited number of well-defined tasks. I had to perform those tasks and was not permitted to do others. I not only had to perform those tasks, I also had to do them in the manner prescribed by the organization; I was not allowed in most cases to come up with idiosyncratic ways of doing them. Furthermore, the general idea at Ford and other bureaucracies is to reduce people to human robots or computers that make few, if any, judgments. Once people have been reduced to this status, it becomes possible to think about actually replacing human beings with machines. This has already occurred to some extent as computers have taken over bureaucratic tasks once performed by people. Once the technology has been developed and priced reasonably, one can anticipate that robots will begin replacing humans in the office.

Similarly, a bureaucracy's clients are also controlled. They may get only certain services from the organization and not others. (For example, the IRS can offer us advice on our tax returns but not on our married lives. As a Ford personnel officer, I could advise employees about work-linked issues but not about family matters.) Clients may receive those services only in a certain way and not in others. (For example, welfare payments, as well as salary payments at Ford, are made by check; the individual cannot receive cash.)

While the Ford bureaucracy (and the IRS), like any bureaucracy, carried with it a number of advantages, what struck me, as one might expect from reading Chapter 7, were its *irrationalities.* I was appalled by the large number of people employed in the Ford bureaucracy and the fact that many of them did relatively little that was essential to the functioning of the automobile company. The organization was slow and cumbersome. Rules dominated and complicated everything. Many of the people in high-ranking positions seemed to be mediocre if not downright incompetent. Many of the able people in the organization occupied marginal or low-level positions. They did much of the organization's work but received little of the credit and few of the rewards. Many of those people were forced to leave the organization or left on their own accord as a result of frustration with the way the organization functioned. In short, although it was designed to be a highly rational structure, the Ford bureaucracy struck me as highly irrational.

I reacted in much the same way to the assembly line at Ford. While I did not work on the line, I often had occasion to visit it either to gather some information or, more likely, to appear busy when I had little or nothing to do. (In fact, it was often the case that I, as well as many of my peers, had little to do, and this is another irrationality of the rational bureaucracy.)

Like the modern bureaucracy, the assembly line was "invented" at the dawn of the twentieth century. It was pioneered in the bureaucratized automobile industry. It is Henry Ford who is generally credited with its invention (although it had precursors in industries such as meat-packing and the automobile assembly line was more a product of Ford engineers than of Henry Ford himself), and it was in the automobile industry that it found its best-known application. The assembly line represented a remarkable step forward in the rationalization of manufacturing and was utilized in many different types of manufacturing operations. Like the bureaucracy and the fast-food restaurant, the automobile assembly line at Ford and the other automobile companies beautifully illustrates the basic elements of formal rationality.

It is an *efficient* system for manufacturing an automobile. It is far more efficient to put a large number of highly specialized unskilled workers along a moving conveyor belt than it is to put a number of craft workers in a room and ask them to build a car. What each worker on the line does (for example, putting a hubcap on each passing car) is highly *predictable,* and one end product is identical to all the others. The assembly line permits the *calculability* of many elements of the production process and maximizes the number of cars that are produced. As was pointed out above, this emphasis on quantity often has negative effects on quality.

The assembly line permits maximum *control* over workers. Workers must do the tasks that are required of them and do them when they are needed. It is immediately obvious when a worker fails to perform the required task on time; if, for example, a worker fails to install a hubcap, it will be missed as the car moves down the line. The limited time allotted for each job makes it necessary that the task be done as specified. There is little or no room for innovative ways of doing a specific task. Assembly lines are nonhuman technologies that, compared to earlier technologies, allow fewer, less skilled people to produce cars. Furthermore, the specialization of each task permits the replacement of human workers with robots. The routine repetitive tasks required on the line are just the kind of work robots were created to handle. We are now beginning to see more tasks on the automobile assembly line being handled by mechanical robots; the human robots are being replaced by mechanical robots. Once tasks have been simplified so that they can be handled by human robots, the stage is set for the replacement of human by nonhuman robots.

As has been well detailed by many observers and as it struck me on my visits to the shop floor, the assembly line carried with it much *irrationality*. There are a number of irrationalities of rationality—inefficiency, unpredictability, and so on—but the main irrationality is dehumanization. The assembly line was clearly a dehumanizing setting in which to work. Human beings, equipped with a wide array of skills and abilities, were asked to perform a limited number of repetitive, highly simplified tasks over and over. Instead of expressing their human abilities on the job, people were forced to deny their humanity and act in a robotlike manner. People did not express themselves in their work; rather, they denied themselves.

Furthermore, the workers seemed to care little about their work or the quality of what they produced. As a result, there were many defects in the finished products. Theoretically, the workers were supposed to be able to start automobiles at the end of the assembly line, and the cars were to be driven off to waiting trucks or railroad cars and delivered to dealers. In fact, because of poor quality control, many cars did not start and had to be pushed off the line. Hordes of workers were then required to descend on those automobiles and repair them so that they could be started. Even then, many quality problems remained and were left to dealers to fix or for customers to be displeased with, perhaps for the life of the car.

After I left Ford, I began studying, and later teaching about the automobile industry. The industry seemed primed for a fall, and that occurred less than a decade after I left Ford. The immediate cause of the fall was the oil crisis of 1973, when gasoline prices were driven up and people began to demand smaller, more fuel-efficient automobiles. American manufacturers had generally ignored small car production and the popularity of the Volkswagen Beetle because there was far more money to be made in the sale of big, gas-guzzling automobiles. However, the Japanese were ready with small cars and the capacity to mass-produce them, and as a result, their share of the American market began to grow after 1973.

At first American manufacturers did not take the Japanese seriously and moved slowly to produce small cars in greater quantities. When they did recognize the threat, they seemed unable to produce a small car that could come anywhere close to the quality of the Japanese cars. For example, the Chevrolet Chevette was hardly a rival to the Toyota Corolla.

Thus began the process that has led to the situation today in the automobile industry. American automobile companies are in deep trouble, with frequent huge losses and a declining share of the domestic market. In contrast, Japanese automobile companies are astride the world market, and there is little on the immediate horizon to threaten their position. Given my views on the American automobile company's bureaucracies and assembly lines, I thought I understood at least some of the sources of this country's competitive problems. However, what were the roots of the Japanese successes?

This question led me to read a great deal on the workings of Japanese automobile companies. It was clear that they had solved many of the problems associated with bureaucratic structures and assembly lines in the United States (see below for a discussion of many of those solutions). However, what most interested me was whether there was an overarching explanation for not only the Japanese successes but the American failures. Once again I was drawn to Weber's theory, and this time I developed the idea of *hyperrationality* to explain the success of the Japanese automobile industry and the corresponding failure of its American counterpart. Let us turn now to this idea, how it was derived from Weberian theory, and how it helps us understand Japan's successes and, as will be discussed at the end of this chapter, this country's failures.

WEBER AND HYPERRATIONALITY

Although Weber claimed not to have an overarching theory that could explain the social world, especially the rise of the West and the failure of the rest of the world to modernize, it is possible to discern, as I have discussed previously, such a theory of rationalization in his work. That is, it was a distinctive process of rationalization that lay at the base of the ability of the West to modernize, while the rest of the world failed to modernize because of major barriers to this process. In fact, it is this process in its more modern guise that is discussed in Chapter 7 under the heading of McDonaldization. Furthermore, it is possible to identify in the work of Weber four types of rationality that lie at the heart of his theory of rationalization (Kalberg, 1980; Levine, 1981). (For an application of Weber's theory of rationalization to the creditcardization of the United States, see the exhibit in this chapter).

The first type—*practical rationality*—is found in day-to-day activities. In their everyday actions, people routinely analyze all the possible means available to them, choose the alternative that best allows them to reach their ultimate end, and then follow that line of action. Most students engage in practical rationality all the time. For example, on the first day of classes in the fall, students look at the alternative routes to the building in which one of their classes meets, choose the most direct path, and then follow it when it is time to go to that class.

Theoretical rationality refers to an effort to master reality through the development of increasingly precise and abstract concepts. This involves an attempt to master the world intellectually, whereas practical rationality involves a pragmatic effort to master the world through action. Again, students commonly engage in theoretical rationality. Each new class represents a new area of study that a student must master intellectually. As the semester proceeds, the student's knowledge base is composed of increasingly precise and abstract concepts. Thus, before you started this course and this book, you had a very vague sense of sociology. Now you have mastered a number of precise and abstract concepts, including rationality, McDonaldization, and now hyperrationality.

Substantive rationality involves value postulates, or clusters of values, that guide actors in their daily lives, especially in their choice of means to ends. This is a rational choice of means to ends guided by larger values. Like practical rationality but unlike intellectual rationality, it is manifested in everyday actions. However, in contrast to practical rationality, which is purely pragmatic, substantive rationality involves action guided by broad human values. Students engage in substantive rationality when they value their university and therefore devote considerable energy to its betterment. Thus, students may put in long hours working in the student government to improve the university. Having bought into the value of the university and having been involved in the choice of specific objectives (for example, raising money for a worthy campus activity, cleaning up the campus) on the basis of that value, students then must choose the most rational means of achieving the goals that have been set by the student government.

Finally, *formal rationality* involves the rational calculation of means to ends guided by universally applied rules, regulations, and laws. Formal

The Beginnings of a Sociological Idea: Creditcardization II

Both the credit card and the fast-food restaurant are major symbols of *both* the twentieth century *and* the role of the United States in its development. Both began to come of age in the 1950s, were almost entirely American innovations, have undergone tremendous growth since that time, and in many ways have come to be symbols of the United States throughout the world. They are products of a mobile society and have contributed greatly to an increase in social mobility. The automobile in particular played a key role in the development of both the credit card and the fast-food restaurant. The need for fast-food restaurants arose as more people found themselves on the move, especially by automobile, for business or pleasure. The ready availability of fast food and later many other goods and services (especially motel rooms) in chains that modeled themselves after fast-food restaurants fueled people's mobility. The same dynamic was at work in the growth of the credit-card industry. As more people found themselves on the road for long periods, cash became increasingly cumbersome and personal checks were unlikely to be honored away from home. The credit card filled this need beautifully. In its turn, the credit card helped people become even more mobile by allowing them to pick up and go with little or no forethought or to remain on the road for longer periods. Of course, the increase of air travel did much the same thing, but on an international scale.

The major similarity between fast-food restaurants and credit cards is that they are both part of the process of rationalization. While I have previously dealt at length with Weber's theory of rationalization, Georg Simmel had a very similar perspective (B. Turner, 1986).

Calculability is reflected in the fact that the credit card permits people to maximize the number of things they can buy and the amount of money they can spend on them. After all, because instant credit is offered up to a predefined but expandable limit, people are able not only to spend all their available money but to go into debt for thousands of dollars. In an effort to increase the debt limit, people often try to maximize their credit limits and accumulate as many cards as possible, each with its own credit limit. In fact, in our society the number of credit cards one has and the upper credit limit of those cards are increasingly important status symbols. Rather than the amount of savings one has, the modern status symbol is how much debt one has and how much more one is capable of incurring.

This emphasis on the quantity of credit-card debt allowed tends to lead to a lessening of interest in the quality of the things one can buy.

With well-defined cash limits, the consumer tends to be more careful, often buying high-quality goods that will have that a long and useful life. However, if things are bought on seemingly ever-expandable credit, there is less emphasis on quality: The emphasis is on buying large numbers of things. After all, if things wear out quickly, they can be replaced, often on the basis of a later and higher limit on one's credit card. Similarly, the ready availability of virtually anything and everything leads to a *leveling* of the value of goods and services. This leveling of everything to a common denominator leads to the cynical attitude that everything has its price, that anything can be bought or sold on the market. Since anything can be bought at any time, people develop a blasé attitude that sees "all things as being of an equally dull and grey hue, as not worth getting excited about" (Simmel, 1907/1978:256). The blasé person has lost completely the ability to make value differentiations among the ultimate objects of purchase. Put slightly differently, the credit card (and before that money) is the enemy of esthetics, reducing everything to formlessness, to purely quantitative phenomena.

The second dimension of rationality—*efficiency*—is manifested in the tendency of the credit card to greatly enhance the efficiency of virtually all kinds of shopping. Instead of carrying large and cumbersome amounts of cash, all one needs is a thin piece of plastic. There is no need to plan for purchases by going to the bank and loading up on cash. One can buy things wherever and whenever one wants as long as the trusty card is sitting in one's pocket.

The credit card makes consumption more *predictable.* That is, it serves to free the consumer from the unpredictability associated with cash flow or cash on hand. The credit card has a *smoothing* effect on consumption. We can purchase things or engage in some form of entertainment even though we do not have cash on hand. We are now better able to avoid painful lulls in consumption or entertainment when we are unable to participate because of a lack of ready cash. This also makes the world of the purveyor of goods and services more predictable.

The credit card is itself a kind of nonhuman technology. More important, it has given birth to a range of technologies that intervene between buyer and seller and serve to constrain both. Most notable here is the vast computerized system that "decides" whether to authorize a given purchase. The shopkeeper and the customer may both want to consummate a deal, but if the credit-card company's computer system says no, there is likely to be no sale. This is part of a general trend in rationalized societies to take decision making away from people and put it in the hands of nonhuman technologies.

A variety of pressures have forced the credit-card industry to pursue ever higher levels of rationalization through new and more sophisticated nonhuman technologies. For example, both the consumer and the shopkeeper want quick authorizations of credit-card sales, and this leads to the need for ever more sophisticated computers and computer programs to make such authorizations possible. Similarly, credit-card companies have a strong interest in seeing charges entered speedily into a customer's account so that bills are paid sooner or, better yet, so that interest can be charged sooner on unpaid balances. As with the desire for quicker authorizations, the search for speedier billing also leads to technological advances. Another pressure pointing in the same direction is the need to decide whether to give someone credit and how much credit to give. The movement is away from leaving this up to a human being to decide on a subjective basis and in the direction of developing computerized systems that come up with scores that allow the computer to make these "decisions."

Perhaps the best example of taking control away from humans and building it into the technology is the movement away from "country club" billing and toward "descriptive billing." In country club billing customers receive with the total bill copies of the actual charge slips used for each purchase. This is an expensive undertaking for credit-card companies, and they have in the main pushed for descriptive billing, in which the consumer merely gets a list of the charges, dates, and amounts and copies of receipts are not provided. The problem here is the loss of control by the consumer. With copies of receipts, the consumer can clearly see whether a purchase has been made. With only lists, often long lists, the consumer must rely on memory or on his or her own record keeping. (As we saw in Chapter 7, this is another characteristic of a rationalizing society—pushing more work onto consumers who do it on an unpaid basis.) People often throw up their hands and assume that the list of bills is correct, surrendering control over this issue to the credit-card companies and their computers.

Finally, there is the *irrationality of rationality* associated with the fact that the credit-card world is one in which people generally interact with nonhuman technologies, their products such as bills or overdue notices, or people whose actions and decisions are constrained if not determined by nonhuman technologies. Horror stories abound of people caught up in the "heavy machinery" of credit-card companies. Pity the poor consumers who get charged for something they didn't buy or are sent a series of computer letters with escalating threats because the computer erroneously considers them to be in arrears. Trying to get satisfaction from these technologies or their often robotlike representatives is perhaps the ultimate in the dehumanization associated with a rationalizing society.

More generally, the irrationality of rationality is a general label for the problems associated with rational systems. For example, credit-card companies tend to discriminate against minorities and women. Women often find themselves in a Catch-22 situation, being unable to get credit cards because they do not have a credit history since their credit cards were in a husband's name. Ironically, credit-card companies also discriminate against those who in the past resisted credit and preferred to pay for what they bought, often in cash.

The largest set of problems is associated with the actions taken by credit-card companies to increase their revenues and profits. For example, these companies have altered their accounting methods so that customers end up paying more in interest. Few customers are knowledgeable enough to understand the implications of such changes in accounting procedures or even to realize that they have been made. The problem, however, is more general than that: "A number of banks took advantage of consumer complaisance by changing annual fees, rates, grace periods, late charges, and other card restrictions without attracting a great deal of consumer attention" (Mandell, 1990:79). Few consumers have the will or ability to carefully oversee the activities of credit-card companies.

Perhaps the most persistent and reprehensible activities of credit-card companies involve their efforts to keep interest rates high even during periods when these rates are low and/or declining. This was most notable in the 1980s, when overall interest rates began to fall from historical highs in the early part of the decade but credit-card companies kept the interest rates they charged their customers high. This continues to this day. As I write in late 1992, interest rates are extraordinarily low but the rates charged by most credit-card companies are several times the prime rate. These companies have kept their rates high because they know that "the segment that revolves credit is not particularly rate sensitive" (Mandell, 1990:79).

Still another irrationality of rationality is the secrecy (Simmel, 1906/1950) associated with the credit-card industry. While cash transactions are relatively, and sometimes completely, anonymous, credit-card transactions are not. Our names are associated with every credit-card purchase we make. The nature and pattern of our purchases are amassed in the computer system. Even more troubling is the fact that in order to get a credit card (as well as other forms of credit) we need to pass a credit check. It is here that credit bureaus and their enormous and often shared files come into play. A wide array of information that we have wittingly or unwittingly given out about ourselves is often accumulated in these files and is brought to the fore and used whenever we seek credit.

This means, of course, that many things about us are no longer private; they are no longer secret. More frighteningly, these files may be used and abused for other purposes. For example, it is said the credit bureaus routinely share information with the government. The problem of privacy is exacerbated by the fact that credit-card companies usually sell their lists as a way to increase their income. The result is that our names come into the hands of groups that we might feel should not have them. Furthermore, groups may request special types of lists, such as those which include people with a certain credit history or a given level of income, and this serves to communicate more specific kinds of information about us to other agencies.

While credit cards permit greater access to information about their users, there is great secrecy associated with the credit-card companies themselves. For example, there is a lengthy list of fraudulent activities undertaken against credit-card companies (Mandell, 1990:67). However, to prevent potential perpetrators from learning from these activities, credit-card companies have sought to conceal the nature and degree of such activities from the public. In addition, these companies have sought to keep their misguided ventures into the credit-card arena, along with their losses from such ventures, from the general public.

---

rationality was both native to and eventually dominated the Western industrialized world, where people came to be guided in their actions by formal rationality. It is based on formalized rules, regulations, and laws and is institutionalized in large-scale structures such as the bureaucracy and the capitalist economy. Thus, in the bureaucracy, people's actions are determined by the rules and regulations of the organization, not by values, intellectual processes, or even pragmatic concerns. Students engage in formal rationality when they unthinkingly follow the rules and regulations of the university.

Formal rationality often leads to decisions that disregard the needs of actors, implying that substantive rationality and the human values involved in it are unimportant. A formally rational system does not take into account the wants and needs of actors. In a formally rational capitalist economy, for example, profits are the primary focus, not issues of humanity. Thus, a capitalist firm may push workers to the edge of human endurance or even beyond in an effort to maximize profits.

Weber saw the bureaucracy as the epitome of formal rationality because it strongly furthered the development of the "rational matter-of-factness," the unconcern for human beings, that he saw as increasingly characteristic of the personality of the professional experts who populated bureaucratic structures. These "experts" possessed a "spirit of formalistic impersonality . . . without hatred or passion, and hence without affection or enthusiasm" (Brubaker 1984:21). In Weber's view, the modern bureaucracy is a distinctive product of the West and was a crucial factor, along with the capitalistic firm, in the rise of the West.

Weber argued that the development of formal rationality largely accounted for the unique development and unprecedented success of the West. While the other types of rationality existed at other times and in other societies, formal rationality was characteristic *only* of the modern West. Weber suggested not only that formal rationality was important in the West but also that it came into conflict with the other types of rationality, especially substantive rationality, and reduced them in importance and ultimately subordinated, if not totally eliminated, *all* of them in terms of their importance to Western society.

While Weber was right in tracing the economic success of the West to formal rationality, it is my view that the Japanese miracle was caused by the ability of the Japanese to import Western formally rational systems after World War II and fuse them with both indigenous formally rational structures and the substantive, theoretical, and practical rationality already in existence. It is the simultaneous and synergistic coexistence of all four types of rationality—*hyperrationality*—that constitutes my explanation of Japan's industrial rise (Ritzer and Lemoyne, 1991). I have labeled such a system of rationality "hyperrationality" because it constitutes an unprecedented level of rationality, a level far greater than that achieved in the West, which is impeded by its nearly exclusive reliance on formal rationality.

Following the Weberian mode of analysis, which emphasizes "ideal types," or exaggerated models for social analysis, here is the ideal type of hyperrationality:

First, hyperrationality involves the simultaneous coexistence of practical, theoretical, substantive, and formal rationality. Second, each of these subtypes exists to a high degree. That is, in a hyperrational system it is not just that all four types coexist but that each of them flourishes; there is a high degree of practical, theoretical, substantive, and formal rationality in a hyperrational system. Third, each subtype is interrelated with all the others. Fourth, out of this interaction a new level and type of rationality emerge; hyperrationality is an emergent phenomenon. This means that there is a synergism among the four types of rationality, allowing for the emergence of the highest possible level of rationality.

Although Weber did not develop a full-fledged theory of the interconnectedness among all four types of rationality and hence a sense of hyperrationality, it is clear that he did recognize a variety of coexistences. By extending Weber's limited thoughts on interconnectedness, one can derive a sense of hyperrationality from his work. The creation of such an idea also allows us to create an alternative to the Weberian "iron cage" thesis that formal rationality will come to dominate and eradicate the other three types. A hyperrational society in general and a hyperrational economy in particular stand in contrast to societies and economies dominated by formal rationality.

It is not just that the Japanese have been able to operate with all four types of rationality; they have been able to develop a high level of rationality within each type. The overall level of rationality has been heightened even further by the synergistic interaction of the four types. That is, out of this interaction a level of rationality has emerged that is greater than the sum of the individual rational parts. Put simply, Japanese industry succeeded because it developed all four types of rationality, developed each to a high degree, *and* created an unprecedented level of overall rationality through the interaction of all four subtypes.

Having delineated a sense of hyperrationality and the way in which it is derived from but extends Weberian theory, I now turn to a demonstration of the fact that hyperrationality is a useful theoretical tool for explaining the rise of Japanese industry. Later, and more briefly, I will suggest that a failure to develop a hyperrational system, a single-minded reliance on formal rationality, similarly accounts for the industrial failures of the United States, especially in the automobile industry.

HYPERRATIONALITY AND THE RISE OF JAPANESE INDUSTRY[1]

In this section I will briefly look at each of the four major types of rationality and a few examples of the way in which they have come to exist in Japanese industry. As I proceed, I will also point to some of the synergism that has been achieved among these four types.

Formal Rationality

At the close of World War II Japanese factories were primitive affairs. Initially they were developed by importing American and European structures, procedures, and technologies (Halberstam, 1986:306). For example, from 1951 through March 1984, Japanese companies entered into nearly 42,000 contracts for the importation of the best Western technology (Abegglen and Stalk, 1985:126). If this transfer had not occurred, no amount of capital and labor could have enabled Japanese industry to reach its current competitive level (Gibney, 1982:42).

The late importation of these ideas and systems into a society that

[1] The following discussion was coauthored by Terri LeMoyne.

already had strong substantive, theoretical, and practical rationality helps explain why formal rationality did not triumph over the other types. It was the formal rationality that was to a large extent foreign, and while it was adopted, it was forced to coexist with the other types.

Not only did Japan import formally rational systems, it also had its own indigenous forms. One such structure is the Ministry of Trade and Industry (MITI), which was first established in 1949 as a result of a merger of the Ministry of Commerce and Industry and the Board of Trade (Johnson, 1982:134). In brief, MITI is a formally rational bureaucratic structure which is responsible for overseeing Japan's industries and ensuring that their individual and collective successes also maximize the interests of the nation as a whole (Johnson, 1982:28–29). It is organized into branches that correspond to the major sectors of that nation's industries, and each branch is responsible for the overall success of companies within its sector (Johnson, 1982:48). MITI is involved in developing guidelines about appropriate actions for companies, restraining the destructive effects of monopolies, and aiding smaller companies to make them viable competitors (Johnson, 1982:26). The MITI bureaucracy is also concerned with creating conditions that will assist industries in meeting specific long-range objectives (Vogel, 1979:65–66; Johnson, 1982:28–29). In essence, this long-range planning involves the extension of formal rationality to future planning, giving Japan an enormous advantage over American industry, where formal rationality has been employed largely to achieve short-term goals.

With MITI, the Japanese have created a second, formally rational system with its own bureaucratic branches, sectors, and hierarchical levels to oversee and assist the formally rational, highly bureaucratized industrial sector. The formal rationality of MITI's operation heightens the formal rationality of Japanese industry. In effect, the coexistence of these two formally rational structures serves to synergistically elevate the overall level of formal rationality in Japanese industry.

Another distinctively Japanese formally rational development is the just-in-time (JIT) system, which involves "producing and delivering finished goods just in time to be sold, subassemblies just in time to be assembled into finished products, fabricated parts just in time to go into subassemblies, and purchased materials just in time to be transformed into fabricated parts" (Schonberger, 1982:16). The JIT system is more formally rational than the Western just-in-case (JIC) system, in which industries in the United States produce and store large quantities "just in case" they are needed (Schonberger, 1982:16). JIT requires a higher degree of calculability, a key dimension of formal rationality (Eisen, 1978), than does JIC because manufacturers must precisely calculate the number of parts needed at every stage of the production process so that there is little, if any, backup inventory (Fucini and Fucini, 1990:36). JIC requires far less calculability because backup inventories exist throughout the entire production process (Alston, 1986:52). As a result, far less money is spent on inventory and inventory maintenance in Japan than in the United States (Abegglen and Stalk, 1985:105; Lincoln and Kalleberg, 1990:55). JIT also reduces the amount spent on interest on capital invested in backup inventory and reduces the floor space needed for inventory by one-third, resulting in lower expenditures on the physical plant (Alston, 1986:52). In turn, as a result of smaller factory size, less money is spent on physical maintenance, heating, and cleaning costs than in the United States (Alston, 1986:54).

Finally, in many ways bureaucratic systems in Japan are more formally rational than their Western counterparts. For example, one must have attended one of the imperial universities (admission is governed by tough entrance examinations) to obtain a management position in one of the premier industrial organizations. Once hired, all new managers move through the bureaucratic hierarchy at the same pace and are regularly rotated to different positions and departments (Johnson, 1982:58–60).

This high degree of formal rationality paradoxically encourages a higher degree of substantive rationality in Japanese industrial bureaucracies. Because they run so smoothly, there is greater flexibility, resulting in fewer status distinctions between managers and subordinates and between white- and blue-collar workers (Rohlen, 1975:188–189). Work responsibilities are less clearly distinguished, and there is more of a blending of roles and positions. Workers are dominated by fewer rules, process less paperwork, and are viewed as people rather than interchangeable bureaucratic parts (Iwata, 1982; Kenney and Florida, 1988:132). While formal rationality tends to overwhelm substantive rationality in the West, it serves to encourage at least some of its manifestations in Japan. Formal rationality in Japan also buttresses practical (quality control circles) and theoretical (dependency on engineers) rationality (see below).

Substantive Rationality

In spite of the importation of Western formal rationality and the development of indigenous formally rational systems, Japanese industry has managed to retain a consistent set of human values and a broad sense of community (Bellah, 1957; Vogel, 1979:98; Gibney, 1982; Ishikawa, 1982; Woodrum, 1985); in other words, it has retained its substantive rationality. These values are apparent, for example, during job indoctrination periods, when new workers are encouraged to view the company as a community to which they are expected to contribute. In making their contributions to this work community, they are also contributing to the welfare of the larger society (Alston, 1986:29; Taylor, 1985).

This communitarianism is derived partly from the value the Japanese place on groupism, in which the goal is for the group and the individual to become one (Iwata, 1982:39). In Japanese, the word *individualism* denotes selfishness, isolation from others, and persons concerned only with their own advantage rather than with working for the welfare of others. The person weakens the group by being individualistic, while everyone gains when all seek to make the group more efficient (Dore, 1986:1). Whether at home or in the work setting, the group typically counts for more than the individual (Taylor, 1985:77; Abegglen and Stalk, 1985:272), leading to intense group pressures within an industry to produce high-quality goods and services (Shimokawa, 1982:291).

Japanese companies also develop ideologies (Rohlen, 1975:208) similar to those of the traditional family (Alston, 1986:27; Fields, 1983:69). As a result, one's friends and colleagues tend to be one and the same. The members of this group are a worker's *nakama,* or buddies, and the group can easily become more important than one's immediate family (Taylor, 1985:70). The company becomes *marugakae* (total embrace), or the primary focus of the worker's life (Taylor, 1985:175).

To foster this sense of community, Japanese companies usually sponsor and pay for overnight trips, weekend recreation, and office parties (Rohlen, 1975:190). One tangible result of this obscuring of the line between work and nonwork is that the Japanese willingly spend their leisure time with business colleagues. Although they may not converse about work, they are reinforcing the work relationship (Taylor, 1985:114). In contrast, Americans tend to have rigidly designated times for work and find it an infringement if they are asked to do anything work-related in their off-hours (Iwata, 1982:81). Thus, in the United States formal rationality is rigidly separated from substantive rationality, making it unlikely for the two to feed off one another as they do in Japan.

Wa, or the quest for harmony, unity, and cooperation (Gibney, 1985:189; Morgan and Morgan, 1991:19–21), is manifested at the level of the industrial organization in consensus-type decision making and a strong respect by each individual for all others (Pegels, 1984:72). Supervisors are responsible for making certain that *wa* supports the company's objectives, and it is not uncommon for a Japanese executive to hang a scroll in his or her office with only one character on it: *wa* (Taylor, 1985:115). The substantive rationality of *wa* helps counter the excesses of formal rationality. For example, unlike in the United States, workers are not depersonalized or treated like machines or appendages to machines (De Vos, 1975:218). Also, the Japanese will not use formally rational techniques if they threaten *wa* (Alston, 1986:124).

Groupism and *wa* have permitted the Japanese to develop their distinctive system of permanent employment, a system which is composed of both formally and substantively rational elements. Permanent employment was offered to employees because of the desire of large businesses to protect their investment in a skilled labor force by reducing the risk that those workers would take their skills elsewhere. While far from universal in Japan, permanent employment has become the predominant pattern in the modern industrial sector and in large commercial organizations (Dore, 1973; Vogel, 1979:132–133; Hill, 1981; Lincoln and Kalleberg, 1990). For workers in these sectors, job security is complete except under extreme circumstances such as bankruptcy (Alston, 1986:223). Permanent employment tends to support and reinforce the substantive rationality of groupism and *wa*. Japanese workers feel that their skills belong to the group rather than to the person (Gibney, 1985:7; Alston, 1986:223). They tend to view themselves as workers for Toyota who happen to be welders. In contrast, Americans see themselves as welders who happen to work for Ford (Osako, 1977; Alston, 1986:223). Clearly, the Japanese system helps engender a far greater commitment to the employing organization.

Permanent employment has certain formally rational characteristics in addition to the substantively rational ones already mentioned. First, standardized examinations are used to select the best employees. Second, periodic wage increases are based on a clearly defined seniority system. Third, pay differences tend to be insignificant because salaries are tied to seniority, which reduces conflict between and within work cohorts. Not only is permanent employment formally rational, it has a number of formally rational by-products. For example, because the employees are permanent, a company can engage in a variety of long-range plans. Also, because of this stable pool of workers, long-range predictions can be made regarding other aspects of its operation. More generally, permanent employment encourages an overall longer-term perspective (Noda, 1975:140; R. Clark, 1979; Vogel, 1979:65–66; Abegglen and Stalk, 1985), while in the United States the likelihood of job change militates against this.

Other aspects of permanent employment encourage heightened practical and theoretical rationality. First, because of their greater security, managers tend to take more risks, experiment with new ideas, and generally act more flexibly than their American counterparts (Alston, 1986:153–154). Second, because they are safe from layoffs, Japanese workers work hard even during bad economic times, while American workers typically feel anger as a result of imminent layoffs, resulting in poor performance (Ross and Ross, 1982:41). Thus, here as elsewhere, the four subtypes of rationality work together in Japan to produce a higher level of overall rationality.

Americans are likely to think that a system of permanent employment will lead people *not* to work hard. That is, from the American perspective, why work hard when your job is assured almost irrespective of your performance? The American assumption is that you work hard because if you don't, you will not be rewarded and may even lose your job. However, for Japanese workers permanent employment helps buttress an already strong belief in the employing organization. The employer believes enough in them to offer them a job for life, and they reciprocate by giving all they've got for the employer.

Theoretical Rationality

At the societal level in Japan, theoretical rationality is apparent in the widely circulated newspapers which impart highly technical information, a well-supported system of educational television, a very active book publishing and translation business (Vogel, 1979:30), a high literacy rate, and a commitment to education and study well beyond the end of formal education (Abegglen and Stalk, 1985:132; Dore, 1986:65; Aguayo, 1990:43). All these factors support a widespread ability to think using highly precise and abstract concepts, the keystone of theoretical rationality. The major examples of the Japanese industrial emphasis on theoretical rationality involve the commitment to engineering (McMillan, 1984:11; Abegglen and Stalk, 1985:134; Alston, 1986:21) and research and development (Kono, 1984:87; Dore, 1986:134–135), both of which involve precise and abstract thinking.

Japan has substantially more engineers in positions of senior management than does the United States, and it graduates more engineers each year than does any Western country (McMillan, 1984:11). For example, Japan graduates 75,000 engineers a year, or 3,000 more than does the United States, even though its university population is one-fifth the size (Morgan and Morgan, 1991:8). In terms of research and development (R&D), in the 1980s (and projected for the 1990s) Japan shifted its focus from exports from industries with a low investment in R&D (textiles, iron, steel, automobiles) to those which require large R&D investments (electronics, production processes, and biotechnology) (McMillan, 1984:95). The number of patents issued to Japan has increased by 350 percent in the last twenty years, while the issuance of patents has fallen by 10 percent in the United States. Japanese applicants received 16,158 American patents in 1988, or 21 percent of the total number received by foreigners. This figure is more than double the 6,352 patents (9 percent of the U.S. total) the Japanese received in 1975 (Morgan and Morgan, 1991:8–9).

At the national level, comparatively little Japanese investment goes into research related to national defense. In 1985 Japan spent 2.5 percent of its gross national product (GNP) on civilian R&D, compared with 1.9 percent in the United States and 2.4 percent in Germany. In terms of basic research, Japan spent $34 billion in 1984 (about the same sum per capita as in the United States), while the United States spent $96 billion on R&D, with nearly one-third of that sum going toward defense (Morgan and Morgan, 1991:7). These investments in defense have produced results that have few commercial applications (*Science and Engineering Indicators*, 1989:128).

The strong emphasis on theoretical rationality is linked to, reinforces, and is reinforced by the other types of rationality. For example, substantively rational groupism and *wa* contribute to the commitment of scientists and engineers to their employers and their willingness to contribute their knowledge to the employers' success. The provision of this knowledge in turn strengthens the collectivity and its *wa*. Permanent employment also plays a role since engineers and scientists are willing to both contribute knowledge and stay abreast of new advances in a continuing effort to enhance an organization that will remain their occupational home throughout their careers. Permanent employment produces a long-range perspective in which engineers and scientists engage in work that may not produce tangible or profitable results for years. MITI, a formally rational structure, also encourages an emphasis on science and engineering by fostering technological developments within designated industrial sectors.

Practical Rationality

One manifestation of Japan's emphasis on practical rationality is its "bottom-up" management philosophy, which allows lower-level managers to define and solve problems. In contrast, the "top-down" approach characteristic of the United States focuses on imposing decisions on lower echelons in the organization (Pegels, 1984:4). On occasions when top-down decisions occur, the Japanese try to disguise them and make them appear to be bottom-up (Gibney, 1982:61).

In most Japanese companies major managerial decisions go through *ringisho* (Ouchi, 1981:35; Alston, 1986:181–183; Marsh, 1990; Morgan and Morgan, 1991:157–158), meaning "decisions in a circle by document" (Gibney, 1985). In *ringi*, a memo is sent out by a junior department head or a member of the planning staff detailing a plan that has usually come from far down within the company. This document then makes its way to all department heads as it moves up the company ladder. By the time the final draft is circulated, everyone's ideas are either on the table or in the last draft. As a result, once the plan reaches the president of the company, there is wide acceptance of it and all that is needed is the president's seal of approval (Gibney, 1982:62). The result is that lower-level managers take the initiative in identifying problems, gathering information, consulting with other groups within the company, calling issues to the attention of higher officials, and drawing up documents summarizing their findings and recommendations (Vogel, 1979:144).

There is a diffusion of managerial responsibility in which all workers are given some managerial duties (Pegels, 1984:20). There is also little need for close supervision in the workplace. Instructions are generally vague, and workers are expected to take the initiative without supervision or directives from management. The situation, not the manager, dictates what action will be taken (Iwata, 1982:25). As a result, employees are able to employ practical rationality in their day-to-day activities.

This bottom-up practical rationality is reinforced by the substantive rationality of groupism and *wa*. Japanese executives can give their employees considerable autonomy because they are assured that the employees will work for the good of the company. In turn, it can be assumed that subordinates will not attack management policies or the manager's authority. Bottom-up management also contributes to the formal rationality of the organization. The ideas of workers help improve a variety of formally rational structures, such as assembly lines and bureaucracies. This is even more apparent in another aspect of Japanese practical rationality, quality control circles.

Rather than relying on Western, formally rational quality control departments, the Japanese have institutionalized a concern for quality in quality control (QC) circles in which every worker is his or her own quality inspector (Alston, 1986:269; Imai, 1986:3–4; Aguayo, 1990:42). This emphasis on quality is derived from the ideas of two Westerners, W. Edwards Deming and J. M. Juran, American exponents of quality control who were largely ignored in the United States (Pegels, 1984:148). These Americans, who became driving forces behind Japan's industrial revival of the late 1940s, taught the Japanese that quality must be built into the production of the product rather than imposed by separate quality control departments that engage in inspection and testing. They taught the Japanese formally rational techniques such as statistical quality control and the use of statistical charts, and the Japanese adapted this system to their needs by combining the functions of quality inspector and production worker. They believed that their workers could inspect products and test them for quality as they were producing them (Pegels, 1984:148).

This emphasis on quality was institutionalized in the quality circle, which consists of a group of workers (usually led by the immediate supervisor) who meet regularly to identify, analyze, and solve quality problems and a variety of other work-related issues (Aguayo, 1990). Because of the substantive rationality of groupism and *wa*, workers willingly meet in quality circles during nonwork hours. The idea behind quality circles is that all workers possess and employ practical rationality and therefore have a host of ideas on how to improve the work process. Quality circles allow all workers to openly express these ideas as well as providing a setting for the generation of new ideas (Pegels, 1984:156). It is clear that the Japanese have exploited the practical rationality of workers, especially those at the bottom of the ladder, while the United States has relied on formally rational systems to suppress it, resulting in the blind conformity of workers to these formally rational systems.

Therefore, practical rationality reinforces and is reinforced by the other types of rationality. The emphasis on knowledge and information characteristic of theoretical rationality supports the effort to utilize the abilities of all workers. Because of the substantively rational groupism and *wa,* one can assume that workers will utilize their abilities for the company rather than for themselves. Both the substantively and formally rational components of permanent employment encourage participation in quality circles, and this reinforces the dedication of workers to the organization. Finally, because of the fast pace of the formally rational JIT, all workers must be vigilant on the issue of quality.

A NOTE ON THE AMERICAN CASE

Hyperrationality gives us a clear sense of why the Japanese automobile industry succeeded, but what does it tell us about the failures of its American counterpart? Briefly, American industry relied almost exclusively on formally rational systems, most notably bureaucracies and assembly lines. In relying on this one type of rationality, Americans failed to utilize the other three types. Indeed, there was an effort to eliminate the other types of rationality from the workplace.

Values were seen as having no role in the workplace, certainly not as a guide to work-related activities. Workers were not expected to exercise intellectual rationality. If that type of rationality had any place, it was among the scientists, technicians, and top managers employed by the organization. Workers were also not expected to exercise practical rationality on the job. Instead, they were expected to do exactly as they were told and what the assembly line demanded of them. If they had any practical ideas for improving day-to-day activities, they were asked to drop them in the "suggestion box." Theoretically, managers were to study those suggestions; in practice, the suggestion slips were often dropped in the wastebasket at the end of the workweek.

Thus, the Americans relied almost exclusively on one type of rationality, while the Japanese employed all four types. Furthermore, the synergism among the four types yielded a level of rationality far beyond what one might have expected from the mere summation of the use of the four types. Thus, put another way, many of the problems of this country's automobile industry are traceable to its failure to develop a hyperrational system like that developed by the Japanese.

CONCLUSION

In this chapter I have offered a theoretically based explanation for the post–World War II success of Japanese industry. In brief, my view is that such an explanation must focus on the issue of rationality. The concept of hyperrationality constitutes the basis of my effort to offer a more complete explanation of Japanese industrial success.

This analysis, like many others, portrays Japan and Japanese industry in a very positive light. While hyperrationality has brought unprecedented economic success to Japan, there is a dark side to it. It can be argued that hyperrationality has produced an unprecedented level of worker exploitation: *hyperexploitation.* For example, Japanese workers are pushed by formally rational systems, motivated by substantively rational systems, and impelled by workplace refinements stemming from theoretical and practical rationality to improve and increase production. In contrast, the pressure on workers in the United States comes largely from formally rational systems. The net result of the hyperrational system is that Japanese workers work far harder than do their American counterparts. In fact, increasing attention is being given to the problem of *karoshi,* or death caused by overwork. This commitment to hard work translates into phenomenal profits for employing organizations and great wealth for the society as a whole. While Japanese workers have certainly profited from this system, most of the gains have gone, as they must in a capitalist economy, to a relatively small number of people.

However, the point of this chapter is neither to criticize the Japanese system of hyperrationality nor to extol its virtues. Rather, as was mentioned previously, my goal has been to use this theoretical tool to help explain sociologically the post–World War II success of Japanese industry.

Returning to the theme of this book, the objective has been to trace the beginnings of the idea of hyperrationality to my work experiences at the Ford Motor Company as well as to my later exposure as a sociologist to Weberian theory. As was true with the concept of McDonaldization in Chapter 7, it is hoped that the development of the concept of hyperrationality will be the beginning of a number of theoretical analyses and empirical studies based on this idea.

CHAPTER 9

New Beginnings: Sociology Today and Tomorrow

In much of this book I have focused on sociology's past. Even Chapters 7 and 8, which dealt with very recent ideas, involved a look backward. I have glanced back in time in order to give the student a sense of sociology through a description of some of its beginnings. However, I do not want to leave the reader with the impression that all this is merely history with little relevance to what is currently occurring in sociology as well as in society as a whole. In fact, *all* the major ideas whose beginnings were discussed in these pages continue to affect and be utilized by sociologists today. To illustrate the contemporaneousness of the material covered in this book and to offer a summary of its main themes, I will discuss a recently published study by Gary Alan Fine (1992a) of restaurants and the cooks who work in them. I will do this by returning to each of the layers covered in this book—sociology itself, biographical factors involved in the work, the school in which it is embedded, its methodological and theoretical orientation, its association with a particular substantive area, and the way in which it relates to some of the concepts discussed throughout this book—and relating each layer to Fine's study.

A CONTEMPORARY CASE STUDY

Most generally and obviously, Fine is operating within the domain of *sociology*. Fine's study would not have been done if it had not been for the existence of the field of sociology and the fact that he was trained in it and was functioning within that intellectual tradition. Fine might have come to look at the restaurant industry anyway, but his work would have been quite different if he had devoted himself to a different discipline. For example, if he had become a journalist, perhaps a food critic for a newspaper, he would have examined the quality of the food, not the nature of social life and social interaction in a restaurant.

In addition, there is a *biographical* aspect to the general approach Fine takes in his study of the restaurant business. While not a graduate of the University of Chicago, Fine has been influenced by the First and Second Chicago Schools since his days as an undergraduate student and is today one of the leading exponents and practitioners of the Chicago approach. Fine's orientation was directly (by Erving Goffman) and indirectly (through the reading of their work) shaped by the ideas of people associated with the two Chicago schools. Let me quote from a letter from Fine (1992b) which was a response to a letter in which I asked him to explain his link to the two Chicago schools. First, Fine describes his undergraduate days at the University of Pennsylvania and the profound influence on him of one of the last major products of the Second Chicago School, Erving Goffman:

> I am not sure how to respond to your request for the Chicago influences on my life and career, but I'll give it a shot. I was an undergraduate at the University of Pennsylvania at the period of time that Erving Goffman moved to Penn. . . . I was fortunate enough to take one of his early graduate courses, even though I was an undergraduate, and I think Erving rather liked the presumption of that. He later let me into a second course from which he excluded all Sociology graduate students. There were 10 of us—myself, three professors, and several students from Anthropology and Communication. This was the period of time at which Erving was composing *Frame Analysis* [a major work of Goffman's], and of course that had a great impact on me (Fine, 1992b).

Fine went on to get a Ph.D. from Harvard and his first teaching job at the University of Minnesota. While at Harvard, he took courses at Boston University and Boston College with theorists whose work had a number of affinities with the Chicago Schools. At Minnesota, as he put it, he "learned" from colleagues who were part of the two Chicago schools and had received Ph.D.s from Chicago. However, like most sociologists who in recent years have associated themselves with the Chicago schools, Fine had to do it largely on his own since both the First and Second Chicago Schools had long since ceased to exist:

> As I mentioned on the phone, I think there is something about those scholars of my generation who are generally within the Chicago School or interactionist orbit that derives from our being trained, in many instances, outside of Chicago. That is to say that we were trained in departments in which Chicago School sociology may not have been a predominant thrust, and we were taught sociology as a whole, rather than being trained in that one perspective. . . . I, for one, was not trained to be

> a member of any particular school, but rather picked up sociology where I found it—in whatever dribs and drabs I could make sense of (Fine, 1992b).

What is most directly manifested in Fine's restaurant study is the influence of the Chicago School's major methodological (participant observation) and theoretical (symbolic interactionism) contributions. Speaking of the methodology involved in his restaurant study, Fine says, "I conducted participant observation in four restaurants in the Twin Cities metropolitan area (St. Paul/Minneapolis and their surrounding suburbs), spending a month [about 75 to 100 hours per restaurant] observing and taking notes in the kitchen of each restaurant during all periods in which the restaurant was open" (Fine, 1992a:1271). While primarily involved in doing a participant observation study, Fine, like many other followers of the Chicago School, employed other methods as well, most notably lengthy interviews with full-time cooks.

Fine's theoretical orientation here, as in most of his work (Fine, 1990), is symbolic interactionism. This is revealed by the fact that while he recognizes external constraints on restaurant workers, especially cooks, he sees them as creating their own worlds on a daily basis. Those worlds are based on a continuing series of negotiations between the cooks and those involved in other aspects of the restaurant business. This emphasis on actors creating their social worlds and maintaining those worlds through ongoing negotiations with others is a hallmark of symbolic interactionism.

Here is the way Fine describes his methodological and theoretical orientations:

> It just seemed that understanding the world in terms of its detailed particulars, while using those particulars to build theory seemed to make sense. I have never considered myself to be a descriptive ethnographer, although I very carefully lay out the descriptive bases of my work so that others can understand the social world (Fine, 1992b).

Fine is making clear not only his use of a descriptive, ethnographic orientation traceable to participant observation but also his desire, shared by most sociologists, to link methods and theories (in this case, symbolic interactionism).

The focus on the cook makes this a study in the sociology of work, and as a result, that layer of sociology, more specifically the early history of the sociology of work at the University of Chicago, is also relevant to Fine's research. In fact, one finds references in Fine's study not only to Everett Hughes but also to important disciples of Hughes (Chapter 6), such as Howard Becker, Rue Bucher, and Anselm Strauss. Furthermore, many of the traditional interests of the Chicago School of occupational sociology are unmistakable in Fine's study.

For example, Fine, like Howard Becker (1963) in his previously discussed study of the jazz musician, is interested in the conflict between worker and client. In Becker's case the conflict is between the jazz musician and the audience, while in Fine's study it is between the cook and the diner. Thus, a cook may prepare a dish that is perfect from his or her viewpoint, but it may be sent back by the customer. For example, a duck breast may be served pink, but the diner may feel that it is undercooked and return it to the kitchen so that it will be cooked further. In sending the food back, the customer is, at least in the eyes of the cook, questioning the cook's judgment. The chef is obligated to cook the duck further because of his or her need to accept the idea that the customer is always right. However, in so doing, cooks believe "they are prostituting themselves" (Fine, 1922a:1280) by compromising their aesthetic judgment and conforming to the expectations of people who lack such taste. In this regard cooks resemble, as Fine explicitly recognizes, Becker's jazz musicians, who similarly felt that they were prostituting themselves when they played what the audience wanted (usually old standards) rather than what they thought should be played. Thus, both the cook and the jazz musician are in conflict with their clients.

Fine also uses Goffman's (1959) dramaturgical ideas (Chapters 1 and 5) to analyze what takes place in the restaurant. Cooking may be seen as the back stage for the room in the restaurant where the food is served to the customers (the front stage). Things go on in the back stage that are unknown in the front stage and that would destroy what is taking place there if they were to become known. For example, "as discomfiting as it may be, when food falls on a dirty counter or floor after being cooked, cooks will wipe or rinse it, and then serve it, with the customer none the wiser" (Fine, 1992a:1281).

I have also previously discussed Bucher's (1962) concept of professional segments (Chapter 6). Fine uses this idea to identify and differentiate among segments within the restaurant industry. For example, Fine studied a haute cuisine French restaurant, La Pomme de Terre, as well as a restaurant in a hotel that was part of a larger chain. The French restaurant was considered to be one of the best not only in Saint Paul–Minneapolis but in the upper Midwest, while the hotel restaurant was "not esteemed for the quality of its cuisine" (Fine, 1992a:1272). The point is that these restaurants operate in very different segments of the restaurant industry, with the result that the occupational realities for cooks in the two settings are quite different. For example, a cook at the French restaurant would feel considerable anger when food was returned to the kitchen, but cooks at the hotel, with few illusions about fine cooking, were far more likely to take such rejection in stride.

Let me offer one more example of continuity between Fine's research and the sociology of work. As we saw in Chapter 6, occupational careers were of great significance to Hughes and his students. Fine relates the realities of cooks' work to their career stages. Those at entry-level positions in their careers are engaged in largely routine manual tasks: They "chop onions, peel potatoes, or destring celery" (Fine 1992a:1286) and are unlikely to be concerned with the aesthetics of their work. However, those who have achieved the position of a high-status head chef, especially at a prestigious restaurant, are far more likely to be concerned with the aesthetics (for example, the artistic way in which food is presented to the diner) of the food they prepare. Another difference is that high-status chefs are expected to be creative in their cooking, while beginners are expected to perform routine tasks and conform to the demands of the chef.

I can also relate Fine's study to the layer of specific sociological ideas, even to the concept of McDonaldization. In the following quotation, Fine compares McDonald's to a famous New York restaurant (Lutece) and analyzes differences between the cooks in the two settings:

> The self-image and market niche of a restaurant affects how workers view the sensory qualities of their production. Although McDonald's and Lutece have aesthetics associated with their work, the cooks at the latter have more autonomy and their aesthetic decisions are more subtle and consequential. McDonald's has corporate aesthetic standards for the "design" of their food, set by the central office. Worker aesthetics at McDonald's involves problem solving of immediate production needs—following the *preset rules* with style, care, efficiency, and coping with customer demands (Fine, 1992a:1286; italics added).

From the point of view of McDonaldization, Fine is demonstrating that "cooks" at McDonald's are controlled by nonhuman technology (the preset rules), while those at Lutece are permitted and even encouraged to be far more independent and creative.

Finally, although he does not explicitly mention it, I can also relate Fine's analysis to the idea of hyperrationality. It could be argued that the cooks at McDonald's, like workers who labor on an American automobile assembly line, are forced to rely almost exclusively on formal rationality. That is, they follow the preset rules laid down by the organization. However, those who cook for restaurants like Lutece come closer to being able to exhibit hyperrationality on the job. There are certainly rules to be followed (formal rationality), but such cooks are far more likely to rely on larger human values such as the production of an aesthetically appealing meal (substantive rationality). Chefs at Lutece also use theoretical rationality (for example, expertise acquired in training schools for chefs) and practical rationality (tricks of the trade picked up on the job). Thus, the differences between McDonald's and Lutece can be traced to the heavy reliance on formal rationality of McDonald's and the ability to utilize all four types of rationality, to be hyperrational, of Lutece.

Thus, Fine's very recent study illustrates all the major concerns of this book. The study demonstrates that the various beginnings discussed throughout these pages are far more than dusty historical remnants; they are living legacies in contemporary sociology. But what of the future of sociology? What does this discussion of the beginnings of new ideas have to with it?

CHALLENGES TO SOCIOLOGY IN THE FUTURE

It may appear from these pages that sociology is already quite old, tracing its formal history back to Auguste Comte in 1822. However, if we were able to look at sociology today from the vantage point of the future, we would see that the field is in its infancy. A century from now, in the 2990s, sociologists will look back on the field in the 1990s and see it as a discipline still in one of its earliest phases.

While still in its infancy, sociology today is well institutionalized not only in the United States but in many other nations. The American Sociological Association has over 12,000 members, and thousands of people from the United States and around the world attend its annual meetings. There are also strong regional societies such as the Eastern, Southern, Midwestern, and Pacific Sociological Societies. Many other nations have strong national associations of sociologists, and there is an increasingly important International Sociological Association. Most colleges and universities offer many sociology courses, and one can major in sociology in the vast majority of those schools. Many universities have graduate programs that offer M.A.s and Ph.D.s in sociology. There is an active job market both in and out of academia for those with graduate degrees in sociology. There are also an increasing number of jobs for professional sociologists in a variety of nonacademic settings such as business, government, and research institutes.

Much of this success, I believe, can be traced to the fact that sociology has generated over its relatively brief life span an enormous number of ideas. In fact, looking back over this book about beginnings, it is striking that almost all of it has been about the generation of ideas.

While sociology has been widely and successfully institutionalized, it is also, like virtually all fields, faced with continual challenges. For example, in the 1990s all indications are that American universities will face a series of adversities and, among other things, be forced to become "lean" organizations (Womack, Jones, and Ross, 1990). The perception is emerging that not all universities, not even the richest and most prestigious Ivy League schools, can do everything. This will mean different things in different universities, but departments and programs will be reduced or eliminated in at least some universities and colleges. While it will not bear the brunt of these reductions, sociology will be faced with its share of them. Already a few sociology departments have been reduced in size or eliminated altogether.

In some ways, sociology in the 1990s is very vulnerable to these cutbacks. Sociology grew dramatically in the late 1960s and early 1970s as a result of the influx of radical, antiwar students and the generally more liberal and progressive mood in the country. Those students found in sociology a vast storehouse of ideas that seemed highly relevant to the problems that beset society. However, the radical 1960s and early 1970s eventually gave way to the conservative Nixon, Reagan, and Bush years; the invasion of Grenada; Operation Desert Storm; and the like. Having flourished in the radical years, student interest in sociology dropped dramatically in the far more conservative decades of the 1980s and early 1990s. This drop in student interest makes sociology vulnerable in an era of cuts in academia.

In fact, the number of bachelor's degrees awarded in sociology peaked in 1973 at 35,996. By 1989 that number had dropped to less than half, 14,393. However, it should be pointed out that this drop is somewhat exaggerated because in the intervening years programs such as criminal justice, urban studies, and women's studies split off, at least in part, from sociology. In the process, they took students with them who are no longer counted as sociology students even though they are learning a great deal of sociology and may even be taught by sociologists in those other programs. In any case, there is some indication that enrollments have improved somewhat since 1989 (Kantrowitz, 1992).

Interest in sociology is likely to ebb and flow depending on the times and the public mood. If the current hard economic realities persist, as many expect, through the 1990s, one can anticipate an increase in interest in sociology as a discipline able to comprehend and offer solutions to the kinds of social problems generated during tough economic times. Continuing problems like poverty, homelessness, racism, sexism, the deterioration of the cities, and inequities in the health care system make it likely that sociology will be with us to stay. More generally, the social world is here to stay and people will always be drawn to it as a field of study as well as to fields that offer insights into it.

Yet sociology cannot afford to grow overconfident. It must continue to demonstrate its relevance and importance to the larger society. One of the ways it can achieve that is to continue to do what has been discussed throughout this book: generate newer and better sociological ideas. As long as those ideas continue to flow, sociology has a bright future.

However, while sociologists have produced many thought-provoking ideas, they have not always demonstrated the usefulness of those ideas to the public and to public officials. As we have seen throughout this book, although sociology has been long on insight, it has been short on ideas for practical programs to deal with the social world in general and social ills in particular. Even if they do have policy ideas, sociologists have little access to those in power and little influence on public policy. Thus, there is no national Council of Social Advisors to complement the Council of Economic Advisors. As the former president of the American Sociological Association, James Coleman, says, "It's extremely important for sociology to demonstrate its utility to society if it's going to be viable in the long run" (cited in Kantrowitz, 1992:55). Sociologists have done much work that is relevant to the larger society and its problems. However, political leaders have not been prone to listen and sociologists have not always been adept in getting their ideas heard. Furthermore, sociologists have not done as well as they might in translating their solid insights into viable and practical programs designed to solve social problems.

In the future, sociology needs to produce ideas that are of more direct relevance to our most pressing social problems. In a recent important book, Coleman (1990:651) says that sociologists must be interested in knowledge not merely for the sake of knowledge but also as part of "a search for knowledge for the reconstruction of society." Furthermore, those who produce ideas for such a reconstruction must become more capable of translating them into terms that can be understood and appreciated by members of the larger society. Also, sociologists have to become more aggressive in seeing to it that their ideas are heard and implemented by those in power. We have seen that sociology is a veritable idea factory. What is now needed is a set of new ideas about how the plethora of sociological concepts can be applied in the larger society. Once this begins on a large scale, sociology will embark on yet another new beginning, this time one involving a movement from a largely academic and intellectual enterprise to one with broader practical relevance and importance.

Bibliography

Abbott, Andrew, forthcoming: "The Sociology of Work and Occupations." *Annual Review of Sociology* 19.

Abegglen, James C., and George Stalk, Jr., 1985: *Kaisha, the Japanese Corporation.* New York: Basic Books.

Adler, Patricia A., and Peter Adler, 1983: "Relationships between Dealers." *Sociology and Social Research* 67:260–278.

Aguayo, Rafael, 1990: *Dr. Deming: The American Who Taught the Japanese about Quality*. New York: Carol Publishing Group.

Albas, Daniel, and Cheryl Albas, 1988: "Aces and Bombers: The Post-Exam Impression Management Strategies of Students." *Symbolic Interaction* 11:289–302.

Alexander, Jeffrey C., 1985: "The 'Individualist Dilemma' in Phenomenology and Interactionism," in S. N. Eisenstadt and H. J. Helle (eds.), *Macro-Sociological Theory*, vol. 1. London: Sage, pp. 25–51.

———(ed.), 1988: *Durkheimian Sociology: Cultural Studies.* Cambridge, UK: Cambridge University Press.

Alston, Jon P., 1986: *The American Samurai: Blending American and Japanese Managerial Practices.* Berlin: Walter de Gruyter.

Amsden, Alice H., 1989: *Asia's Next Giant: South Korea and Late Industrialization.* New York: Oxford University Press.

Anderson, Nels, 1923/1961: *The Hobo.* Chicago: University of Chicago Press.

———,1975: *The American Hobo: An Autobiography.* Leiden, Netherlands: E. J. Brill.

———, 1983: "A Stranger at the Gate: Reflections on the Chicago School of Sociology." *Urban Life* 11:396–406.

Antonio, Robert, and Patrick Akard, 1986: "Militarism and International Political Economy," in George Ritzer, *Social Problems,* 2d ed. New York: Random House: 563–609.

Azadarmaki, Taghi, 1992: *An Analysis of the Roots of Ibn Khaldun's Social Theory: A Case Study in Metatheorizing*. Doctoral dissertation, University of Maryland, College Park.

Baran, Paul, and Paul Sweezy, 1966: *Monopoly Capital: An Essay on the American Economic and Social Order.* New York: Monthly Review Press.

Barron, James, 1989: "Please Press 2 for Service; Press ? for an Actual Human." *New York Times,* February 17, pp. A1, B2.

Becker, Howard S., 1963: *Outsiders: Studies in the Sociology of Deviance.* New York: Free Press.

———(ed.), 1964: *The Other Side.* New York: Free Press.

———, Blanche Geer, David Riesman, and Robert Weiss (eds.), 1968: *Institutions and the Person: Essays Presented to Everett C. Hughes.* Chicago: Aldine.

Bellah, Robert, 1957: *Tokugawa Religion: The Values of Pre-Industrial Japan.* Glencoe, Ill.: Free Press.

Berger, A. A., 1983: "Berger vs. Burger: A Personal Encounter," in Marshall Fishwick (ed.), *Ronald Revisited: The World of Ronald McDonald.* Bowling Green, Ohio: Bowling Green University Press, pp. 125–128.

Besnard, Philippe, 1983: *The Sociological Domain.* Cambridge, UK: Cambridge University Press.

Beyer, Andrew, 1990: "Lukas Has the Franchise on Almighty McDollar." *Washington Post,* August 8, pp. F1, F8.

Biggart, Nicole Woolsey, 1989: *Charismatic Capitalism: Direct Selling Organizations in America.* Chicago: University of Chicago Press.

Blauner, Robert, 1964: *Alienation and Freedom.* Chicago: University of Chicago Press.

Blumer, Herbert, 1969: *Symbolic Interaction: Perspective and Method.* Englewood Cliffs, N.J.: Prentice-Hall.

Boas, Max, and Steve Chain, 1976: *Big Mac: The Unauthorized Story of McDonald's.* New York: NAL, 1976.

Boles, Jacqueline, and A. P. Garbin, 1974: "Stripping for a Living: An Occupational Study of the Night Club Stripper," in Clifton Bryant (ed.), *Deviant Behavior.* Chicago: Rand McNally, pp. 312–335.

Brewer, John, and Albert Hunter, 1989: *Multimethod Research: A Synthesis of Styles.* Newbury Park, Calif.: Sage.

Brubaker, Rogers, 1984: *The Limits of Rationality: An Essay on the Social and Moral Thought of Max Weber.* London: Allen & Unwin.

Bruyn, Severyn, 1966: *The Human Perspective in Sociology.* Englewood Cliffs, N.J.: Prentice-Hall.

Bucher, Rue, 1962: "Pathology: A Study of Social Movements within a Profession." *Social Problems* 10: 40–51.

———, and Anselm Strauss, 1961: "Professions in Process." *American Journal of Sociology* 66:325–334.

Bulmer, Martin, 1984: *The Chicago School of Sociology: Institutionalization, Diversity, and the Rise of Sociological Research.* Chicago: University of Chicago Press.

Burman, Patrick, 1988: *Killing Time, Losing Ground: Experiences of Unemployment.* Toronto: Wall and Thompson.

Butler, Suellen, and William Snizek, 1976: "Waitress-Diner Relationships." *Sociology of Work and Occupations* 3: 209–221.

Charon, Joel, 1985: *Symbolic Interaction: An Introduction, an Interpretation, an Integration,* 2d ed. Englewood Cliffs, N.J.: Prentice-Hall.

Choate, Pat, 1990: *Agents of Influence: How Japan's Lobbyists in the United States Manipulate America's Political and Economic System.* New York: Knopf.
Clark, Rodney, 1979: *The Japanese Company.* New Haven, Conn.: Yale University Press.
Clark, Terry, 1973: *Prophets and Patrons: The French University and the Emergence of the Social Sciences.* Cambridge, Mass.: Harvard University Press.
Cohen, Richard, 1990: "Take a Message—Please!" *Washington Post Magazine,* August 5, p. 5.
Coleman, James, 1990: *Foundations of Social Theory.* Cambridge, Mass.: Harvard University Press.
Collins, Randall, 1980: "Weber's Last Theory of Capitalism: A Systemization." *American Sociological Review* 45: 924–942.
———, 1985: *Weberian Sociological Theory.* Cambridge, UK: Cambridge University Press.
Colomy, Paul (ed.), 1990: *Functionalist Sociology.* Brookfield, Vt.: Elgar.
———, and J. David Brown, forthcoming: "Progress in the Second Chicago School," in Gary Fine (ed.), *A Second Chicago School?*
Comte, Auguste, 1830–1842/1974: *The Positive Philosophy.* New York: AMS Press.
———, 1851–1854/1976: *The System of Positive Philosophy.* New York: Burt Franklin.
———, 1891/1973: *The Catechism of Positive Religion.* Clifton, N.J.: A. M. Kelley.
Cook, Karen, Richard M. Emerson, Mary R. Gillmore, and Toshio Yamagishi, 1983: "The Distribution of Power in Exchange Networks: Theory and Experimental Results." *American Journal of Sociology* 89: 275–305.
Cooley, Charles H., 1902/1964: *Human Nature and the Social Order.* New York: Scribner's.
Cooper, Kenneth J., 1991: "Stanford President Sets Initiative on Teaching." *Washington Post,* March 3, p. A12.
Cressey, Paul G., 1932: *The Taxi Dance Hall.* Chicago: University of Chicago Press.
Davis, Kingsley, and Wilbert Moore, 1945: "Some Principles of Stratification." *American Sociological Review* 10: 242–249.
De Vos, George A., 1975: "Apprenticeship and Paternalism," in Ezra Vogel (ed.), *Modern Japanese Organization and Decision-Making.* Berkeley: University of California Press, pp. 210–227.
Dore, Ronald, 1973: *British Factory, Japanese Factory: The Origins of Diversity in Industrial Relations.* Berkeley: University of California Press.
———, 1986: *Flexible Rigidities: Industrial Policy and Structural Adjustment in the Japanese Economy 1970–1980.* Stanford, Calif.: Stanford University Press.
———, 1987: *Taking Japan Seriously: A Confucian Perspective on Leading Economic Issues.* Stanford, Calif.: Stanford University Press.
Douglas, Mary, 1986: *How Institutions Think.* Syracuse, N.Y.: Syracuse University Press.
Drucker, Peter, 1981: "Behind Japan's Success: Defining Rules for Managing in a Pluralist Society." *Harvard Business Review,* January–February, pp. 83–90.
Durkheim, Émile, 1893/1964: *The Division of Labor in Society.* New York: Free Press.
———, 1895/1964: *The Rules of Sociological Method.* New York: Free Press.

———, 1897/1951: *Suicide.* New York: Free Press.
———, 1912/1965: *The Elementary Forms of Religious Life.* New York: Free Press.
———, 1928/1962: *Socialism.* New York: Collier Books.
Egan, Timothy, 1990: "Big Chains Are Joining Manhattan's Toy Wars." *New York Times,* December 8, p. 29.
Eisen, Arnold, 1978: "The Meanings and Confusions of Weberian 'Rationality.'" *British Journal of Sociology* 29: 57–70.
Eisenstadt, S. N., 1965: *Modernization, Protest and Change.* Englewood Cliffs, N.J.: Prentice-Hall.
Emmott, Bill, 1989: *The Sun Also Sets: The Limits to Japan's Economic Power.* New York: Random House/Times Books.
England, Paula, 1992: *Comparable Worth: Theories and Evidence.* Chicago: Aldine DeGruyter.
Erikson, Kai, 1961: "Notes on the Sociology of Deviance." *Social Problems* 9:307–317.
Farhi, Paul, 1990: "Domino's Is Going to School." *Washington Post,* September 21, p. F3.
Faris, Robert E. L., 1970: *Chicago Sociology: 1920–1932.* Chicago: University of Chicago Press.
Feagin, Joe R., and Clairece Booher Feagin, 1993: *Racial and Ethnic Relations,* 4th ed. Englewood Cliffs, N.J.: Prentice-Hall.
Fields, George, 1983: *From Bonsai to Levi's: When West Meets East: An Insider's Surprising Account of How the Japanese Live.* New York: Macmillan.
Fine, Gary, 1990: "Symbolic Interactionism in the Post-Blumerian Age," in George Ritzer (ed.), *Frontiers of Social Theory: The New Syntheses.* New York: Columbia University Press, pp. 117–157.
———, 1992a: "The Culture of Production: Aesthetic Choices and Constraints in Culinary Work." *American Journal of Sociology* 97: 1268–1294.
———, 1992b: Personal Communication to the author.
———, forthcoming: "Introduction: A Second Chicago School?" in Gary Fine (ed.), *A Second Chicago School?*
Fitzgerald, Ellen, 1990: *Endless Crusade: Women Social Scientists and Progressive Reform.* New York: Oxford University Press.
Foote, Nelson, 1953: "The Professionalization of Labor in Detroit." *American Journal of Sociology* 58: 371–380.
Freidson, Eliot, 1960: "Client Control and Medical Practice." *American Journal of Sociology* 65: 374–382.
———, 1970: *The Profession of Medicine.* New York: Dodd, Mead.
———, 1975: *Doctoring Together: A Study of Professional Social Control.* New York: Elsevier.
Friedman, Jon, and John Meehan, 1992: *House of Cards: Inside the Troubled Empire of American Express.* New York: Putnam.
Frisby, David, 1984: *Georg Simmel.* Chichester, UK: Ellis Horwood.
———, 1992: *Simmel and Since: Essays on Georg Simmel's Social Theory.* London: Routledge.
Fucini, Joseph J., and Suzy Fucini, 1990: *Working for the Japanese: Inside Mazda's American Auto Plant.* New York: Free Press.

Geison, Gerald L. (ed.), 1983: *Professions and Professional Ideologies in America*. Chapel Hill: University of North Carolina Press.

Gerth, Hans, and C. Wright Mills (eds.), 1946: *From Max Weber: Essays in Sociology*. New York: Oxford University Press.

Gervasi, Susan, 1990: "The Credentials Epidemic." *Washington Post*, August 30, p. D5.

Gibney, Frank, 1982: *Miracle by Design: The Real Reason behind Japan's Success*. New York: Time Books.

———, 1985: *Japan: The Fragile Superpower*. New York: Penguin.

Gilbert, Margaret, 1992: *On Social Facts*. Princeton, N.J.: Princeton University Press.

Glaser, Barney, and Anselm Strauss, 1971: *Status Passage*. Chicago: Aldine/Atherton.

Goffman, Erving, 1959: *The Presentation of Self in Everyday Life*. Garden City, N.Y.: Anchor.

———, 1961: *Encounters: Two Studies in the Sociology of Interaction*. Indianapolis: Bobbs-Merrill.

———, 1963: *Stigma: Notes on the Management of Spoiled Identity*. Englewood Cliffs, N.J.: Prentice-Hall.

Gold, Raymond, 1969: "Roles in Sociological Field Observations," in George McCall and J. L. Simmons (eds.), *Issues in Participant Observation*. Reading, Mass.: Addison-Wesley, pp. 30–39.

Guillain, Robert, 1970: *The Japanese Challenge*. Philadelphia and New York: Lippincott.

Haas, Jack, and William Shaffir, 1982: "Taking on the Role of Doctor: A Dramaturgic Analysis of Professionalization." *Symbolic Interaction* 5: 187–203.

Habermas, Jurgen, 1984: *The Theory of Communicative Action*. Vol. 1, *Reason and Rationalization of Society*. Boston: Beacon Press.

———, 1987: *The Theory of Communicative Action*. Vol. 2, *Lifeworld and System: A Critique of Functionalist Reason*. Boston: Beacon Press.

Halberstam, David, 1986: *The Reckoning*. New York: Avon.

Hall, Richard, 1983: "Theoretical Trends in the Sociology of Occupations." *Sociological Quarterly* 24: 5–23.

Hanlin, Li, Fang Ming, Wang Ying, Sun Bingyao, and Qi Wang, 1987: "Chinese Sociology, 1898–1986." *Social Forces* 65: 612–640.

Haug, Marie, 1975: "The Deprofessionalization of Everyone?" *Sociological Focus* 8: 197–213.

Hawthorn, Geoffrey, 1976: *Enlightenment and Despair*. Cambridge, UK: Cambridge University Press.

Heilbron, Johan, 1990: "Auguste Comte and Epistemology." *Sociological Theory* 8: 153–162.

Hendrickson, Robert A., 1972: *The Cashless Society*. New York: Dodd, Mead.

Hill, Stephen, 1981: *Competition and Control at Work*. Cambridge, Mass.: MIT Press.

Hochschild, Arlie, 1983: *The Managed Heart: Commercialization of Human Feeling*. Berkeley: University of California Press.

Hockstader, Lee, 1991: "No Service, No Smile, Little Sauce." *Washington Post*, August 5, p. A12.

Hong, Lawrence K., and Robert W. Duff, 1977: "Becoming a Taxi-Dancer: The

Significance of Neutralization in a Semi-Deviant Occupation." *Sociology of Work and Occupations* 4: 327–342.

Hoselitz, Bert, 1960: *Sociological Aspects of Economic Growth.* Glencoe, Ill.: Free Press.

Hsu, Frances L. K., 1983: *Rugged Individualism Reconsidered.* Knoxville, Tenn.: University of Tennessee Press.

Hughes, Everett, 1958: *Men and Their Work.* Glencoe, Ill.: Free Press.

———, 1970: Personal communication to the author.

Imai, Masaaki, 1986: *Kaizen: The Key to Japan's Competitive Success.* New York: McGraw-Hill.

Ishikawa, Akihiro, 1982: "A Survey of Studies in the Japanese Style of Management." *Economic and Industrial Democracy* 3: 1–15.

Iwata, Ryuahi, 1982: *Japanese-Style Management: Its Foundations and Prospects.* Tokyo: Asian Productivity Organization.

Jacobs, Jerry A. (ed.), 1992: "Sex Segregation and Gender Stratification," *Work and Occupations* 19: 339–486.

Janowitz, Morris, 1960: *The Professional Soldier: A Social and Political Portrait.* New York: Free Press.

Jay, Martin, 1973: *The Dialectical Imagination.* Boston: Little, Brown

———. 1986: *Permanent Exiles: Essays on the Intellectual Migration from Germany to America.* New York: Columbia University Press.

Johnson, Chalmers, 1982: *MITI and the Japanese Miracle: The Growth of Industrial Policy, 1925–1975.* Stanford, Calif.: Stanford University Press.

Johnson, Dirk, 1986: "Vacationing at Campgrounds Is Now Hardly Roughing It." *New York Times,* August 28, p. B1.

Kalberg, Stephen, 1980: "Max Weber's Types of Rationality: Cornerstones for the Analysis of Rationalization Processes in History." *American Journal of Sociology* 85: 1145–1179.

Kamata, Satoshi, 1980: *Japan in the Passing Lane: An Insider's Account of Life in a Japanese Auto Factory.* New York: Pantheon.

Kammeyer, Kenneth, George Ritzer, and Norman Yetman, 1992: *Sociology: Experiencing Changing Societies,* 5th ed. Boston: Allyn & Bacon.

Kantrowitz, Barbara, 1992: "Sociology's Lonely Crowd," *Newsweek,* February 3, p. 55.

Kenney, Martin, and Richard Florida, 1988: "Beyond Mass Production: Production and the Labor Process in Japan." *Politics and Society* 16: 121–158.

———, 1991: "Transplanted Organizations: The Transfer of Japanese Industrial Organization to the U.S." *American Sociological Review* 56: 381–398.

Kintzele, Jeff, 1986–1987: "The Logic of Credit as the Logic of Modernity." *Revue de L'Institut-de-Sociologie* 3–4: 139–151.

Kitahara, Michio, 1986: "Commodore Perry and the Japanese: A Study in the Dramaturgy of Power." *Symbolic Interaction* 9: 53–65.

Kitsuse, John, 1962: "Societal Reaction to Deviant Behavior: Problems of Theory and Method." *Social Problems* 9: 247–257.

Klegon, Douglas, 1978: "The Sociology of the Professions: An Emerging Perspective." *Sociology of Work and Occupations* 5: 259–283.

Kleinfeld, N. R., 1986: "The Ever-Fatter Business of Thinness." *New York Times,* September 7, pp. 1ff.

Kohn, Melvin (ed.), 1989: *Cross-National Research in Sociology.* Newbury Park, Calif.: Sage.

Kono, Toyohiro, 1984: *Strategy and Structure of Japanese Enterprise.* Armonk, N.Y.: Sharpe.

Kowinski, William Severini, 1985: *The Malling of America: An Inside Look at the Great Consumer Paradise.* New York: William Morrow, 1985.

Kurtz, Howard, 1991: "Slicing, Dicing News to Attract the Young." *Washington Post,* January 6, p. A1.

Kurtz, Lester, 1984: *Evaluating Chicago Sociology.* Chicago: University of Chicago Press.

Landesco, John, 1929: *Organized Crime in Chicago.* Chicago: University of Chicago Press.

Langer, Gary, 1990: "Computers Reach Out, Respond to Human Voice." *Washington Post,* February 11, p. H3.

Lavin, Carl H., 1989: "Automated Planes Raising Concerns." *New York Times,* August 12, pp. 1, 6.

Lemert, Edwin, 1951: *Social Pathology.* New York: McGraw-Hill.

Lengermann, Patricia, 1979: "The Founding of the *American Sociological Review.*" *American Sociological Review* 44: 185–198.

———, and Jill Niebrugge-Brantley, 1992: "Contemporary Feminist Theory," in George Ritzer, *Sociological Theory,* 3d ed. New York: McGraw-Hill, pp. 447–496.

———, forthcoming: *Feminist Sociological Theory.*

Lenzer, Gertrud (ed.), 1975: *Auguste Comte and Positivism: The Essential Writings.* New York: Harper Torchbooks.

Lev, Michael, 1990: "California McDonald's to Cut Menu Prices." *New York Times,* December 21, p. D3.

Levine, Donald, 1981: "Rationality and Freedom: Weber and Beyond." *Sociological Inquiry* 51: 5–25.

Lincoln, James R., and Arne L. Kalleberg, 1990: *Culture, Control, and Commitment: A Study of Work Organization and Work Attitudes in the United States and Japan.* Cambridge, UK: Cambridge University Press.

Lukes, Steven, 1972: *Emile Durkheim: His Life and Works.* New York: Harper & Row.

Madge, John, 1962: *The Origins of Scientific Sociology.* New York: Free Press.

Mandell, Lewis, 1990: *The Credit Card Industry: A History.* Boston: Twayne.

Manuel, Frank, 1962: *The Prophets of Paris.* Cambridge, Mass.: Harvard University Press.

Marsh, Robert M., 1976: "Research and Development Functions in a Japanese Firm." *Studies in Comparative International Development* 11: 25–35.

———, 1990: "Bottom-Up Decision-Making in Japanese Factories." International Sociological Association, 12th World Congress of Sociology, July 9–13, Madrid.

———, and Hiroshi Mannari, 1975: "The Japanese Factory Revisited." *Studies in Comparative International Development* 10: 30–44.

Marx, Karl, 1867/1967: *Capital: A Critique of Political Economy,* vol. 1. New York: International Publishers.

———, 1859/1970: *A Contribution to the Critique of Political Economy.* New York: International.
———, 1932/1964: *The Economic and Philosophic Manuscripts of 1844,* Dirk J. Struik (ed.). New York: International.
———, and Friedrich Engels, 1848/1948: *Manifesto of the Communist Party.* New York: International.
Matthews, Fred, 1977: *Quest for an American Sociology: Robert E. Park and the Chicago School.* Montreal: McGill University Press.
McIlwee, Judith S., and J. Gregg Robinson, 1992: *Women in Engineering: Gender, Power and Workplace Culture.* Albany: State University of New York Press.
McLellan, David, 1973: *Karl Marx: His Life and Thought.* New York: Harper Colophon.
McMillan, Charles J., 1984: *The Japanese Industrial System.* Berlin: Walter De Gruyter.
Mead, George Herbert, 1934/1962: *Mind, Self and Society: From the Standpoint of a Social Behaviorist.* Chicago: University of Chicago Press.
Merton, Robert K., 1949/1968: "Manifest and Latent Functions," in R. K. Merton, *Social Theory and Structure.* New York: Free Press, pp. 73–138.
Mid-American Review of Sociology 1991: Special Issue, 15.
Miller, Stephen, 1964: "The Social Base of Sales Behavior." *Social Problems* 12:15–24.
Mills, C. Wright, 1959: *The Sociological Imagination.* New York: Oxford University Press.
Mitzman, Arthur, 1970: *The Iron Cage: An Historical Interpretation of Max Weber.* New York: Grosset and Dunlap.
Morgan, James C., and J. Jeffrey Morgan, 1991: *Cracking the Japanese Market: Strategies for Success in the New Global Economy.* New York: Free Press.
National Public Radio, 1990: *Morning Edition,* October 3.
Newsweek, 1984: "Country-Club Campgrounds." September 24, p. 90.
———, 1985: "The McDonald's of Teaching." January 7, p. 61.
Noda, Kazuo, 1975: "Big Business Organization," in Ezra Vogel (ed.), *Modern Japanese Organization and Decision-Making.* Berkeley: University of California Press, pp. 115–145.
Oberschall, Anthony, 1972: "The Institutionalization of American Sociology," in A. Oberschall (ed.), *The Establishment of Empirical Sociology: Studies in Continuity, Discontinuity and Institutionalization.* New York: Harper & Row, pp. 187–251.
Osako, Masako, 1977: "Technology and Social Structure in a Japanese Automobile Factory." *Sociology of Work and Occupations* 4: 397–426.
Ouchi, William G., 1981: *Theory Z: How American Business Can Meet the Japanese Challenge.* Reading, Mass.: Addison-Wesley.
Park, Robert E., 1925: "The City: Suggestions for the Investigation of Human Behavior in the Urban Environment," in R. E. Park and E. W. Burgess (eds.), *The City.* Chicago: University of Chicago Press.
———, 1927/1973: "Life History." *American Journal of Sociology* 79: 251–260.
———, and Ernest W. Burgess, 1921: *An Introduction to the Science of Sociology.* Chicago: University of Chicago Press.

Parsons, Talcott, 1966: *Societies*. Englewood Cliffs, N.J.: Prentice-Hall.

Pegels, Carl C., 1984: *Japan vs. the West: Implications for Management*. Boston: Irvington.

Platt, Jennifer, forthcoming: "Research Methods and the Second Chicago School," in Gary Fine (ed.), *A Second Chicago School?*

Postman, Neil, 1992: *Technopoly*. New York: Knopf.

Prichard, Peter, 1987: *The Making of McPaper: The Inside Story of USA Today*. Kansas City: Andrews, McMeel and Parker.

Ramirez, Anthony, 1990: "In the Orchid Room . . . Big Macs." *New York Times*, October 30, pp. D1, D5.

Reskin, Barbara F., and Patricia A. Roos (eds.), 1990: *Job Queues, Gender Queues: Explaining Women's Inroads into Male Occupations*. Philadelphia: Temple University Press.

Ritzer, George, 1972: *Man and His Work: Conflict and Change*. New York: Appleton-Century-Crofts.

———, 1975: *Sociology: A Multiple Paradigm Science*. Boston: Allyn & Bacon.

———, 1977: *Working: Conflict and Change*, 2d ed. Englewood Cliffs, N.J.: Prentice-Hall.

———, 1981: *Toward an Integrated Sociological Paradigm: The Search for an Exemplar and an Image of the Subject Matter*. Boston: Allyn & Bacon.

———, 1983: "The McDonaldization of Society." *Journal of American Culture* 6: 100–107.

———, 1989: "The Permanently New Economy: The Case for Reviving Economic Sociology." *Work and Occupations* 16: 243–272.

———, 1991: *Metatheorizing in Sociology*. Lexington, Mass.: Lexington Books.

——— (ed.), 1992: *Metatheorizing*. Newbury Park, Calif.: Sage.

———, 1993: *The McDonaldization of Society*. Newbury Park, Calif.: Pine Forge Press.

———, forthcoming: *Buy Now, Pay Forever: The Credit Card in the United States and the World*.

Ritzer, George, and Terri LeMoyne, 1991: "Hyperrationality: An Extension of Weberian and Neo-Weberian Theory," in George Ritzer, *Metatheorizing in Sociology*. Lexington, Mass.: Lexington Books, pp. 93–115.

———, and David Walczak, 1986: *Working: Conflict and Change*, 3d ed. Englewood Cliffs, N.J.: Prentice-Hall.

———, 1988: "Rationalization and the Deprofessionalization of Physicians." *Social Forces* 66: 1–22.

Rock, Paul, 1979: *The Making of Symbolic Interactionism*. Totowa, N.J.: Rowman and Littlefield.

Rodgers, Joseph, and M. D. Buffalo, 1974: "Fighting Back: Nine Modes of Adaptation to a Deviant Label." *Social Problems* 22: 101–118.

Rohlen, Thomas P., 1975: "The Company Work Group," in Ezra Vogel (ed.), *Modern Japanese Organization and Decision-Making*. Berkeley: University of California Press, pp. 185–209.

Romero, Mary, 1992: *Maid in the U.S.A.* London: Routledge.

Rosenberg, Morris, 1979: *Conceiving the Self*. New York: Basic Books.

Ross, Joel E., and William C. Ross, 1982: *Japanese Quality Circles and Productivity.* Reston, Va.: Reston Publishing Company.

Roth, Julius, 1963: *Timetables: Structuring the Passage of Time in Hospital Treatment and Other Careers.* Indianapolis: Bobbs-Merrill.

———, 1974: "Professionalism: The Sociologist's Decoy." *Sociology of Work and Occupations* 1: 6–23.

Roy, Donald, 1954: "Efficiency and 'the Fix': Informal Integroup Relations in a Piecework Machine Shop." *American Journal of Sociology* 60: 255–266.

———, 1959–1960: "'Banana Time': Job Satisfaction and Informal Interaction." *Human Organization* 18: 158–169.

———, 1968: "The Union-Organizing Campaign as a Problem of Social Distance: Three Crucial Dimensions of Affiliation-Disaffiliation," in Howard S. Becker, Blanche Geer, David Riesman, and Robert Weiss (eds.): *Institutions and the Person: Essays Presented to Everett C. Hughes.* Chicago, Aldine, pp. 49–66.

———, 1974: "Sex in the Factory: Informal Heterosexual Relations between Supervisors and Work Groups," in Clifton Bryant (ed.), *Deviant Behavior.* Chicago: Rand McNally, pp. 44–66.

Runcie, John, 1980: "By Day I Make the Cars." *Harvard Business Review* 58: 106–115.

Salomon, Albert, 1945: "German Sociology," in George Gurvitch and Wilbert F. Moore (eds.), *Twentieth Century Sociology.* New York: Philosophical Library, pp. 586–614.

Samuelson, Robert J., 1989: "In Praise of McDonald's." *Washington Post,* November 1, p. A25.

Scaff, Lawrence, 1989: *Fleeing the Iron Cage: Culture, Politics and Modernity in the Thought of Max Weber.* Berkeley: University of California Press.

Scholastic News, 1991: "Super Soup Cooks Itself," January 4, p. 3.

Schonberger, Richard J., 1982: *Japanese Manufacturing Techniques.* New York: Free Press.

Schwartz, Pepper, 1990: "Research on Relationships," in Bennett Berger (ed.), *Authors of Their Own Lives.* Berkeley: University of California Press, pp. 363–380.

Science and Engineering Indicators, 1989: "Industrial R&D and Technology." Washington, D.C.: National Science Board, pp. 128–144.

Seidensticker, Edward, 1985: "Preface," in Jared Taylor, *Shadows of the Rising Sun: A Critical View of the "Japanese Miracle."* New York: Quill.

Shapiro, Eben, 1990: "Ready, Set, Scan That Melon." *New York Times,* June 14, p. D1.

Shapiro, Laura, 1990: "Ready for McCatfish?" *Newsweek,* October 15, pp. 76–77.

Shimokawa, Koichi, 1982: "Entrepreneurship and Social Environment Change in the Japanese Automobile Industry: On the Key Elements of High Productivity and Innovation." *Social Science Information* 21: 273–300.

Sica, Alan, 1988: *Weber, Irrationality and Social Order.* Berkeley: University of California Press.

Simmel, Georg, 1906/1950: "The Secret and the Secret Society," in Kurt Wolff (ed.), *The Sociology of Georg Simmel.* New York: Free Press, pp. 307–376.

Simmel, Georg, 1907/1978: *The Philosophy of Money*, Tom Bottomore and David Frisby (eds. and trans.). London: Routledge and Kegan Paul.

———, 1908/1971: "The Stranger," in Donald Levine (ed.), *Georg Simmel*. Chicago: University of Chicago Press, pp. 143–149.

———, 1950: *The Sociology of Georg Simmel*, Kurt Wolff (ed. and trans.). New York: Free Press.

Simon, David, and D. Stanley Eitzen, 1992: *Elite Deviance*, 4th ed. Boston: Allyn & Bacon.

Singer, Peter, 1975: *Animal Liberation: A New Ethics for Our Treatment of Animals*. New York: Avon.

Smigel, Erwin, Joseph Monane, Robert B. Wood, and Barbara Randall Nye, 1963: "Occupational Sociology: A Re-Examination." *Sociology and Social Research* 47: 472–477.

Smith, R. J., 1983: *Japanese Society: Tradition, Self and the Social Order*. Cambridge, UK: Cambridge University Press.

Sokoloff, Boris, 1975: *The "Mad" Philosopher Auguste Comte*. Westport, Conn.: Greenwood Press.

Solomon, David, 1968: "Sociological Perspectives on Occupations," in Howard S. Becker, Blanche Geer, David Riesman, and Robert Weiss (eds.), *Institutions and the Person: Essays Presented to Everett C. Hughes*. Chicago: Aldine, pp. 3–13.

Spencer, Maryellen, 1983: "Can Mama Mac Get Them to Eat Spinach?" in Marshall Fishwick (ed.), *Ronald Revisited: The World of Ronald McDonald*. Bowling Green, Ohio: Bowling Green University Press, pp. 85–93.

Starr, Paul, 1982: *The Social Transformation of American Medicine*. New York: Basic Books.

Sutherland, Edwin, 1937: *The Professional Thief*. Chicago: University of Chicago Press.

Taylor, Jared, 1985: *Shadows of the Rising Sun: A Critical View of the "Japanese Miracle."* New York: Quill.

Thomas, W. I., and Dorothy Swaine Thomas, 1928: *The Child in America: Behavior Problems and Programs*. New York: Knopf.

———, and Florian Znaniecki, 1918–1920: *The Polish Peasant in Europe and America*. Chicago: University of Chicago Press.

Thurow, Lester C. (ed.), 1985: *The Management Challenge: Japanese Views*. Cambridge, Mass.: MIT Press.

Tiryakian, Edward A., 1962: *Sociologism and Existentialism: Two Perspectives on the Individual and Society*. Englewood Cliffs, N.J.: Prentice-Hall.

———, 1979: "The Significance of Schools in the Development of Sociology," in William Snizek, Ellsworth R. Fuhrman, and Michael K. Miller (eds.), *Contemporary Issues in Theory and Research*. Westport, Conn.: Greenwood Press, pp. 211–233.

———, 1986: "Hegemonic Schools and the Development of Sociology: Rethinking the History of the Discipline," in Richard C. Monk (ed.), *Structures of Knowing*. Lanham, Md.: University Press of America, pp. 417–441.

Toffler, Alvin, 1970: *Future Shock*. New York: Random House.

Toren, Nina, 1975: "Deprofessionalization and Its Sources: A Preliminary Analysis." *Sociology of Work and Occupations* 2: 323–337.

Tuchman, Barbara W., 1980: "The Decline of Quality," *New York Times Magazine*, November 2, pp. 38ff.
Turner, Bryan, 1986: "Simmel, Rationalization and the Sociology of Money." *Sociological Review* 34: 93–114.
Turner, Jonathan, 1985: "In Defense of Positivism." *Sociological Theory* 3: 24–30.
——— (ed.), 1989: *Theory Building in Sociology: Assessing Theoretical Cumulation*. Newbury Park, Calif.: Sage.
———, 1990: "The Past, Present and Future of Theory in American Sociology," in George Ritzer (ed.), *Frontiers of Social Theory*. New York: Columbia University Press, pp. 371–391.
———, and Stephen Turner, 1990: *The Impossible Science*. Newbury Park, Calif.: Sage.
Turner, Ralph, 1968: "Social Roles: Sociological Aspects." *International Encyclopedia of the Social Sciences*. New York: Macmillan.
Visser, Margaret, 1989: "A Meditation on the Microwave." *Psychology Today*, December, pp. 38ff.
Vogel, Ezra F., 1979: *Japan as Number One: Lessons for America*. New York: Harper & Row.
Vogler, Conrad C., and Stephen E. Schwartz, 1993: *The Sociology of Sport: An Introduction*. Englewood Cliffs, N.J.: Prentice-Hall.
Wallerstein, Immanuel, 1974: *The Modern World System: Capitalist Agriculture and the Origins of the European World-Economy in the 16th Century*. New York: Academic Press.
———, 1980: *The Modern World-System II: Mercantilism and the Consolidation of the European World-Economy, 1600–1750*. New York: Academic Press.
———, 1989: *The Modern World-System III: The Second Era of Great Expansion of the Capitalist World-Economy, 1730–1840*. New York: Academic Press.
Wallich, Henry C., and Mable I. Wallich, 1976: "Banking and Finance," in Hugh Patrick and Henry Rosovsky (eds.), *Asia's New Giant: How the Japanese Economy Works*. Washington, D.C.: Brookings Institution, pp. 249–316.
Wall Street Journal, 1989: "The Microwave Cooks Up a New Way of Life," September 19, p. B1.
Washington Post Health, 1989: "Big People, Big Business: The Overweight Numbers Rising, Try Nutri/System," October 10, p. 8.
Weber, Marianne, 1975: *Max Weber: A Biography*, Harry Zohn (ed. and trans.). New York: Wiley.
Weber, Max, 1903–1906/1975: *Roscher and Knies: The Logical Problems of Historical Economics*. New York: Free Press.
———, 1903–1917/1949: *The Methodology of the Social Sciences*, Edward Shils and Henry Finch (eds.). New York: Free Press.
———, 1904–1905/1958: *The Protestant Ethic and the Spirit of Capitalism*. New York: Scribner.
———, 1916/1964: *The Religion of China: Confucianism and Taoism*. New York: Macmillan.
———, 1916–1917/1958: *The Religion of India: The Sociology of Hinduism and Buddhism*. Glencoe, Ill.: Free Press.
———, 1919/1946: "Politics as a Vocation," in Hans Gerth and C. Wright Mills

(eds.), *From Max Weber: Essays in Sociology.* New York: Oxford University Press, pp. 129–156.

———, 1920/1946: *From Max Weber: Essays in Sociology.*, Hans Gerth and C. Wright Mills (eds.). New York: Oxford University Press.

———, 1920/1952: *Ancient Judaism,* Hans Gerth and Don Martindale (eds.). New York: Free Press.

———, 1921/1958: *The Rational and Social Foundations of Music.* Carbondale, Ill.: Southern Illinois University Press.

———, 1921/1963: *The Sociology of Religion.* Boston: Beacon Press.

———, 1921/1968: *Economy and Society,* 3 vols. Totowa, N.J.: Bedminster Press.

———, 1921/1978: *Economy and Society: An Outline of Interpretive Sociology,* 2 vols., Guenther Roth and Claus Wittich (eds.). Berkeley: University of California Press.

———, 1927/1981: *General Economic History.* New Brunswick, N.J.: Transaction.

Weinstein, Deena, 1992: *Heavy Metal: A Cultural Sociology.* New York: Lexington Books.

Wilensky, Harold, 1960: "Work, Careers and Social Integration." *International Social Science Journal* 12: 543–560.

———, 1964: "The Professionalization of Everyone?" *American Journal of Sociology* 70: 137–158.

Wiley, Norbert, 1979: "The Rise and Fall of Dominating Theories in American Sociology." in William Snizek, Ellsworth R. Fuhrman, and Michael K. Miller (eds.), *Contemporary Issues in Theory and Research.* Westport, Conn.: Greenwood Press, pp. 47–79.

———, 1986: "Early American Sociology and *The Polish Peasant.*" *Sociological Theory* 4: 20–40.

———, 1988: "The Micro-Macro Problem in Social Theory." *Sociological Theory* 6: 254–261.

Witz, Anne, 1992: *Professions and Patriarchy.* London: Routledge.

Wolinsky, Fredric, 1988: *The Sociology of Health: Principles, Practitioners, and Issues,* 2d ed. Belmont, Calif.: Wadsworth.

Womack, James P., Daniel T. Jones, and Daniel Roos, 1990: *The Machine That Changed the World.* New York: Rawson Associates.

Woodrum, Eric, 1985: "Religion and Economics among Japanese Americans: A Weberian Study." *Social Forces* 64: 191–204.

Woronoff, Jon, 1982: *Inside Japan, Inc.* Tokyo: Lotus Press.

———, 1986: *Japan Syndrome: Symptoms, Ailments, and Remedies.* New Brunswick, N.J.: Transaction Books.

Wright, Gordon, 1960: *France in Modern Times.* New York: Rand McNally.

Zeitlin, Irving, 1990: *Ideology and the Development of Sociological Theory,* 4th ed. Englewood Cliffs, N.J.: Prenctice-Hall.

Zoglin, Richard, 1988: "Get Ready for McRather." *Time,* April 11, p. 78.

Name Index

Subject Index